Los Angeles
Boulevard

PRAISE FOR THE FIRST EDITION

"*Los Angeles Boulevard*, Suisman's concise and shamefully under-appreciated 1989 study of the history and design of the boulevards, remains the most important take on this gigantic subject."

- CHRISTOPHER HAWTHORNE, ARCHITECTURE CRITIC, LOS ANGELES TIMES

"Suisman's work contributes to a larger understanding of the city both through his careful analyses and through the visual imagery he deploys. He has created a lyrical cartography of Los Angeles's geopolitical form."

- PAULETTE SINGLEY, "SHAPING THE CITY: STUDIES IN HISTORY, THEORY AND URBAN DESIGN"

"By turns poetic, by turns forensic, Doug Suisman proves that the boulevards of Los Angeles are the true source of our social vigor. No one demonstrates with a keener eye nor with more affectionate insight how these arteries fuel our urban life and why we must care for them as the highest expression of the desire to make the city in our own image."

- GREG GOLDIN, ARCHITECTURE AND DESIGN MUSEUM

"I think I have learned more about Los Angeles from this monograph than I have in all my prior reading on Los Angeles."

- ALEX KRIEGER, CHAIRMAN, URBAN DESIGN PROGRAM, HARVARD UNIVERSITY

"Suisman's fuselage concept is a very useful tool for the design and analysis of thoroughfares in all their complexity."

- ANDRES DUANY, "THE NEW CIVIC ART"

"In his seminal pamphlet *Los Angeles Boulevard*, urbanist extraordinaire Doug Suisman has been credited with opening the topic of the urban street to discussion among Los Angeles architects. He approached the subject, unlike Reyner Banham, with the idea of inciting action and affecting the built environment."

- JESSE BRINK, EDITOR, LOS ANGELES ARCHITECT

"An excellent short history of the Los Angeles street system."

- THOMAS S. HINES, "THE GRAND AMERICAN AVENUE"

"*Los Angeles Boulevard*, by Doug Suisman, is that rare specimen: a literate, beautifully crafted publication by an architect. He argues that the boulevards are the armature of the city's public space, and as such must be understood both as they have developed historically and as the are today...No finer introduction to, and critical analysis of, L.A.'s legendary boulevards exists."

- DIANE GHIRARDO, DESIGN BOOK REVIEW

"Who is the most influential (living) architect in L.A.? In the realm of the city's infrastructure: Doug Suisman...Although there are relatively few places in L.A. that one can point to and say 'Doug Suisman designed that', Doug nonetheless may be the most influential urban designer / architect practicing in the city today. His long-term research, thinking, and extensive involvement with L.A.'s commercial corridors, districts, and transit systems have resulted in a kind of pervasive presence within L.A.'s very infrastructure."

- ALAN LOOMIS, EDITOR, "LOS ANGELES: BUILDING THE POLYCENTRIC REGION"

Los Angeles **Boulevard**

Eight X-Rays of the Body Public

by Doug Suisman

FOREWORD BY
Christopher Hawthorne

25th Anniversary Edition

ORO EDITIONS

ORO EDITIONS

Publishers of Architecture, Art, and Design
Gordon Goff: Publisher

www.oroeditions.com
info@oroeditions.com

ISBN: 978-1-941806-42-5

Color Separations and Printing: ORO Group Ltd.

Printed in China

This is an expanded version of *Los Angeles Boulevard: Eight X-Rays of the Body Public*, first published in 1989 by The Los Angeles Forum for Architecture and Urban Design

Designed by Doug Suisman

Library of Congress Cataloging-in-Publication Data information available upon request.

Then: the original edition of *Los Angeles Boulevard* was dedicated to the memory of Reyner Banham, whose words on Los Angeles inspired these.

Now: this anniversary edition is dedicated to Moye, Claire and Teddy, whose lives in Los Angeles inspire mine.

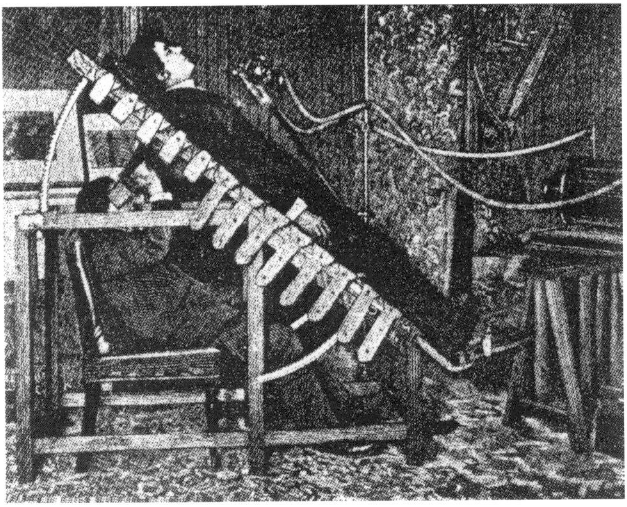

The boulevard and
the body public
under radiological
examination

Contents

Front cover: Wilshire Boulevard
Back cover: Sunset Boulevard

Foreword

by Christopher Hawthorne

In early 2011, I launched a year-long series at the *Los Angeles Times* that was as much personal challenge as research project or statement of critical principles. I decided to read—in some cases re-read—the canonical books on Southern California architecture and urbanism, in chronological order, and write short essays about each one. The goal was to bring some new energy and clarity to my writing about the architectural present and future of Los Angeles by digging more deeply into its past. I called the series "Reading L.A."

In order to keep the task from getting too unwieldy, I attached to it certain rules. No fiction. No anthologies. And, where possible, no books that were out of print or tough to find in local libraries. I didn't conceive of "Reading L.A." as a book club in the traditional sense, but I did want to give readers the chance to follow along if they wanted.

It was this last guideline, more than any other, that kept Douglas Suisman's *Los Angeles Boulevard: Eight X-Rays of the Body Public* off my list. (As it was I wound up including 27 titles—leaving me scrambling, as the year wound down, to keep up the reading and writing schedule I'd assigned myself.) For a time, as I worked on the series, I regretted not including Suisman's study. Though "Reading L.A." wound up confirming my enthusiasm for the big, beefy and ambitious books on L.A.—studies by Carey McWilliams, Reyner Banham, and Mike Davis in particular—a complementary pleasure was discovering shorter and lesser-known volumes that deserve a far wider audience. And that is certainly a fair way to describe *Los Angeles Boulevard*, published by the Los Angeles Forum for Architecture and Urban Design (and distributed by Princeton Architectural Press) in 1989.

I quickly made up for the omission in a fairly substantial way: I dedicated much of my work at the *L.A. Times* the following year, 2012, to a study of Southern California boulevards, producing essays and videos on six major streets, including Crenshaw, Sunset, and Lankershim boulevards. As I began my research for the series, I was surprised to discover how little had been written on the subject. There are essays and even complete books on Wilshire and Sunset boulevards, but hardly anything about the Southern California boulevard as an urban typology or progenitor of a certain kind of architecture, or as part of a wide network of streets that give Los Angeles a huge, loose, and permissive grid where Manhattan has a tight and controlling one.

Los Angeles Boulevard was in that sense a lifeline for me. This was particularly true in the careful historical studies it provided of how dusty cattle trails along the edges of the large ranchos grew over the course of the 19th and 20th centuries into some of the most famous streets in the world. And it examined L.A.'s streets against the broader backdrop of architectural and urban theory.

What I didn't fully appreciate the first time I read *Los Angeles Boulevard* was how personal and even quixotic it must have seemed when it was new, how willing to cut against the grain of contemporary scholarship about Los Angeles. Southern California was still in throes of a long love affair with the car in 1989, when Suisman's title appeared. We were building our first subway and light-rail lines of the post-war period at that moment, but there was little of the support for new bike and pedestrian infrastructure that is remaking the streets of Los Angeles now (and whose growth was part of the reason I began my own series on the boulevards). The city was also beginning to favor especially dark and gloomy self-portraits. Suisman, then in his early 30s, was writing his study of the boulevards at the same time that Davis was writing the legendary *City of Quartz: Excavating the Future in Los Angeles*. That book, published in 1990, provides a steady drumbeat of dystopian warnings about what Davis called the growing "spatial apartheid" of Los Angeles.

The acclaimed architecture of the period was similarly barbed, either reflecting the growing fissures of L.A. culture and politics or girding itself against them; by the late 1980s the work of the architects who would go on to become known as the L.A. School—Frank Gehry, Thom Mayne, Michael Rotondi, Eric Owen Moss and others—was beginning to strategically fray, to pull itself apart in an effort to expose not just architectural truths but societal ones. It was fragmented and disaffected architecture for what many observers were describing as an increasingly fragmented and disaffected town.

To be clear: there is nothing naïve or sweetly optimistic about *Los Angeles Boulevard*. The tone is closer to patiently analytical; Suisman's study, an intellectually generous one, is a more restrained complement to *City of Quartz* than an argument against it, and shares with the work of the L.A School architects a willingness to accept and examine Los Angeles on its own terms. It begins with Suisman's admission that when he arrived in Los Angeles he found—as so many other writers have found—that the city, at least to judge by appearances, was hardly a city at all. What he discovered instead was "a sad suggestion of abandonment, as if the city had once throbbed, butnow barely fluttered."

And yet with a single insight he was able to shrug off that thin cloak of pessimism—and in doing so to change the scholarship about the built environment in Southern California in a significant way. Suisman's crucial conclusion was that even if everything Mike Davis and other writers were saying were true—even if the architecture of Los Angeles was turning into a landscape of sealed-off privilege—it didn't change the fact that we had in the flowing spaces along our boulevards a great reservoir of public space waiting to be redefined and reactivated. Perhaps, in fact, the city's growing taste for exclusionary architecture made rediscovering and re-defining the boulevards more important than ever.

Suisman, in his introduction to *Los Angeles Boulevard,* wrote that L.A.'s great streets made up "the irreducible armature of the city's public space, and as such are charged with a social and political significance that we can hardly ignore. Public space by definition must allow for the widest range of activities and behavior for the widest possible group of people; anything short of this means that some authority is restricting the use of the space in ways that strip it of its liberating and revelatory function."

This is heady writing by the standards of 2013; by those of the late 1980s it must have felt like shouting into the wind. Among many architects and scholars, the focus then was how the city was closed, not how it might be more open than we realized—or made more open. Even now we continue to ignore some of the basic lessons that *Los Angeles Boulevard* lays out. We think of Los Angeles as having significant public or civic space only at the periphery: along the beaches and in the hilly recesses of Griffith Park. We spent much of the 20th century forgetting that in a city threaded together by great boulevards—some of them twice the length of Manhattan—we have an abundance of public space waiting to be claimed and used, if we can just bring ourselves to think of our built environment that way.

After the police officers who beat Rodney King were acquitted in a Simi Valley courtroom in April 1992, setting off weeks of violence and unrest in Los Angeles, many observers declared that Mike Davis and the bleak pessimism of *City of Quartz* had been validated. Davis won a MacArthur Grant, the so-called "Genius Award," and later applied his thesis of exclusionary urbanism, born of L.A., to places as diverse as Dubai and Lima.

But what if it turns out that history has confirmed Suisman's ideas about the boulevards too? Consider what has happened, after all, in Los Angeles since 1989. Where did the Rodney King unrest play out? On the street. The same is true of the massive immigration-rights protests—collectively known as the "Gran Marcha"—of 2006. And the Occupy protests of 2011. And the 2012 marches in Orange County against a series of shootings by Anaheim police. These marchers, these masses of people imagining or demanding a different future for their cities and their families, were relying on an almost defiantly classical definition of the city and of the public realm as they filled the streets and boulevards. In doing so they turned a number of seemingly immovable clichés about Los Angeles—principally that it has no public realm to begin with—on their heads while also prefiguring more recent protests in Cairo and Istanbul.

And it wasn't just protest or political activity more broadly that has redefined the boulevards or shone fresh light on their potential. In the last decade, and especially in the last five years, the boulevards of Los Angeles have finally managed to throw off the influence of the freeway system and reassert themselves as the place where the full spectrum of urban life—Suisman's "widest range of activities and behavior for the widest possible group of people"—has the chance to play out.

For much of the post-war period, every time we changed the design of a major Los Angeles street it was to make more room for car traffic; indeed we widened so many boulevards so aggressively that for a time it seemed we were trying to turn them into miniature freeways. But now nearly every change to an L.A. street is made in favor of the user who is not in a private car: the pedestrian, the cyclist, the commuter on a bus or train. New parks are being carved out along our boulevards. The car is finally being forced to share the road – and in a broader sense the L.A. street is being remade in a tremendously encouraging way. We are beginning to see it (again) as a place for gathering and for politics and not just as a conduit for moving cars from point A to point B.

This change is part of a major shift in the way Los Angeles thinks of itself. The city of the single-family residence is barely building standalone houses any longer; in recent years between 95 and 98 percent of the new residential units constructed in L.A. have been condominiums or apartments. At the same time, the city of the private car is no longer in the business of building new freeways and is expanding its mass-transit network into a comprehensive system for the first time since the heyday of the electric trolley car nearly a century ago.

We can find some of the earliest evidence of that change in *Los Angeles Boulevard.* Suisman's study combines the interests of an urban planner and architect with those of a scholar; it is an unusual hybrid of detailed history, urban theory, and prescriptive analysis. It is even stronger in the third category now that Suisman has added to it examples of his firm's work in Los Angeles, Pittsburgh, Hartford and the Palestinian territory, among other locations. But perhaps most of all *Los Angeles Boulevard* was and continues to be an efficient and elegantly written clarion call, a reminder that sitting at our feet, or under our wheels, is all the public space that a great city requires.

Introduction to the New Edition

by Doug Suisman

It has been twenty-five years since the work on *Los Angeles Boulevard* began. In 1987, I was a 32-year-old architect (born and educated on the East Coast) trying to make sense of the urbanism of Los Angeles. The city's urban form and particular way of urban life struck me as fascinating, baffling, inspiring, dismaying, and challenging. I was particularly intrigued by the main commercial avenues, generally called boulevards, which seemed both urban and suburban, intense and dispersed, exciting and deserted, all at once. My response was to begin a methodical study of the city and its boulevards—driving and walking along them, observing them, researching them, reading about them, writing about them, drawing them.

Based on these initial studies, in 1988 while teaching architecture at U.S.C., I presented an academic paper called "The New Boulevard: Parking and Public Life in Los Angeles," which established some of the main themes that interested me: the history of the city's urban form, the shape of its public space and the price of its privatization, the role of the automobile and public transport, and the array of architectural responses to these conditions.

At the same time, a new organization called the Los Angeles Forum for Architecture and Urban Design had begun a pamphlet series, beginning with Craig Hodgett's "Swimming to Suburbia." The Forum was supportive of my efforts, and in 1988 applied for and received a grant from the National Endowment for the Arts to cover the cost of publishing a new pamphlet based on the boulevard research. A year of writing, drawing and graphic design resulted in the 1989 publication of 1,500 copies of *Los Angeles Boulevard: Eight X-Rays of the Body Public.*

The pamphlet, distributed by Princeton Architectural Press to its various retail outlets, was well received and quickly sold out. This was long before the days of PDF files and the internet, so that once depleted, further distribution was limited. But the pamphlet's black-and-white content and standard size (an open spread was 8.5" x 11") made it easy and inexpensive to photocopy. For many years, I continued to see stapled photocopies being passed around by architecture students, or even handed out by their professors. Though the type and images grew increasingly fuzzy and scratched as copies were copied, I was pleased that the pamphlet seemed to have a life of its own as an urban design *samizdat*.

I kept a small number of originals for my office and personal use, but these were gradually given away, and eventually I found myself without a single copy left. Our office would regularly receive requests for a copy or inquiries as to where to get one. We finally decided to prepare a new master by photocopying the printer's proofs, and from that we were able to produce a fairly legible facsimile. We handed out a number of these, perhaps forty or more. But as the firm grew and our attention turned to real design problems and projects, the pamphlet came to seem less important—merely an early theoretical roadmap for the work that followed.

On several occasions the Los Angeles Forum raised the possibility of reissuing the pamphlet, and while I was very open to the idea, the press of current work always seemed to sidetrack us. So the project languished. Then in 2011, we quietly celebrated the 20th anniversary of Suisman Urban Design, and thought once again about a new edition. By coincidence, Christopher Hawthorne, the architecture critic of the *Los Angeles Times*, contacted me in early 2012 about a year-long project he was launching to take a fresh look at the boulevards. Perhaps the moment for a second edition had really arrived. Working with Robert Barrett, a long-time publications editor at Hennessey & Ingalls bookstore, we developed the text you have in your hands.

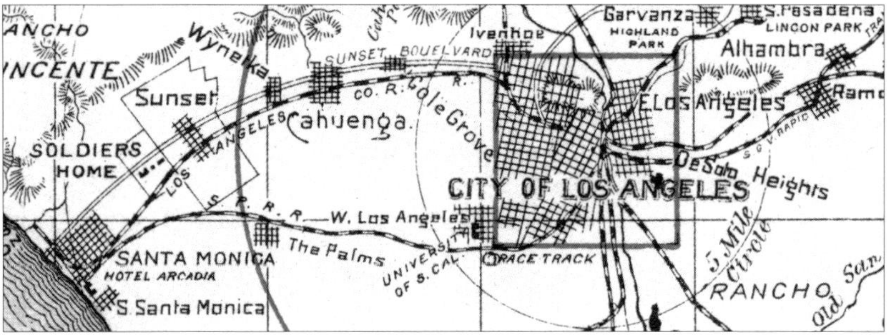

Map details showing the concept for Sunset, the first Los Angeles boulevard (Lankershim Ranch Land & Water Company Map, 1888)

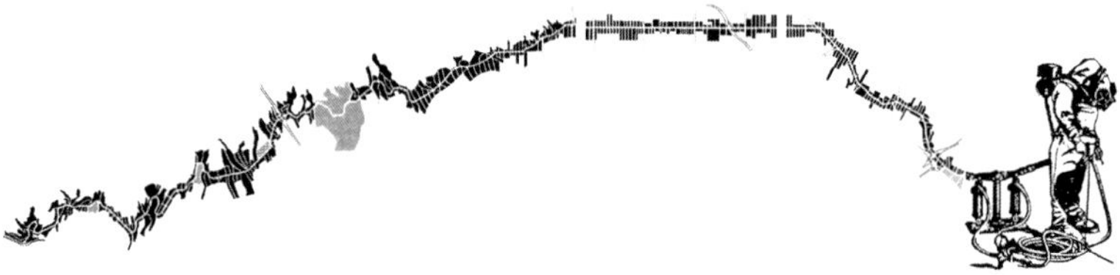

Figure-ground plan of Sunset Boulevard, shown as configured today and interpreted as umbilical infrastructure

Following Christopher Hawthorne's new foreword and this new introduction, you will find the original introduction and the eight "x-rays" —or chapters— of the pamphlet. The typography has been refreshed, but the words and images are nearly identical to the original, with just a few exceptions. One is the addition (at left) of a key detail from the elegant 1888 Lankershim Ranch map of Los Angeles. It is probably the first cartographic representation of any Los Angeles boulevard, in this case Sunset before it was actually built, presented with the striking misspelling of "bouelvard." The other key exception is the new front cover, which includes a heretofore unpublished axonometric diagram of the western half of Wilshire Boulevard. The companion drawing on the back cover is from the original pamphlet and shows the eastern half of Sunset Boulevard.

The second section begins with "Boulevard in Practice," a concise portfolio of ten boulevard projects or project groups that my firm has worked on from 1991 to 2012. Given the strong opinions expressed by the young but inexperienced author in 1989, it seemed appropriate to examine the extent to which theory survived as it transformed into practice over the following two decades. The lesson I draw from this body of work—aside from the durability of my love for cities, streets, public spaces, and cafés with strong coffee—is that each project has taught me something new about public space, and I focus on these lessons in the commentary.

The subject of streets and boulevards is really the inexhaustible subject of urban form and city living—the place where, in the terms Jane Jacobs used, the order of art and the order of life intersect. Those intersections, both literal and metaphorical, are the places where I have had the joy and good fortune to practice the art I know—making city places. I hope the reader will take equal pleasure. This work is never done alone, but almost always in a framework of noisy, passionate, contentious, creative collaboration. How else could cities, the most complex human artifacts, arise? This edition is dedicated to the many colleagues, clients, and citizens with whom and for whom, over two decades, we have had the privilege of designing boulevards.

Acknowledgements

For the 1989 first edition

My thanks to The Los Angeles Forum for Architecture and Urban Design for creating the original pamphlet series, and the Forum's Christian Hubert and Aaron Betsky for their help and support in getting the project published; the Design Arts Program of the National Endowment for the Arts for funding the project; the late Klaus Herdeg, Richard Ingersoll, Mary McLeod, Robert Harris, the late Catherine Brown, and William Morrish for their support in obtaining the NEA grant; and Deborah Brochstein, Lorrain Wild, Jodee Kulp, the staff at Graphic Arts Services, and Marsha Burgeson, for their help in the book design and production; Robert Freem, former Los Angeles City archivist, for help in researching the first boulevards; former student Tony K.H. Jen for research and some of the figure-ground plans; my former students at the University of Minnesota for their boulevard studies; and the late Lee Buckley for her generous editing, support, and encouragement throughout. This publication was supported by two grants from the Design Arts Program of the National Endowment for the Arts: an Organization Grant to the Los Angeles Forum of Architecture and Urban Design, and an Individual Advancement Grant to the author.

For the 2014 second edition

I would like offer heartfelt thanks to the following: The Los Angeles Forum for Architecture and Urban Design and Tom Marble for encouraging me to produce a second edition; Janet Sager for her sustained help in making the project happen; my editor Robert Barrett for his expertise and encouragement; Greg Goldin and the Architecture + Design Museum for their interest in boulevards and this project; Christopher Hawthorne for his revival of interest in the boulevards and his extraordinary support of this project; Eli Garsilazo at Suisman Urban Design for his exceptional design work on many of the boulevard projects and his patient support of this effort; our many Suisman Urban Design co-workers and colleagues across twenty-three years for taking on the challenge of boulevard design; James Mary O'Connor for his three decades of friendship and encouragement on all things boulevard, including this book; finally at home, Moye Thompson for her loving, sustained encouragement and her enthusiasm for the book and its return to print, and Claire and Teddy, who share with me their experience of Los Angeles boulevards in a way I never can...as natives.

For 25 years of boulevard partnership and collaboration

Peachtree Street
Heather Clendenin
Turk Kaufman
Mark Treib
Greg Tung
Mary Comerio

Electric Trolley Bus
Nick Patsaouras
ICF Kaiser Engineers
DMJM
Olin Partnership
Barrio Planners

Hill Street
ZGF
Melendrez Associates
Charles Loveman
Tom Gilmore

Market Court
Melendrez Associates
Brian Mitchell
Ann Mueller Peaks
Filomena Eriman
Gloria Uchida

Civic Center
Dan Rosenfeld
Melendrez Associates
Johnson Fain
RAW Architects
Rolan Wiley
Steve Lewis

Grand Avenue
Olin Partnership
Francis Krahe
Kim Yasuda
Ayahlushim Hammond

Metro Rapid
Rex Gephart, Metro
Russ Chisholm, TMD
Julie Silliman
Martha Welborne

Hollywood Media District
Mary Lou Dudas
Tim Mahoney
Helmi Hisserich

First Street
Ed Avila
Campbell & Campbell
Rios Clementi Hale
Karen Yamamoto

La Plaza de Cultura y Artes
Ed Avila
Rios Clementi Hale
Chu + Gooding

Allegheny City
Pittsburgh Children's Museum
Jane Werner
Chris Siefert

The Arc
RAND Corporation
Michael Rich
Ross Anthony
Steve Simon
Mary Vaiana
Michael Schoenbaum
Glenn Robinson
Ann Kerr
Hiba Husseini
Arthur Winter
Chris Tucker
Jerry Green
Guilford Glazer
Diane Glazer
Jihad El-Wazir
Bassem El-Wazir
James Bennet

iQuilt Plan
Ronna Reynolds
David Fay
Tyler Smith
Michael Vergason
Beata Corcoran
Doug Hayes
Domingo Gonzalez
Nancy Lok
Bill Richter
Norman Garrick
Kevin Perry
Jarret Walker
David Panagore
Jonas Maciunas
Bonnie Malley
Jackie Mandyck
Bob Patricelli
Oz Griebel
Mayor Pedro Segarra
Mike Stotts
Suzanne Hopgood
Susan Talbott
Kim Reynolds
Patty Hickson
Matt Poland
Richard Frieder
Sally Whipple
Michael Zaleski
Joe Marfuggi
Carl Bard
Eric Daniels
Andy Bassette
Tom Luszczak
Chuck Sheehan
William DiBella
Shep Holcombe
Tom Nenortas
Terry Gellin
Sam Schrager
Walter Wick
Caitlin Narkawicz
Kat Niedmann
Sally Taylor
Jennifer DiBella

Suisman Urban Design
Miriam Bartoli
Alan Chan
Eli Garsilazo
Steve LaRocque
Erick Rodriguez
Janet Sager
Mark Stankard
Doug Suisman

Manuel Barrios
Alexis Bennett
Aron Carcamo
Amanda Carlson
Helen Choi
Sean Christensen
Peter Drasnin
Bill Duncan
Robert Franklin
Gabriel Golden
Javier Gomez
Thurman Grant
Jack Hartley
Mette Heide
Tony K.H. Jen
Robin Kim
Zhiwei Liao
Jamie Meyer
Armando Mtz-Celis
Lisa Padilla
Tony Paradowski
Alpana Prajapati
Tarek Qaadumi
Guoping Shi
Kevin Short
Bianca Siegl
Kate Spanbock
Cliff Spencer
Tulasi Srinivas
Alexis Taylor
Deborah Torres
Daniel Windsor
Ashley Zarella
Mazen Zoabi

Los Angeles Boulevard

Eight X-Rays of the Body Public

Introduction

For a long time, my most cherished assumption about urbanity was that it was something you could see. I depended on those glimpses of urban streets and the blurred hustle of people on the sidewalks to produce that potent mix of anxiety and excitement we call city life. Sounds and smells played a part of course... the peculiar two-note braying of European sirens or the mossy fragrance of New York's sidewalk steam could conjure up vivid and detailed streetscapes. But these served mainly to intensify an essentially visual drama, played out between the immobility of stone and the mesmerizing flicker of human activity.

This personal axiom of visible urbanity was abruptly challenged six years ago when I first saw the boulevards of Los Angeles. Along their edges, dense with architectural trash and treasure, the absence of an equally vibrant sidewalk activity evoked for me a sad suggestion of abandonment, as if the city had once throbbed, but now barely fluttered. Even with Reyner Banham's sunny reassurance that Wilshire Boulevard was "one of the only great streets in the world where driving is a pleasure", and his warning not to measure it against the "sacred Labyrinths" of older cities[1], I soon found myself obsessed by L.A.'s great riddle: can a city be a city without appearing to be one? I've been looking for answers on the boulevard.

The fact that the boulevards are barely recognized by their mother city does not make this search any easier. In the world according to the Los Angeles Department of Public Works, the city is comprised of major and secondary highways, collector streets, and service roads – but no boulevards.[2] The street naming policy adopted by the City and County in 1967 requires that all new east-west thoroughfares be called "avenues", all north-south thoroughfares "streets".[3] Even for existing roads, the County's policy is that "the use of suffixes such as Drive, Place, Way, Boulevard, Street or Avenue should not be considered as part of the basic name." The mellifluous category of boulevard is thus reduced to an irrelevant "suffix." And no wonder. As great public corridors, the boulevards themselves have been all but abandoned, delivered without apparent regret to the splintering effects of technical and economic determinism. Consider the boulevard's cross-section, balkanized beyond recognition into the following domains: overall width (Department of City Planning), roadbed surface (Bureau of Engineering), traffic lanes, lighting, signals, and parking structures (Department of Transportation), underground and overhead utilities (Department of Water and Power), trees and planting (Department of Parks and Recreation), sidewalks and adjoining building heights and setbacks (Building Department), building use and general character (private banks, brokers, and developers), building materials and specific character (private engineers and architects). There is no single authority responsible for the integration of all these forces, and thus no official conception of what it means to be a boulevard in the nation's largest and soon most populous city.

This pamphlet is an attempt to champion the boulevards as significant urban creations – with their own histories, their own architecture, their own politics – and to address some of the thorny formal and social questions which they raise. In some respects this is working backwards, for the boulevards have often been regarded...indeed have often been...the mere resultants of the various urban pressures brought to bear on them. I want to reverse this conception, and imagine the boulevard not as the passive and invisible receptor of inexorable forces, but as the stage on which we explicitly debate – through construction – the nature of the modern city, especially in the ongoing experiment called Los Angeles.

That the boulevards exist in the minds of many people is beyond doubt, despite the demurring of the agencies mentioned above. I have so far counted over ninety major thoroughfares which are clearly labeled "boulevard" on everything from cocktail napkins to freeway exits, which would suggest an empirically definable species, albeit a species characterized – like almost everything related to the physical environment of Los Angeles – by roughly equal measures of sparkling regularity and riotous inconsistency. Some streets called boulevards hardly live up to the name, and others designated as mere avenues have clearly been short-changed, but in general, we can tell a Los Angeles boulevard when we see one because it: 1) makes arterial connections on a metropolitan scale, 2) provides a framework for civic and

BOULEVARDS

Adams
Alondra
Artesia
Avalon
Balboa
Balboa (Newport)
Baldwin Park
Barham
Beach
Bellflower
Beverly
Brand (Glendale)
Brand (S.Fernando)
Burbank
Cahuenga
California
Canada
Centinela
Century
Chatauqua
Colorado
Compton
Crenshaw
Culver
Del Amo
East Orange Grove
El Segondo
Exposition
Foothill
Garden Grove
Gateway
Glendale
Griffith Park
Hacienda
Harbor
Harbor (Newport)
Hawthorne
Hollywood
Jamboree
Jefferson
La Cienega
La Mirada
La Tijera

Lakewood
Lankershim
Laurel Canyon
Lincoln
Lomita
Long Beach
Los Feliz
MacArthur
Magnolia
Manhattan Beach
Martin Luther King
National
Newport
Norwalk
Ocean Park
Olympic
Pacific
Paramount
Pico
Ramona
Redondo Beach
Reseda
Robertson
Roscoe
San Vicente
San Vicente (S. Monica)
Santa Monica
Sawtelle
Sepulveda
Sierra Madre
Sunland
Sunset
Topanga Canyon
Torrance
Tweedy
Valley
Ventura
Victory
Washington
Washington (Pasadena)
Westwood
Whittier
Wilshire
York

commercial destinations, and 3) acts as a filter to adjacent residential neighborhoods.

On this basis it is easy to distinguish boulevards from freeways, which have no destinations, and from strips, which have no neighborhoods. When viewed as an integrated system, the boulevards establish the city's overall physical structure, a fact which will come as a surprised to the million of honest people who have been misled into thinking that Los Angeles is a city organized by its freeways; Los Angeles is a city whose freeways have been organized by its boulevards. The freeways respectfully cut under or bridge over them, curve to avoid them, extend ramps down to them, and announce their names on large illuminated signs. As a good subway system serves the avenues, the freeways serve the boulevards.

But the boulevards do more than establish an organizational pattern. They constitute, I believe, the irreducible armature of the city's public space, and as such are charged with a social and political significance that we can hardly ignore. Public space by definition must allow for the widest range of activities and behavior for the widest possible group of people; anything short of this means that some authority is restricting the use of the space in ways that strip it of its liberating and revelatory function. This definition surely lays to rest the occasional claims that in Los Angeles, the public realm is to be found on the freeways and beaches. The freeways may be publicly financed and owned, but they are among the most highly controlled environments in the world. The miles of beautiful beaches are a source of great pride, and in their egalitarian mix of people and open access to virtually anyone, they are truly public places; but they are no more the public realm of Los Angeles than Central Park is the public realm of New York. Urban parks, whether downtown or by the shore, are only specialized recreational extensions of the public domain of the city, and do not even begin to approach the full measure of a city's public life.

This "public life" is difficult to define, but it suggests the spontaneous dramatization of who we are as a people. Some have suggested that this social portraiture has less and less to do with physical places in the city, and ever more to do with the electronic media. Certainly political and social debate takes "place", for most Americans, in the print media and especially on television. Television is extraordinarily efficient and broad in scope, but it interposes a screen – the medium itself – between experience and interpretation, and is thus highly vulnerable to manipulation. Indeed the more television pervades, the more important the public environment becomes as a touchstone for measuring the real. We cling, and properly so, to the idea that even if we have heard of some circumstance on television, we can still reserve judgment until we go and "see for ourselves." Such direct sight, indeed such insight, is forever embedded in the concept of a public realm.[4] As technology continues to dematerialize our activities and thereby erodes the functioning of physical places, it becomes all the more important to recognize the boulevard as the critical thread of an endangered public realm.

The history of public streets shows, however, that such high-minded social and political purpose rarely provides the impetus for street development. Technical, economic and authoritarian goals are usually the real engines of intervention, despite claims of social or aesthetic intent. The boulevards of Paris, admired today for their beauty and social vitality, were largely the result of a stagnant economy, working-class insurrection, and a series of cholera epidemics. In the same way, the boulevards of Los Angeles are primarily shaped by concerns for fire and seismic protection, security against crime, automobile traffic and parking, and the elbowing of an unfettered market economy. It often seems that the boulevard has so many economic and technical tasks to satisfy that to hope it will foster democratic behavior, reflect the true conditions of limits. We have come to view the boulevard like an airplane, on which the exigencies of safety and technique are so obviously compelling that we willingly sacrifice our political principles, social habits and aesthetic satisfaction in exchange for simply getting somewhere in one piece.

Occasional protests against this reduction of the street to utilitarian status, or of the public realm to economic servility, are usually dismissed as either naïve or reactionary, standing in the way of history. Should we therefore let the public space of the boulevards slowly expire as the last vestige of an outdated urban form, or even try, as did Le Corbusier and others, to kill it once and for all? I wonder. The history of urban technology reveals that in almost every instance, the enthusiasm for the new is soon tempered by unanticipated consequences of change, both in physical and moral terms. In our own time, the trend is towards privatization – of police power, of public works, of public space. The pseudo-public streets seen in many commercial and residential developments are deeply troubling, for they give the illusion of public space when in fact individual behavior is restricted by forces – often camouflaged – of private control. If we are in fact going to abandon public space as the proving ground of free behavior and the most reliable mirror of social conditions, then such and abandonment ought to be a matter of explicit public policy rather than the product of an insidious erosion, always justified on technical or economic grounds.

Architects play a key role in this process, but I am afraid that as a profession we contribute, wittingly or not, to the decline of the boulevards as public realm. In one way or another, all architecture is public architecture. Our awareness grows daily of the interdependence of all material systems, and it is hard to conceive of an architectural project which has virtually no impact on some aspect of the collective environment. And yet, while lawyers are exhorted to uphold justice and doctors to care for the public's health, architects are rarely encouraged to do more than seek the private satisfactions of the artist on the one hand, or of the businessman on the other. It should come as no surprise that the public regards the profession with a certain distrust. Until we are explicitly relieved of the responsibility, the guardianship of the public environment ought to be the architect's highest calling. From the largest-scale planning projects to the smallest renovation, the architect has the unique capacity to satisfy all technical and economic claims and still reinforce the free and open nature of public space.

A first step is the careful formal analysis of the structure of that public space, especially in the problematic form it has taken in the American automotive city. As a tentative step in that direction I have tried, in the eighth and final essay entitled "Fuselage: Cross-Sections of the Public Realm", to suggest ways of looking at the interrelationship of street, building, and car, and its effect on public space. That essay is preceded by seven other which attempt to chart, in a somewhat overlapping chronology, notable developments in the history of the boulevards. All the essays are, at best, highlights of a complex evolution, a comprehensive treatment of which has yet to be written. They are starting points, a handful of radiological snap-shots which, like all x-rays, only tell part of the story.

1 Suture

The Pueblo/Rancho Landscars

> **"Confusion is a word we have invented for an order which is not understood."**
>
> —HENRY MILLER

> **"Wounds heal and become scars. But scars grow with us."**
>
> —STAINISLAW LEC, "UNKEMPT THOUGHTS"

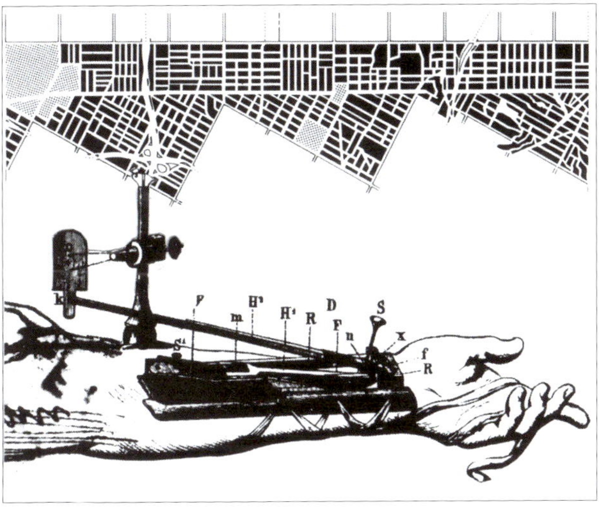

The birth of the boulevards did not occur on virgin terrain. If the surface of a landscape is a kind of skin on which incisions are made by human settlement, then the archeological sites of cities are often comprised of little more than the scars of such incisions, the cicatrix that remains after all the layers of construction and civilization have crumbled and blown away. In inhabited cities, theses old scars may be enmeshed in a more recent intaglio, but they are seldom completely hidden. The Spanish were the first Europeans to carve up and distribute the lands of greater Los Angeles under a system of public and private land ownership, and the ground-scars of their activity still engrave the city. In many places, the boulevards of modern Los Angeles are the most tangible record of that surgical legacy.

By the time the Spanish arrived in the area to establish a new pueblo—or civil settlement—in 1781, they had nearly three centuries of experience in the subjugation and settlement of the hemisphere.[1] Los Angeles was simply one of the last, most remote, and least important exercises in the Spanish imperial art of town-founding. Established for no other reason than to raise food for the royal troops garrisoned in the region, it was nonetheless laid out according to the same 1573 Laws of the Indies which had shaped virtually every one of the thousands of Spanish colonial villages, towns and cities, from Chile to California: a rectangular plaza in the middle, a church and government house on the plaza's perimeter, a roughly orthogonal grid of streets spreading outward from the plaza, and a square pueblo boundary of two leagues (5.25 miles) per side.[2] In California, this administrative stamp – which was to remain under Spanish control for only forty years, and then under Mexican control for another twenty-five – generally ignored the territorial claims of the native American tribes.

When American forces arrived to take control of Los Angeles after the defeat of Mexico in 1848, they found a frontier pueblo that was little more than a ramshackle village floating in the center of its huge 28-square-mile frame.[3] A young lieutenant named Ord was charged with the task of surveying this new American property and imposing on it some kind of blueprint for growth. Ord had to work with what little he had, fixing the still unsurveyed pueblo boundaries from a center point at the front door of the plaza church, and extending the town to the north and south with two separate grids which were slightly skewed to accommodate existing street irregularities – the small grid to the north is the framework for today's Chinatown, the much larger grid to the south for almost all of what now constitutes "Downtown". The most significant fact is that Ord passed up the opportunity to realign the city grid on a true north-south compass which would have simultaneously made the streets parallel to the pueblo boundary and brought them in to conformance with standard practice for American townships. Thus the original plaza's diagonal orientation – prescribed by the 1573 Laws as a Vitruvian technique for breaking prevailing winds – set into motion the sequence of diagonal grid planning efforts which, in their cumulative effect, were still powerful enough in the 1960's and 70's to force the reorientation of virtually all of the major freeways as they pass through the downtown area.

Ord's two grids covered only a small area of the pueblo...given the town's anemic character in 1848, he may have justifiably concluded that it would take decades for the gridded areas to fill up. But a mere five years later, another Army surveyor named Hancock was called upon to map out the land all the way to the pueblo boundaries. The famous Hancock Survey

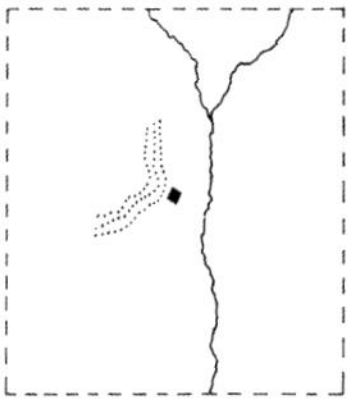

1781
Pueblo Founding

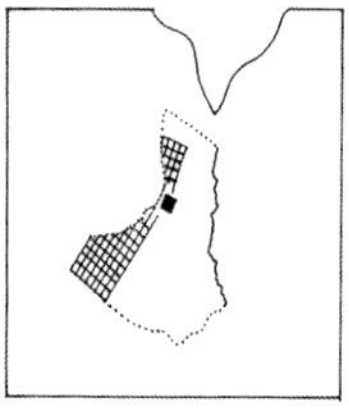

1848
Ord's Survey

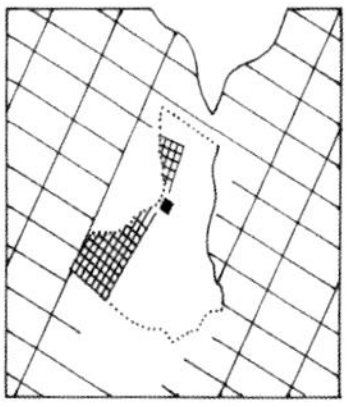

1853
Hancock's Survey

realigned and extended Ord's grid just as Ord had done with the Spanish grid. But while Ord's blocks and lots had closely matched the fine grain of the existing town, Hancock's grid was on the super scale of U.S. Land Survey which had been in effect since 1783: streets every half-mile in one direction and every mile in the other. The resulting super-blocks were far too big for direct subdivision, and would all require a later superposition of a finer mesh of streets and blocks before actual building lots could be sold off. In this way, Hancock planted the first real seeds of the boulevard system, whose large-scale intervals would prove perfectly suited to a city with so much territory to cover.

The scar of each of these operations is still apparent, and not only to someone with a map. Most of the major boulevards on the periphery of downtown conform to Hancock's plan, as do certain unusual streets like Micheltorena, which follows the path laid down by Hancock straight up into the hills with San Franciscan stubbornness, making it one of the steepest streets in the city. The effects of both the Ord and Hancock plans are particularly apparent at their boundaries: the critical downtown section of the Harbor Freeway was built in a large gap between the two surveys, while the kink in Figueroa at Pico marks the point where the street passes from one system to the other. Along Hoover Street, which marks the western boundary of the pueblo, the diagonal streets and obliquely disposed buildings of the east side belong to Hancock's survey, while the neat perpendiculars of the west side owe their disposition to the township grid subsequently imposed on the old common lands just beyond the pueblo boundary.

These areas outside the pueblo have a different story. Virtually all of the territory of the region—other than the exceptional areas set aside as missions—was either designated as common land for the exclusive use of the pueblo, or as a rancho to be conferred as property to individuals by grant, initially from the Crown itself, but later from vice regal or gubernatorial authorities.[4] Most of the City of Los Angeles and indeed of the entire County is stamped by the pattern of these entities far more than by the pueblo itself, whose once vast surface of nearly 28 square miles now accounts for a mere 6% of the total area of the city proper. The history of the boulevards, which run for miles across the basin, is one of a laborious stitching together of this triple Spanish legacy of pueblo, rancho, and common land.

The layout of the ranchos did not usually follow the same principles of geometric regularity as the pueblo itself.[5] While very little was left to chance in the Spanish Empire, it appears that regulations concerning the form of large-scale agricultural lands were somewhat fluid, varying from region to region. In Los Angeles, the pattern of rancho designation was based more on local topological conditions and the limitations of surveying technology than on any theoretical planning system. Most large-scale land divisions are a combination of straight lines and existing natural edges; the larger the area and the more irregular its topography, the more technically difficult it becomes to impose a boundary that is both simple and verifiable. Many of the ranchos were even larger than the pueblo, and the pre-settlement terrain of the region was deceptively complex: the absence of soil-stabilizing vegetation combined with torrential rains produced a land surface that was furrowed with gulleys and washes, so that even in relatively flat areas, Cartesian geometry often fell before nature. Of the fifty-three Spanish and Mexican ranchos, only tiny Escorpion in the western San Fernando Valley is a perfect rectangle; virtually all fifty-two others are defined by boundaries of varying irregularity. As for the common lands, they were, under Spanish law, not for sale, and as a result they remained relatively free of private development until well after the American takeover. By that time, American surveying standards and technology permitted the imposition of the highly regular U.S. Land Survey system of division over large areas of previously undivided land.

West of the pueblo, this regularity lasts only for the clear mile and a half or so before the rancho lands begin, when, like a perfect jet formation suddenly buffeted by turbulence, the boulevards begin to take off in erratic directions. One look at the overall map of the Ranchos explains why, for here in the center of the zone between the pueblo and the sea was the region's densest concentration of small ranchos. With their inconsistent configurations and sometimes rapid succession of different owners, the ranchos were developed at different periods and often with entirely different patterns. The boulevards therefore tend to traverse the different ranchos in one of two ways: either by twisting to conform to changing street grids, or by following the boundary lines between them, where pre-existing development was usually the lightest. Hence Pico Boulevard runs straight from the Pacific for almost three miles, precisely conforming to the shared boundary of four different ranchos, while an extended central section of Wilshire Boulevard marks the boundary of Rancho La Brea to the north and Rancho Las Cienegas to the south, accounting for the marked difference of block patterns on either side. And much of San Vicente Boulevard, whose exceptions diagonal position suggests a far more important arterial connector, is simply following the diagonal southeastern boundary of the Rancho La Brea.

The formal correspondence of the city's modern boulevards to historic patterns of settlement could be dismissed as a mere footnote to the grander metropolitan text of freeways and decentralization, especially in the light

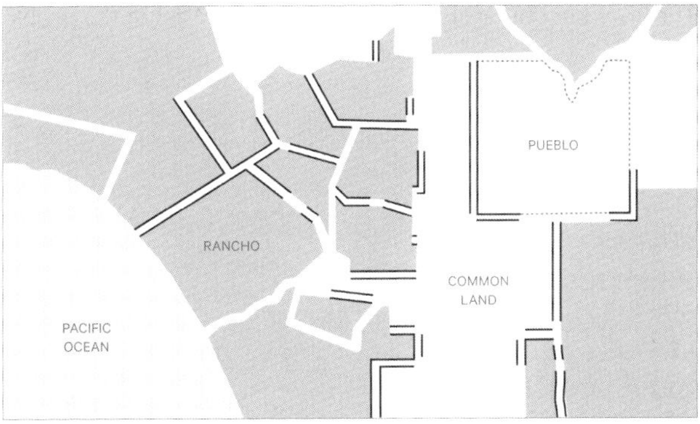

Segments of existing boulevards which correspond to rancho or pueblo boundaries

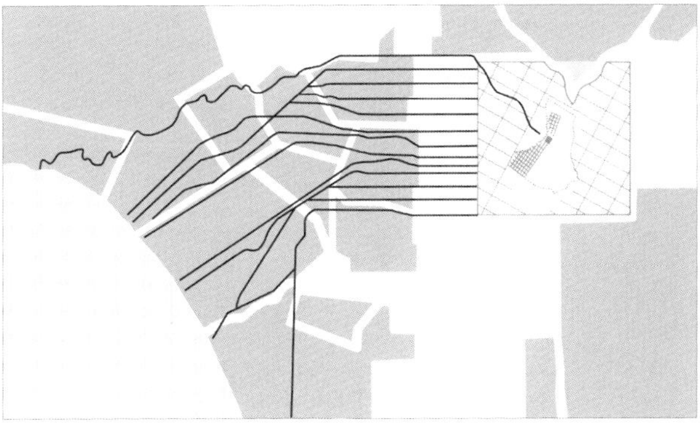

Modern conditions, showing the major east-west boulevards in relationship to the rancho boundaries and the pueblo street grid

of newer, non-physical conceptions of the urban realm. But the material record of daily life in Los Angeles finds us moving—on foot and in motor vehicles—along urban corridors whose very position of the land we cannot explain without a knowledge of conditions which have long disappeared from view. This would suggest a radiological view of the urban landscape in a city far better known for its dermatoplasty. By looking through the surface both for persistent structures and catalytic events, the ostensible confusion and randomness of the pattern of boulevards is instead revealed as a (mostly) logical consequence of historical conditions. Far from a post-Second World War phenomenon, the boulevards reflect tensions dating back almost 150 years, when an aggressive mercantile culture began to impose its stamp on the agrarian province of a dying empire. The pattern which has emerged is, in Venturi's words, one whose "order is not obvious".[6] A combination of quilt and collage, it is characterized by operations of both joinery and overlay. As they move across pueblo, rancho, and common land, the boulevards bind up the wounds of space and time.

It was all prices to them: they never looked at it: why should they look at the land? they were Empire Builders: it was all in the bid and the asked and the ink on their books.

—ARCHIBALD MACLEISH, "WILDWEST"

2 Umbilical

The Spawning of Sunset Boulevards

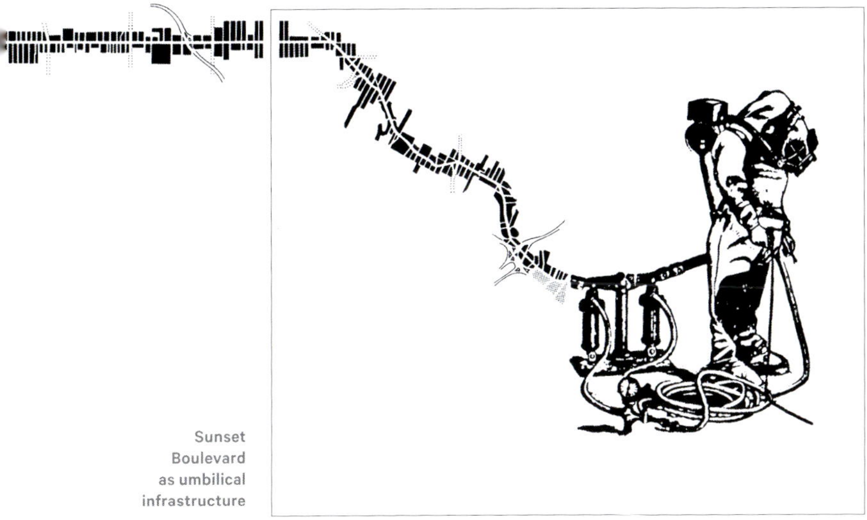

Sunset Boulevard as umbilical infrastructure

For over half a century, from 1870 to 1920, the detailed business of the Los Angeles City Council was painstakingly transcribed by hand in nearly one hundred heavy leather-bound folios, each weighing as much as a small sack of cement. This whole elephantine collection is now stored in a rather bleak warehouse structure that serves as the city archives; and as you lift open the covers and begin to scan the broad pages, now somewhat brittle and musty, the impression emerges of an incipient twentieth century metropolis struggling with the limited tools of a provincial municipal apparatus. Each page is organized into neatly spaced lines of black ink for regular business and red ink for adopted ordinances. The elegant script, which was produced with a rhythmic alternation from ink well to paper, surges to ornate flourishes on the capital letters which begin each paragraph, evidence of a rather ceremonial administrative sensibility. The whole work is broken down into daily entries, with each new date written large on the top of a fresh page, like chapter headings in a Victorian diary. Half way down the page entitled "November 14th, 1892", the following terse entry appears: "From Geo. H. Smith et. al. asking that a street be established 100 feet wide to be called Sunset Boulevard". There was apparently little interest in the proposal, for no discussion is recorded, and the matter does not reappear in the City Council minutes for almost a year. But this inconspicuous notation of 1892 is very likely the first use of the term "boulevard" in the official proceedings of a city which would eventually endow the trans-metropolitan boulevard with a character and a scale it had never possessed before.

That such a momentous development should emerge from an obscure initiative on the part of a group of private citizens seems perplexing until you correlate an 1889 property map of Los Angeles with the site description which accompanied the proposal: "...commencing at the junction of Beaudry Avenue with Bellevue Avenue, along Elysian Park Avenue, along Reservoir Street, along the railroad track, thence by the most suitable line to the city line". The Smith group's strategy was to combine several existing railroad and street right-of-ways with a limited amount of new street construction in order to create an important new link between the central business district and the northwest corner of the city; any property along it would significantly increase in value. Only someone entirely unfamiliar with the city's tempestuous history of unrestrained land speculation will be surprised to discover that the two major undeveloped tracts along the boulevard are labeled on the map as the property of "Geo. Patten & G.H. Smith", and "G.H. Smith" respectively. The scheme for the city's first boulevard appears to have sprung to life not from city planning authorities with a grand vision, but from private landowners looking for high profit at low risk.

It turns out, however, that although Smith and friends were the first to propose a boulevard within the Los Angeles municipal limits—i.e. within the old pueblo boundary—they were in 1892 only the latest in a series of regional developers who had seized on the idea of a street called Sunset Boulevard. The name seems to have come into existence a full five years earlier in 1887, during the middle of what has been called "the largest land boom in America history".[1] It was catalyzed mainly by the recent arrival of the Santa Fe Railroad, the city's first direct link to the rest of the country (the Southern Pacific had arrived nine years earlier but it went north through San Francisco before heading east). Much of the boom centered on the frenzied acquisition and subdivision of the huge Spanish and Mexican ranchos which surrounded the municipality on all sides. To accomplish this enormous task, the patient art of mapmaking was pressed into emergency service by property salesmen anxious to blur the line between real estate and reality: a vast tract of rancho grazing land with little more than scattered shacks and barns would be quickly surveyed, platted, numbered, mapped and christened to imply—with two-dimensional ambiguity—the existence of an elegant resort town with tree-lined avenues and a grand hotel. Over one hundred of these "paper towns" blossomed during the boom, with the majority eventually fading into the same void from which they sprang.[2] One of these was "The Town of Sunset", the creation of a group called the Sunset

Development Company, which had purchased intact the thousands of acres of the old Rancho Santa Fe de Buenos Ayres. Though four miles distant from the setting sun at the coast, the town was ostensibly endowed with magnificent homes, a ravishing central hotel, and a principle avenue called, naturally, Sunset Boulevard. The venture failed, but it established a conceptual precedent for the later development of Westwood. The particular winding path of the Town of Sunset's main boulevard now corresponds to Wilshire Boulevard passing through Westwood, but the origins of both the name and the idea of a Sunset Boulevard appear to lie in this aborted developer's dream.

This Sunset Boulevard may have been the first, but it was not the last. In the same year, an east-west road called Sunset Boulevard showed up on the subdivision maps of at least two other 1887 boom towns, one of them a paper town called "Cahuenga" (in the area where West Hollywood now stands) and the second a more successful development called "Hollywood". Sunset Boulevards were apparently popping up everywhere, and yet do not show up on official maps of the period. Did these Sunset Boulevards exist, or were they "paper" boulevards?

A good portion of these roads in plan appear to have existed in reality, although they may have been little more than dusty bridle paths. Of great importance, however, is that they appear to have been fragments of an existing urban scheme of remarkable simplicity and power. In 1888, an extraordinary

Diagrammatic plan showing the various proposals for Sunset Boulevards around 1892

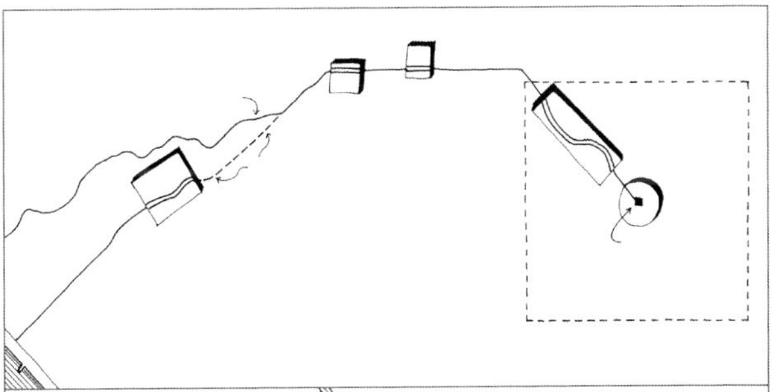

A map of Broadway in New York for scale comparison

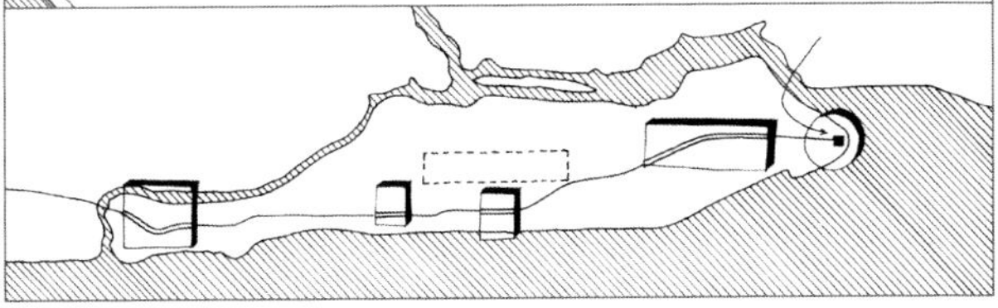

map was distributed by another development group, the Lankershim Ranch Company in the San Fernando Valley.[3] The map was not the usual promotional subdivision plan (although the Lankershim Ranch was quite understandably high-lighted in red), but rather a diagrammatic representation of the entire Los Angeles region, one year after the boom had collapsed. With great clarity it showed almost all of the towns of the region, both existing and projected, connected by a network of interurban rail lines... at a smaller scale it could have been the subway map of a major European capital. But while these railroad connections were emphasized, the map also presented two – and only two – surface roads, both originating in downtown Los Angeles. The eastbound road formed a connection to Pasadena; the westbound road connected downtown to the sea in a single sweeping arc of striking geometric grace. It was labeled "Sunset Boulevard" (see p. 16). Somewhere in the city, someone had conceived of an urban boulevard which curved across the open landscape for nearly fifteen miles.

The Sunset Boulevard of the Lankershim map corresponds quite closely to the path of the Sunset Boulevards of the Smith proposal and the three towns of Hollywood, Caheunga, Sunset, and it therefore seems likely that the planning of each of these developments was based on some awareness of a proposed overland link. Arrayed like pearls on a bowstring, the towns were also connected—on paper at least—by a rail line which ran parallel to the boulevard, but which tended

WHAT'S A BOULEVARD?

Originally neither a street nor French, boulevard derives from the German "bulwark", whose literal meaning was "plank-work", referring generally to any defensive wall; in Dutch it became "bolwerc", and subsequently "belouart" in Old French. Its meaning gradually changed from the wall itself to the ground-plane just outside it, always kept clear in order to deprive an enemy of cover. The city of Paris had been surrounded for centuries by such walls, but in 1670, Louis XIV made the momentous decision to turn his capital into an open city by demolishing the circle of protective ramparts. On the open boulevards, now even wider with the walls removed, the king ordered the planting of trees in regular rows to create an avenue, with "contre-allées", or parallel paths, on either side; the old gates in the walls were replace with freestanding triumphal arches. In this way, the boulevard was finally transformed from a wall to the ground-plane to a green, monumental street corridor. Two hundred years later, Haussmann and Napoleon III simply updated the royal model and imposed it all over the city, often in places where no wall had ever stood. The boulevard was reborn as a portable tool of urban transformation.[4]

to pass through a more southerly part of each town. The railroad would apparently provide the "heavy-duty" service link, while the boulevard promised a tree-lined artery for pleasure and prestige... it was usually the boulevard, and not the railroad track, which passed in front of the fancy resort hotels. Together they created a kind of double umbilical cord, connecting the "mother" pueblo to urban offspring, and linking all of them to the vital force of the sea.

For all the economic logic of these proposals, it is still difficult to know how wildcat real estate men in a remote western town could have alighted on the notion of a boulevard. In 1997, a boulevard was virtually synonymous with Paris (see Inset). Haussmann had completed his work less than twenty years earlier, and engravings of the new capital of the western world were widely disseminated in illustrated magazines; but would these have been well known in California? And why would such an image have taken hold in Los Angeles, when even cosmopolitan San Francisco had not worked up the presumption to rename its major thoroughfares boulevards? A partial explanation may lie at the corner of Main and 3rd Streets where, at least as early as 1889, there stood a rarely mentioned but exceptional structure. A voluminous 16-sided polygon rising to three-stories, it was L.A.'s own version of that quintessential 19th century phenomenon, the panorama.[5] In its archetypal form, the panorama was comprised of a central structural tower containing a staircase which provided public access to the ring-shaped viewing balconies. From there, audiences could survey the surrounding interior walls, smoothly curved, rising to the height of operatic stage sets, and covered by a hand-painted, meticulously rendered 360 degree view of a great urban or natural landscape. Some panoramas actually anticipated cinematography by rotation the scene around the viewers. The experience of even an immobile panorama created a sensation because of its scale

Paris in L.A.: view of the Panorama on Main Street in downtown Los Angeles c. 1889

and verisimilitude—Queen Victoria reportedly felt seasick while viewing a maritime panorama in London[6]—and would have been especially mesmerizing for the residents of a prosperous but remote frontier town. At the Los Angeles panorama of 1889, this nearly magical form of representation was devoted not to prairie landscapes of the Plains or the streets of an East Coast city, but to the 1870 Battle of Paris.[7] Through the smoke and cannon fire, a vivid image of Haussman's Paris must have emerged. Any curiosity aroused might well have been augmented by the rater surprising presence of a significant French community, whose prosperity and influence extended as far as the creation of a French hospital in the city.[8]

In such an urban atmosphere, at once crude and sophisticated, provincial and cosmopolitan, who knows what urban visions might have been inspired. Certainly any suggestion of outdoor cafes and the shady luxury of tree-lined sidewalks would have seemed climatically transferable. The formality of Parisian urbanity—both social and physical—may strike us as an almost comically inappropriate model for such a freewheeling city, but in 1889 Los Angeles had not yet embraced iconoclasm in all its forms. It was struggling with a more tentative dialectic between, of one hand, a centralized provincial city of solid masonry public buildings, modern cable cars, and bursting civic ambition; and, on the other, a regional constellation of independent towns dependent on some form of linear attachment. The Parisian boulevard may well have jumped off the walls of the Panorama like a revelation: a lushly green and sophisticated instrument for the loose binding of center and satellites. That the catalyst of the regional boulevard was more likely entrepreneurial self-interest rather than enlightened civic administration hardly devalues what must be acknowledged as a strikingly early recognition of a new kind of dispersed urbanism. Urban scholars at the close of the 20th century are trying to come to terms with the "new" city, the vast, polynucleated metropolis of our day; one hundred years ago, a glimpse of that new city had already been imagined along the umbilical of Sunset Boulevard.

3 Spine

Piecemeal Grandeur on Wilshire

When fortune surprises us by giving us an important position, without having led us to it by degrees, or without our being elevated to it by our hopes, it is almost impossible for us to maintain ourselves suitably in it, and appear worthy of possessing it.

—LA ROCHEFOUCAULD

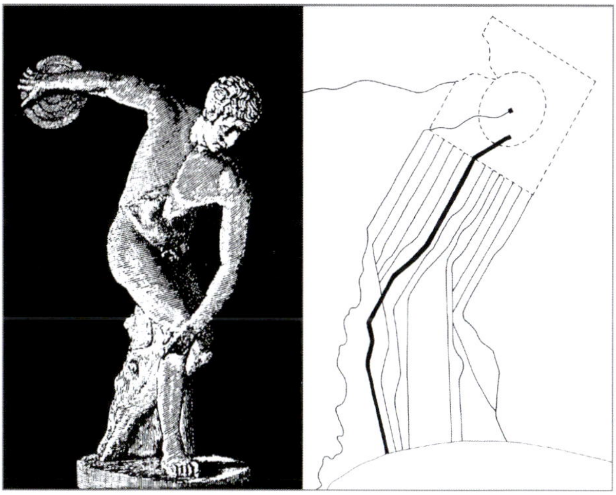

Discobulus and the spine of Wilshire Boulevard

The New World has often proceeded impatiently, and on a strictly empirical basis, with ideas and theories propounded in the Old, and this was the case with the boulevards. In 1886, one year before the earliest proposals for Sunset Boulevard, the Spanish engineer Arturo Soria y Mata had proposed his "Linear City" for Madrid, in which he fused streetcars, free-standing houses, and landscaping into an archetypal long distance boulevard that would tie together the fragments of an emerging regional metropolis. "The plan of symmetry, sexuality, and progression which characterizes the superiority of animals over vegetable forms", he declared, "should also manifest itself in the evolution of urban form...(It is this) plan which determines the superiority of the Linear City—in the form of a vertebrate animal—over modern 'point cities', 'organic cities', and especially invertebrate cities".[1] Soria y Mata's central metaphor of the vertebral column suggested that cities should grow along narrow lines rather than in concentric circles, and that such growth should occur in increments. His plan, which has been called "the last utopia of the 19th century",[2] never took hold in Madrid, but along Wilshire Boulevard in Los Angeles it was given perhaps its most extensive, if unwitting, trial run.

Soria y Mata expected the Linear City to function in one of three ways: 1. as a green suburban belt around a traditional capital city: 2. as an overland link between existing towns or cities; or 3. as an instrument for "colonizing" and repopulating the underused countryside. At one time or another, Wilshire Boulevard would operate under all three guises: as a secluded and park-like suburban district on the periphery of downtown; as a long-distance roadway between Santa Monica, Beverly Hills, and Los Angeles; and as an incubator for development along the open barley fields and pastures of the rancho lands which lay in between. Wilshire's development as a civic spine and its emergence as the city's most prestigious boulevard was not, however, the result of the kind of utopian premeditation intended by Soria y Mata, but of an almost accidental confluence of several ambitious, unrelated private initiatives. That such a singular and powerful urban structure could emerge without the benefit of an overall plan or public leadership is a remarkable emblem of Los Angeles urbanism, both in its achievement and its unfulfilled promise.

Wilshire Boulevard is a 17-mile spine that began at its two ends and grew towards the middle for almost fifty years before completion. The first growth occurred at the base rather than the skull. In 1875 John Jones, a United States senator from Nevada, undertook the development of a new oceanside resort town to be called Santa Monica, after the Rancho San Vicente y Santa Monica in which it lay. Within its rectangular boundaries on a plain sloping gently towards the sea, he established a highly regular grid plan, divided roughly in half by a pair of main avenues running perpendicular to the coastline. The avenues, named California and Nevada, reflected the Senator's divided state loyalties and created between them a band of parks, hotels and public buildings which were to be the civic backbone of the town.[3] By 1887, twelve years later and fifteen miles away, a new road had appeared in downtown Los Angeles named Orange Street, which connected the central business district with a new suburban park name Westlake (now MacArthur), one mile west of downtown. Two of these streets, Nevada Avenue at the shore and Orange Street downtown, conceived and built in almost completer isolation from each other, would eventually be re-christened Wilshire Boulevard; but they would not actually be connected in an uninterrupted line until 1934, when a publicly funded causeway across the lake in Westlake Park filled the last remaining gap between the pueblo and the sea.

Gaylord Wilshire: candidate, schemer, developer

This was an ironic location for the final link of the whole 17-mile chain of Wilshire, because it was the absence of such a route through Westlake Park which had given the adjacent area its secluded atmosphere and helped persuade Gaylord Wilshire to build there a new four-block boulevard bearing his name. Wilshire was a publisher, occasional Socialist political candidate, financial schemer and real estate developer who had a reputation as a publicity seeker; he does not appear to have been held in especially high esteem by his peers.[4] In 1895 Wilshire, along with his brother and father, purchased one of the original large Donation Lots of Hancock's Survey. It was a triangular plot wedged between the diagonal western edge of Westlake Park and the pueblo boundary along Hoover; the northern and southern boundaries were 6th and 7th Streets, which provided the critical connections to downtown. Anticipating the need to subdivide the property with more roads, Wilshire conceived a modest development scheme which now appears as a sly dialectic for his conflicting political and financial instincts. In an 1895 petition to the City Council, he offered to donate part of his property to the city: "a strip of land 120 feet wide by 1200 feet long for a boulevard"; in turn, the city would merely dedicate a strip of public land of equal size along the property's western edge for a second boulevard.[5] The resulting "T"-shaped pair of roads would provide the infrastructure for development; the cross-bar of the "T" running north-south would be called Wilshire Boulevard, the other would be named Benton Boulevard. In one stroke, Wilshire would both increase the value of his property while appearing to share some of it with the public. It took the Council only two weeks to approve. A short time later, for reasons that are unclear, Wilshire switched the names of the two roadways. This apparently minor change put Wilshire Boulevard, rather than Benton, on the east-west path of the city's later development, with the result that the family name of a controversial private citizen was attached to what would become Los Angeles's most important street. Few other cities can lay claim to that kind of civic inadvertence.

Wilshire's conception of a boulevard bore little resemblance to the long, intra-urban Sunset Boulevard then being assembled to the north and west. His two boulevards would not be regional thoroughfares, but grand streets of a few blocks in length, lined with stately homes for the wealthy. Westlake Park and its lake seemed to guarantee a permanent buffer against any commercial intrusion from downtown, but Wilshire apparently decided he needed it in writing, and three months after his initial petition he returned to the Council to obtain an amendment to the agreement. The Council was asked—and agreed—to dedicate Wilshire as "an open boulevard, along which no railroad franchise shall ever be granted or laid thereon... nor that wagons carrying merchandise or any heavy trucking be permitted".[6] Wilshire's strategy paid off when Colonel Otis, the editor and owner of the Los Angeles Times and one of the city's most prominent citizens, became Wilshire's first customer and built a mansion at the corner of Wilshire and Park View (today the site of Otis/Parsons), this insuring the boulevard's success as the main avenue of a fashionable new district.

At its other end, the 1200-foot boulevard diagonally abutted the city limits at the old pueblo boundary, an intersection now straddled by Lafayette Park. At that point, the boulevard happened to coincide with an important old roadway that headed west past the La Brea tar pits and beyond. Wilshire may well have taken this coincidence into account: while the park blocked commercial encroachment from downtown, this roadway would permit—with some strategic realignment—the boulevard's gradual westward extension. The boulevard and its expensive homes did in fact spread westward through the first decades of the century, a few blocks at a time. In the 1910's the mix of building types began to grow richer, as the large houses were slowly joined by expensive apartment buildings, private clubs, and churches. By the 1920's this upper middle class apparatus extended as far west as Western Avenue, placing it directly and conveniently south of Hollywood and this encouraging many of the film industry's

The Ebell Club on Wilshire Boulevard, opened in 1928

early stars and directors to take up residence among Wilshire's wealthy landowning, oil and publishing families.[7]

But in those same twenty years, the first commercial production and distribution of automobiles would soon bring to an end the boulevard's extension on Linear City terms, for Soria y Mata's model—completed one year before Daimler invented the combustion engine—was predicated on the interdependence of residential patterns and fixed rail transit. Los Angeles had a renowned streetcar system, but one which found itself increasingly in competition with automobiles and their much greater freedom of movement. Wilshire Boulevard's hold on residential prestige was being pried loose by new, automobile-based developments like Beverly Hills, established in 1907, and by secluded retreats in the previously inaccessible Hollywood hills. At the same time, as the automobile began to modify residential patterns, it was unhinging fixed commercial habits as well, as merchants slowly began to follow their dispersing clientele. In the late teens and early 1920's, the downtown business district, which had grown and prospered without competition for almost forty years, received the first threats to its civic and commercial hegemony.

In 1924, a developer named A.W. Ross assessed the shifting conditions and concluded that while Wilshire's survival as a fashionable residential address was unlikely; it had extraordinary potential as an automobile-based commercial thoroughfare. Toss began buying up property along a central segment between La Brea and Fairfax Avenues—still open fields in many places—for a project he called "Wilshire Boulevard Center".[8] The site was very much the geographical center of a vast and growing residential area, but in operation it would be nothing like traditional central shopping districts with their web of intersecting streets. Instead, shops would be strung out along a "district" that was a mile long and only two blocks wide. Stores could easily be spotted by drivers, who would then turn off the boulevard and proceed to the nearly continuous band of parking behind the buildings. Ross managed to persuade a few adventurous merchants to relocate to his new district, but soon ran into a serious obstacle when the area, previously unincorporated, became part of Los Angeles in 1925. Under existing city zoning regulations, Wilshire was still restricted to residential use. Ross's efforts to change the zoning designation—which lasted

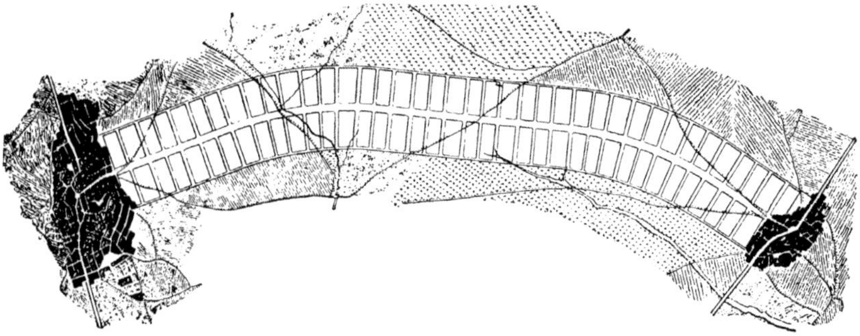

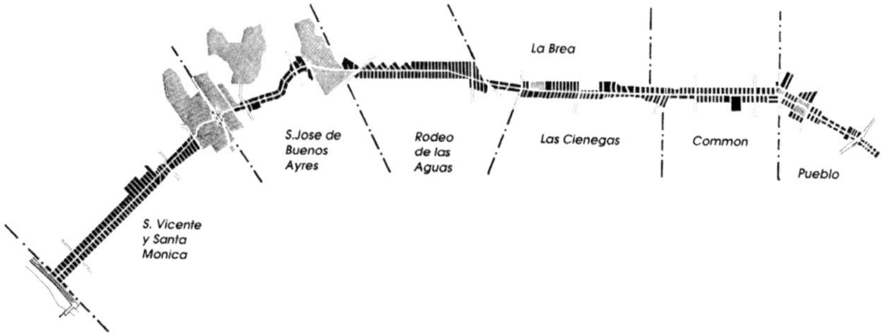
La Brea
S.Jose de Buenos Ayres
Rodeo de las Aguas
Las Cienegas
Common
Pueblo
S. Vicente y Santa Monica

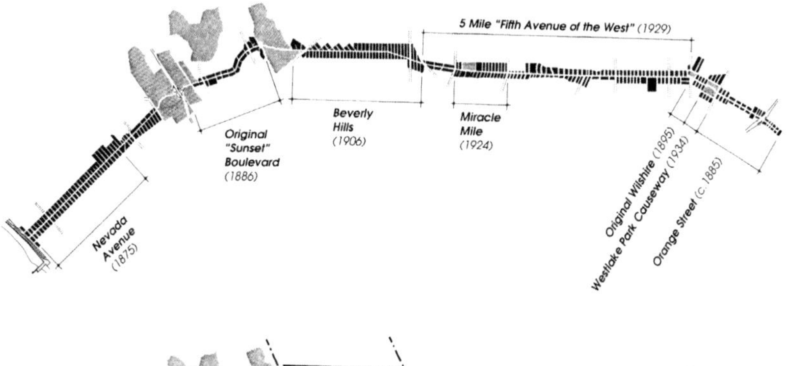
5 Mile "Fifth Avenue of the West" (1929)
Original "Sunset" Boulevard (1886)
Beverly Hills (1906)
Miracle Mile (1924)
Nevada Avenue (1875)
Original Wilshire (1895)
Westlake Park Causeway (1934)
Orange Street (c.1885)

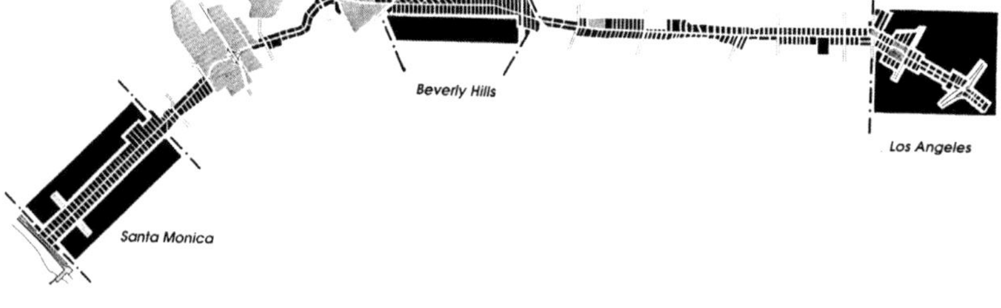
Beverly Hills
Los Angeles
Santa Monica

several years and included a citywide referendum and an appeal to the state Supreme Court—were violently opposed by the downtown business community. Its leaders instead backed a plan—never executed—to widen Wilshire to 200 feet and to "keep it the wonderful thoroughfare it is, a street of handsome homes and stately gardens" i.e. safe from retail competition.[9] They must have suddenly realized with alarm that the disconnected vertebrae of Wilshire were on the verge of fusing into a powerful commercial backbone, one which could drain the life out of downtown like a spinal tap.[10]

Diagram of Soria y Mata's 1886 proposal for the Linear City, shown connecting two existing municipalities

Despite Ross's defeat in the 1926 referendum and in the courts, he was able—on the accepted principle of highest use—to obtain commercial "spot zoning" for one project at a time. Before the Depression could take hold, commercial development was booming along Wilshire Boulevard, even on older sections near downtown, where in 1928 Bullocks Wilshire opened the first major department store outside of downtown. The Los Angeles Times reported in 1929 that along Wilshire's five-mile stretch from Westlake to Fairfax, there were now 108 retail shops, compared to ten only five years earlier. Wilshire Boulevard, the paper noted, was "now being heralded as the Fifth Avenue of the West". The especially striking success of Ross's one-mile stretch led to the nickname of Miracle Mile, which stuck. But it was less a miracle than a harbinger of an entirely new urban dynamic, whose consequences were only beginning to come into focus.

Wilshire Boulevard and its relationship to the pueblo, the common lands to the west, and five ranchos

Miracle Mile and segments of the other four miles back to Hoover became, during the 30's and 40's, the most active commercial, cultural, and social area of the city. Reyner Banham would later dub it "the world's first linear downtown".[11] It contained a rich mix of restaurants, hotels, publishing and insurance companies, parks, theaters, clubs, churches, apartment houses, department stores, galleries and boutiques, and much of the architectural legacy of that era is still visible. But just as central Wilshire had overtaken downtown, it was soon overtaken itself. In part mid-Wilshire suffered from the same linear migration which had given it birth, a migration which continued—during the 1950's and 60's—westward along Wilshire into Beverly Hills and Westwood. But to an even greater extent, Wilshire's role in the city diminished when the full impact of the automobile—and the decline of the mass transit system—was finally manifest.

Chronology and names of the various segments of development along Wilshire

Wilshire as a vertebral connector of three independent municipalities

Wilshire had emerged as the city's earliest and most conspicuous example of linear extension, and to urban observers it must have seemed logical that the old dominance of a central point (downtown) with its regional-town satellites in orbit, would now be replaced by the dominance of a single line. The planetary model would simply give way to the vertebrate one. But the controlling spine turned out to be only a transitional rather than definitive urban form. All over the metropolitan area, many other areas of urban activity were developing in a kind of spontaneous generation. Some were like mini-downtowns, organized around compact networks of streets which we might call "nets"; while others were like incipient Wilshires, strung along the boulevards in "strands". The freeway construction of the 60's and 70's did not so much create these urban forms as put them on an equal footing, undermining old hierarchies of primacy and dependence. The central city and the linear city had become the network city, in which hierarchical position—with respect to prestige, density, activity, or any other category—was fragmentarily distributed in many directions, and subject to change on an almost daily basis.

In this setting of confederated nets and strands, the notion of a dominant spine may be entirely anachronistic, like some enormous femur trapped in the tar at La Brea. A Wilshire address still counts for something in business, although for residential prestige it is now simply something you have to be north of. But the vertebral metaphor is a persistent one, and we can detect its atavism in the thinking behind the new subway system. Sixty years after the first subway was proposed to protect downtown's urban monopoly against the threat of Wilshire Boulevard, the new version finds downtown and Wilshire in alliance against the scattered nets and strands. The routing of the first line will be a virtual re-enactment of the spinal extension all the way out to Fairfax. If the subway spawns residential and commercial development along its route, and if current radical proposals to reduce air pollution and traffic are enacted, Soria y Mata's Linear City, now in its second century, may find its second wind.

4 Girdle

The Studios Face the Boulevards

Before I built a wall I'd ask to know/ What I was walling in or out...

—ROBERT FROST
"MENDING WALL", 1914

Fox Studios entrance on Santa Monica Boulevard west of Beverly Hills, late 1920s

Virtually every studio founded in Los Angeles in the first two decades of the movie industry attached itself to one of the region's major boulevards. This conformity of address may represent nothing more than conventional site selection based on the availability of commercial property and the convenience of streetcar lines. But the physical history of the studios suggests that something more subtle and intangible was at work than mere efficacy, for if the studios had calculated like any other light industry turning out a manufactured product, they might have opted for less expensive properties in more obscure industrial or rural districts, where their operations could be conducted with least interference.

It appears instead that the early filmmakers were at least subliminally aware that the potentially threatening character of their revolutionary product made it necessary to forge an unprecedented social contract with the city that had been selected as its incubator. For their product was not only material but cultural; not a mere utilitarian object but a devastatingly accurate mirror of kinetic reality. Other types of cultural production had already developed their characteristic urban forms and structures: music was produced in auditoria with the status of civic monuments, plays in proscenium theaters clustered in theater districts, paintings and sculpture in schools of art and ateliers on the tops and north sides of buildings, books in scattered printshops and binderies, and furniture, clothing, and decorative objects in workshops and small factories on the urban fringe. But the urban requirements for the production of moving pictures were only gradually coming into focus: clusters of large, dark, and cavernous sheds, like theaters emptied of their seating; outdoor stages with full-scale sets replicating streets and buildings; ranks of small workshop structures for the care of filming equipment, storage of costumes, construction of sets, and editing of film; and finally the availability of “real” sets actual streets with vehicles and people, beaches and hillsides with sand and trees—in the surrounding urban and natural landscape. The development of this new productive typology would require the cooperation and goodwill of the host metropolis.

Such hospitality was by no means taken for granted, for many of the filmmakers had left the east coast under duress, fleeing the uncooperative weather, a contemptuous cultural establishment, and patent detectives in the service of Thomas Edison.[1] In Los Angeles, they were not always welcomed warmly. The Town of Hollywood, which had been founded on principles of Christianity and Temperance, harbored a degree of hostility, based on a general cultural suspicion of those in the profession of acting, and perhaps a more subliminal uneasiness with a technology that threatened to reveal so much.[2] Under such circumstances, the early studio founders might well have opted for a secretive and invisible urban presence, but chose instead to engage the general public on the common and highly visible ground of the boulevards. There the studios would both define a new kind of architectural presence in the city, and slowly acculturate the local population to a radical new window of perception.

The characteristic form which emerged was the walled precinct, with a sharp disparity between inside and out.[3] The perimeter was often defined on at least two sides by major boulevards, and some times on all four; in this way the linear force of the region boulevards then being pieced together was locally redirected into a girdling force for the bounding precincts, an atavistic echo of their original role at the borders of the great ranchos. Along this girdle the studios erected one form of barrier or another: a row of cheery Tudor storefronts (Charlie Chaplin), a rancho-recalling Spanish wall with red tile coping (Fox), or the un-fenestrated Deco flanks of sound studios (RKO).

Partial chronological listing of the movie studios in the Los Angeles region, year of founding, and the boulevard fronted by their main entrance

Studio	Year	Boulevard	At
Christie/Nestor	1911	Sunset	Gower
Universal	1912	Sunset	Gower
Essanay	1912	Sunset	Hoover
Kalem	1913	Sunset	Hoover
Lasky	1913	Vine (St.)	Selma
Majestic	1914	Sunset	Hollywood
Fine Arts	1915	Sunset	Hollywood
Universal	1915	Lankershim	Universal City
Vitagraph	1916	Hollywood	Talmadge
William Fox	1916	Western (Av.)	Sunset
Warner	1918	Sunset	Bronson
Charlie Chaplin	1919	La Brea (Av.)	Sunset
Pickford-Fairbanks	1922	Santa Monica	7200 (Formosa)
Fox	1923	Santo Monica	Westwood
Metro Goldwyn Mayer	1924	Washington	Overland
Warner Brothers Vitaphone	1925	Hollywood	Talmadge
CBC (Columbia)	1926	Gower (St.)	1438
Famous Players/Lasky	1926	Melrose (Av.)	Van Ness (Av.)
Paramount	1927	Melrose (Av.)	Van Ness (Av.)
United Artists	1927	Santa Monica	7200 (Formosa)
Warner Brothers	1928	Barham	Burbank
RKO Radio Pictures	1931	Melrose (Av.)	Gower

Theses barriers were then interrupted with some form of gateway, whose seductive charm was magnified by its contrast with the exclusionary walls. The paired miniature gatehouses at Pickford Fairbanks Studio, with their small-paned windows and salt-and-pepper-shaker friendliness, seemed to promise direct admission to the dreamscapes of the fairy tale. At the original Universal City, a bridge crossed the Los Angeles River on axis with a Churriguerresque archway, flanked by a pair of flapping flags, and shadowed by a crenellated medieval turret, all set against the dramatic profile of the Hollywood Hills; the fact that once past the river the roadway swerved to the right and continued around the studio probably did little to displace the initial illusion of a ritual moat-crossing, and the imminent penetration of a castle precinct. This emphatic closure should be contrasted with the open, garden-like campus planning preferred for certain kinds of institutions like colleges and hospitals.

In almost every case, the controlled physiognomy of these public faces was reductive, converting the complex internal apparatus of the studios into simple and subliminal messages, much the way the inner workings of a watch are covered with decorative faces. Each studio stood on the boulevard like a recounted dream, whose underlying psychic power overcame the "contaminating" presence of ordinary commerce, traffic and strangers. Even today the gateway at Paramount frames the view of an impossibly beautiful sky painted on a vast wall, juxtaposed with the real sky which surrounds it; the message is clearly: we improve on nature. To the passing public, this benign architectural propaganda offered a tantalizing visual scent of the fantasy production within, like a fragrance of jasmine wafting out of a factory of perfumes.

This fugue of the real and the fantastic continued on the inside. The studios were often conceived as walled cities in miniature, with a diminutive grid of streets and alleys, and single buildings making up entire blocks. Indeed Carl Laemmle moved his studio to leased ranchlands in 1915, and actually founded a new municipality called Universal City, which his publicity flyers proclaimed "the most wonderful city in the

Typical studio arrangement, with sound studios, outdoor sets, and continuous perimeter buildings

world, where every person is engaged in some capacity in making Universal Moving Pictures" [4] – the strength of this conceit may well have influenced the Italian film industry to call its headquarters "Cinecittá".

The internal public life of these studio cities took place in the canteens, back lots, executive offices and screenwriters' bungalows. The architecture was a no-nonsense synthesis of simple, rectangular forms and off-white stucco finishes; often the only memorable architectonic feature was the high profile of the roof trusses which provided large, column-free interiors for the sound studios. The overall impression of large-scale sobriety and discipline bore a strong resemblance to another version of micro-city, the military base, with its relentless uniformity and grudging gestures to architectural style.

This posture of cool and permanent reserve stood in sharp contrast to the great outdoor back lots, where every detail of exotic streetscapes was recreated at full scale on huge sets, visibly propped up from behind by elaborate scaffolding. The presence of an architecturally convincing "Old West Main Street" just around the corner from a "Street Scene in Constantinople" must have lent a deep note of ambiguity, even anxiety, to the studio environment. When colored by intense economic pressures, fantasy may quickly lose its charm.

As part of the emerging tacit contract between studios and city, the citizenry were cautiously invited to pass through the successive screens of illusion at the studios—at least some of them. Universal was one of the first to establish a regular visiting policy: grandstands were set up outdoors where, for twenty-five cents, the public could watch a movie being made; after the filming, visitors were invited to spend a little more time (and money) at lunch in a restaurant called Dine with the Stars. The public life of the boulevards was in this way carefully brought inside to the very altar of the new religion and apprized of its rituals, which turned out to be less mysterious than imagined from without. As studio visits became more popular, the backlot streets and interior sets of the studio entered the ancient tradition of the Roman Imperial stage building, the Renaissance perspective theater, and the 19th century panoramas, all of which involved the recreation and reflection of urban public life within controlled interiors.

This interaction with the public entered a new phase in 1916, when D.W. Griffith erected his enormous sets for the film Intolerance directly on Sunset Boulevard. Resembling Carthage from the front and oil rigs from behind, they loomed over the boulevard and the adjacent neighborhood for nearly four years, a daily reminder of the city's growing entanglement with filmmaking. In a kind of subcultural exhalation, the studios began to spawn other such fantasy realms outside the studio enclaves, directly on the boulevards. The Café de Paris recreated an arcaded Parisian boulevard with the Eiffel Tower on axis; at the Seven Seas, water continuously showered on the tin roof to simulate a tropical downpour.

These concentric environmental layers of phantasm and materiality must have occasionally produced something like a schizophrenic swoon. But they reflected very well the unsettling nature of the medium itself, for no cultural product had ever distilled the human imagination into such a brilliant vapor, one that was obviously intangible and yet vividly, breathtakingly real. By locating their laboratories directly on the boulevards, by spawning other fantastic architectural realms on the boulevards, and by permitting the crowds on the boulevards to peek inside the girdle of the studio walls, the studios had injected their alchemy into the marrow of the city's public life.

The interaction with the boulevard continued for some time, even when technological developments brought forth new building types. The early radio and television studios of the 30's and 40's were also located on the boulevards, and whether rendered in high eclectic fantasy or sober International Style, most of them honored traditional principles of urban design, including a respect for the street wall, prominent corner siting, and highly articulated entry sequences. Industry-related nightspots like the Mocambo and Hollywood Canteen continued to choose boulevard locations, as did picketers during labor disputes, a tradition unbroken right through the 1988 Writers' strike.

But this healthy dialectic between the public realm and the realms of imaginative production was decisively undermined by post-War developments like Disneyland. Completely isolated from the daily life of the city, Disneyland subsumed the public realm by fabricating an artificial Main Street that was not an explicit part of film production, but rather a permanent substitute for the boulevard. It helped lead the way to the pseudo-streets of internalized malls, "marketplaces", office complexes and gated residential compounds which have proliferated all over the city; even the studios themselves have moved in this direction in their recent architectural activities. All of these types manifest a preference for the ease of exclusion over the challenges of interaction. Though they share the girdling walls and gates of the early studios, they have crossed the line from precincts to enclaves, draining blood from the city's public life.

5 Phosphor

Day for Night on Hollywood Boulevard

The city man, in his neon and mazda glare, knows nothing of nature's midnight. His electric lamps surround him with synthetic sunshine. They push back the dark. They defend him from the realities of the age-old night.

—EDWIN WAY TEALE

While the national headquarters of the film studios were scattered along the various boulevards of the city, their flagship retail outlets were concentrated on a ten-block strip of Hollywood Boulevard. Because these move theaters brought to the local public not the filmmaking process but its commercial product, their urban and architectural program developed along very different lines than the studios. While the processes of production needed to be carefully guarded within an architecture of enclaves, the product itself required aggressive salesmanship and gave rise to a highly extroverted style of expression. Architectonic forms of exaggerated plasticity and hyper-exoticism, forecourts laid out wide and welcoming to the boulevards, groves of palm trees and lush planting, gaudily bedecked interiors and ever larger signs all brought extravagant attention to otherwise utilitarian buildings of great programmatic simplicity. Compared to traditional theaters, they required little of that excruciating mediation between sight lines and intimacy, since images could be enlarged whereas live actors could not; nor were there any of the elaborate requirements of workshops, dressing rooms, flyspaces and wings, since all of this supporting apparatus had been displaced to the studios. Nevertheless these large sheds were dubbed palaces by a dazzled public and gladly vaunted as such by the industry's public relations departments. In many respects the theaters were able to displace the public's unquenchable curiosity about the studios by providing a heavily costumed facsimile; the theaters became a kind of transubstantiation of the public's murky dreams about the studios themselves. In many ways they served the same function as the public chapels of the great monasteries, where outsiders could come and partake in a substitute ritual that was merely representative of the real mysteries within the cloister.

The illusionistic craftsmen of the soundstages and back lots were conveniently at hand for the construction, ex studio, of theses boulevard pseudo-sets. Of even greater significance than the carpenters of temple roofs and the painters of gilded garlands, however, were the studio magicians of light, for in light itself lay the ultimate mystery of cinematography. The very object of veneration was an image that had been galvanized in light but could only reappear in darkness, an optical inversion well captured by the cinematic term "day for night", which the French call La Nuit Americaine. The earliest nighttime nickelodeons were limited to a fairly Victorian repertoire of glass globes and Braille-like tattoos of tiny white bulbs; into this American night came the head and tail lights of the new automobile sweeping the sidewalks with their paired beams; the filling of glass tubes with neon gas, permitting the bending and coloring of light to almost any shape and hue; and the invention of oscillators and sequential switches which subjected light to rhythmic modulation. This display reached its luminous crescendo with the wheeling in of dozens of klieglights, the powerful carbon-arc brainchild of the America brothers Kliegl, apostles of the new electric lighting science.

Klieglights in front of movie theaters on Hollwood Boulevard in the 1940's

Billeted like soldiers outside the entrances of every theater, these beautiful and frightening white blades of light slashed at each other across the inky sky, and epic sword-fight without the metal.

By the mid-1920's, all of these technologies—urban stagecraft, surface décor, and lighting—appeared on Hollywood Boulevard as if the studios had been turned inside out. All that was missing was stage direction, which eventually appeared in the forecourt of Grauman's Chinese Theater, the site of two revealing rituals: the daytime casting of celebrated hand- and footprints in wet concrete pavement, and the pageantry of the premiere, in which the latest industrial offspring was given a kind of triumphal entry into the city, hailed by a neck-craning public. The pavement ritual showed the industry's diurnal business face, all hustle and press agents and shaking hands, with the selected star brought down from studio Olympus (or at least the Hollywood Hills) before a public audience in broad daylight, a scene which recalls Alexander Chase's observation that "the movie actor, like the sacred king of primitive tribes, is a god in captivity". The premiere which was inconceivable before nightfall, imbued the nocturnal boulevard and sidewalk with a glamour it had never known, as a breathless parade of beauty and glory passed in public before the citizenry with all the splendor of a royal wedding. The ceremony has probably been the most widely photographed subject in the whole widely photographed landscape of this city; its latent psychic tension was seized upon by Nathaniel West, who revealed the incipient riot lurking behind the ritual. Embedded like a phosphor in the city's collective memory the premiere glows with all the false promises of the night.

By the late 20's, the nightly display of klieglights and periodic lighting frenzies of the premieres was visible for miles across the then clear skies of the basin, just at a moment when the city was trying to make up its mind—in the form of transit systems—whether to shore up the hegemony of its downtown or open the floodgates of decentralization. When viewed from downtown or settlements at the shore, the distant lights on Hollywood Boulevard must have given an early hint of the unprecedented spread and scale of the emerging city, and may well have offered observers a kind of thrilling and persuasive incentive to create a new kind of metropolis on the territorial scale of sea and mountains. With its ability to literally gather the eyes of millions across an area of hundreds of square miles, the klieglight may have been the most significant new invention of urban focus and identity since the bell tower.

The legacy of these developments was a tacit collusion between the boulevards and the night. An addiction to the boulevard's potent nocturnal landscape could easily foster a nagging dissatisfaction with its daytime reality, in which the ephemeral often turned out to be the merely shabby. But with the right moody lighting, even the tawdriest precinct could take on a certain vitality and style; to this day one feels much more likely to elicit favorable comment from a visitor if the tour takes place after sunset. From a high vantage point, what can appear during the day as a demoralizing spread of humanity capped by smog becomes—at night—a glittering diagram of metropolitan geometry on the scale of aviation; indeed the aerial lights of the long line of airplanes waiting for landing clearance is like a watery reflection of one of the boulevards, hanging in the sky and visible for a dozen miles in every direction. The orange sodium vapor glow of the boulevards, rushed like torches across the landscape, contains both the warm promise of company, and the darker threat of its own shadows.

Back in Hollywood, the night-lights act as a kind of live x-ray of the city, a reverse image revealing its substructure. On the quiet residential streets the enshrouded lamps in living rooms and flickering blue of televisions suggest introverted life, its back turned warily from the street, where half-hidden streetlamps cast worrisome shadow on the sidewalks and moist lawns. On Hollywood Boulevard itself, extroversion prevails. Wig shops and boutiques for lingerie that were discreetly hidden by the glare of sunlit glass are now illuminated from within like display cases in a wax museum. An uncanny luminous integration of store windows and automobiles, billboards and airplanes, street lights and signage obscures the underlying fragmentation. The big signs blink like heartbeats, and the theater marquees still glow, but the klieglights are gone. The phosphorescence has shifted to the undulating folds of the Sunset Strip, where the great illuminated billboards hover brilliantly in the dark, like floats in a move screen parade. Detached from the studios, detached now ever from cinema's retail palaces, they are but precariously tethered to the last boulevard of the night.

6 Torrent

The Boulevards Accelerate

Motors in all directions, going at all speeds. I was overwhelmed, an enthusiastic rapture filled me... its power is like a torrent swollen by the storms; a destructive fury.

—LE CORBUSIER

The dirt paths, which preceded the boulevards between the Los Angeles River and the sea, bore the markings of a repetitive stomping by the human foot. These would kick away the tumbleweed and crush the seedlings which, as nature's relentless front line, were forever trying to reclaim the path from men. When the Spanish appeared with their sharp leather heels and horses hooved in iron, the paths were soon marked by an even more emphatic stamp, and eventually became boundaries for the ranchos. In some places rude wooden fences confirmed the outlines of a newly furrowed landscape. This staccato pounding of foot and hoof was soon accompanied by the continuous rolling pressure of wheels, first wood and then iron, weighted down with freight and human cargo. But for all the energy of this road-clearing parade, a single downpour could convert the trails into a cementitious trap; the day's sun might then harden the quagmire into peaks and ruts, a miniature volcanic protest against humanity's quest for smoothness, and a constant brake on desired speeds.

The ancient solution to this challenge of surface transport had been to replace loose soil with tightly fitted stones, creating a roadbed whose hard and pulsating ride was compensated by its great reliability; but it was an operation which required a large work force and nearby quarries, and early Los Angeles had neither. In general, roadbeds remained unpaved, and overland rides sin horse-drawn carriages were expected to be rough—in 1885 the L.A. Times wrote, "It is during but a few days of the year that the need of pavements is noticed".[1] Los Angeles was only slightly worse than average in a nation which by 1880 had paved only half of its urban streets, even as the first skyscrapers began to rise.[2]

The rapid improvement, on the other hand, in the production of iron rails and specially fitted wheeled vehicles provided the first hint of a seductive new mobility with which architecture would soon have to reckon. By the 1860's sophisticated horse-drawn machines were available to clear wide swaths across the landscape while workers dug up two parallel trenches, their spoils hauled away in carts pulled by donkeys. In the trenches were then laid down perpendicular rows of wooden ties to carry the new iron rails which, like feudal lords walking across the backs of prostrate serfs, never actually touched the ground. In 1869, the region's first inter-urban rail line was inaugurated for a coal-burning steam locomotive connecting downtown to its port at San Pedro. By 1874, a small network of rails were laid downtown for the city's first primitive form of local rail transit, the horsecar, a specially designed vehicle set upon the rails and lurched into motion by a team of horses or mules; the going on the Spring & Sixth Street Rail Road Company line was slow, but smoother than the horse-drawn omnibuses on pavement.[3]

In the same year in San Francisco, Andrew Hallidie had conducted the first successful experiments in drawing streetcars along a rail by means of an under-ground cable system. Within ten years, a dozen American cities had established extensive cablecar networks. The first in Los Angeles was opened in 1884, on a section of 2nd Street too steep for animal teams. In an iron conduit buried between the two rails, a very long cable was attached to enormous pulleys a considerable distance away, but still capable of pulling thousands of pounds up the hill. Within a few years, cable cars were in wide use downtown even where the topography did not require it. The consequences for the architecture of

Steel wheels, steel rail, and underground cable-traction mechanism

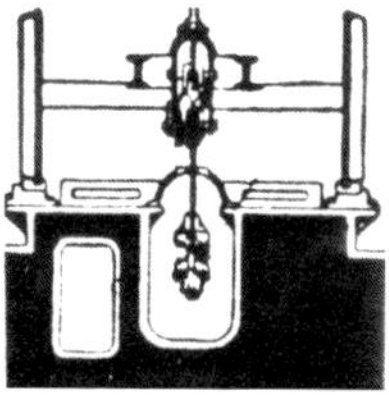

the boulevards was negligible, for the source of mechanical traction was almost magically concealed, and the new cable vehicles were barely larger (or faster) than the old horse-drawn ones.

But more radical changes were imminent, as the use of cable traction gave way, both in Los Angeles and elsewhere, to a new source of motive power. Los Angeles had generated its first electricity in 1881, and by 1886 the new technology was harnessed to rail transport to produce the region's first electric trolley line. It was a financial failure, and it would be another five years before someone would try again, but the precedent was established and would eventually dominate all other forms of transport. Throughout the 1890's, a relentless transformation took place in which all the existing lines that had depended on horses, cable or steam power were converted to electric locomotion, while new lines were extended across the county. In 1895 the important link between down town and Pasadena was electrified, as was—a year later—the even more critical line which ran northwest to Hollywood and then southwest all the way to Santa Monica.

The first architectural evidence of this revolution could be seen on the commercial streets downtown, where widely spaced colonnades of wooden utility poles were embedded in the sidewalk a foot or so from the curb. Initially supporting telegraph and telephone wires only, they were soon laced with electric wires in the service of "the great triad": heat, light, and motion. The poles were often as tall as the office buildings; by virtue of this height and their freestanding position, they introduced a radical new scale and texture to the urban streetscape, competing for effect with Georgian cupolas and Italianate cornices. The presence of this powerful new utility was later made even more conspicuous by the veritable net of overhead wires which powered the new electric trolley cars—so called because of the small pulley mechanism which "trolled" the wires as the cars proceeded. The actual source of motive power, which had always been apparent with the horse and steam engine, and then concealed in sub-surface cables, now dramatically reappeared on the street in a kind of proto-functionalist essay on the exposition of working parts.

On the ever-lengthening boulevards outside downtown, a different but no less assertive cross-section was employed: centered between the familiar pair of trenches for the rails, a small, deep hole would be dug to receive the carefully skinned trunk of a local tree. Near its top, the pole would be fitted like a patriarchal cross with two transverse bars, a short wooden one carrying the different utility lines, and a long, elegant steel one, whose ends—directly centered over the two parallel tracks—held the electric line that powered the streetcars. These would soon appear from both directions at twenty miles per hour, unprecedented for intro-urban transit. In many cases, this physical armature of pole, wire, and rail constituted the architecture of the boulevards, sometimes bordered by trees transplanted to form a windbreak and perhaps to lend a note of dignity to an otherwise utilitarian corridor. Like barnacles multiplying on a submerged chain, freestanding buildings would soon attach themselves to theses corridors. Following the typical furrowed pattern of the streetcar suburb, subsequent development occurred in successive parallel layers, usually no further back than a brisk five-minute walk. For about twenty

Horse-drawn cart, streetcars, pedestrian, and bicyclist in downtown Los Angeles

years after the formation of the Los Angeles Consolidated Electric Railroad Company in 1894, the boulevards were the site of a stable choreography, with streetcars rumbling by from 10 to 20 miles per hour, bicycle prima donnas floating through at a more leisurely 5 to 10, while a chorus of pedestrians criss-crosssed at varying paces with about as much predictability as clouds. Even the appearance of the automobile, of which there were 200 in all of Southern California in 1900, added nothing more than an occasional note of sputtering buffoonery to the urban ballet.

But by the end of the First World War, the pastoral dancing had come to resemble a battle scene, as the urban stage was overwhelmed by sheer numbers and heavy equipment. The Automobile Club of Southern California, begun in 1900 as a genteel association for its 46 members, had by 1923 grown to a membership of 23,000 [4]. As the number of automobiles grew, so did the size and number of streetcars, trying to keep up with the city's unprecedented population boom. The most intense confrontations were downtown, where all of the gains in speed and smoothness of the previous half century were rather ironically defeated by a new kind of streetscape, one that was literally clogged with idling machinery, fuming and lurching forward to grab a few feet of progress; through the chaos pedestrians had to pick their way with great care. This highly visible thwarting of the dream of unimpeded high-speed movement convinced everyone that the old integrated choreography was no longer possible. Even independent real estate developers like Harry ("Culver City") Culver were calling for concerted public action: "Unless citizens, taxpayers, and business interests heed the warning Los Angeles is doomed. Its growth will be stunted, progress retarded, traffic stopped and streets blocked".[5] His comments of 1924 are remarkably similar to those of Le Corbusier in the same year: "Such cities as do not adapt themselves to the new conditions of modern life will stifle and perish...the conservative forces at work in great cities obstruct the development of transport, congest and devitalize activity, kill progress and discourage initiative".[6] To many it seemed that the three-part phenomenon of population growth, automobiles and decentralization had precipitated the century's first urban crisis.

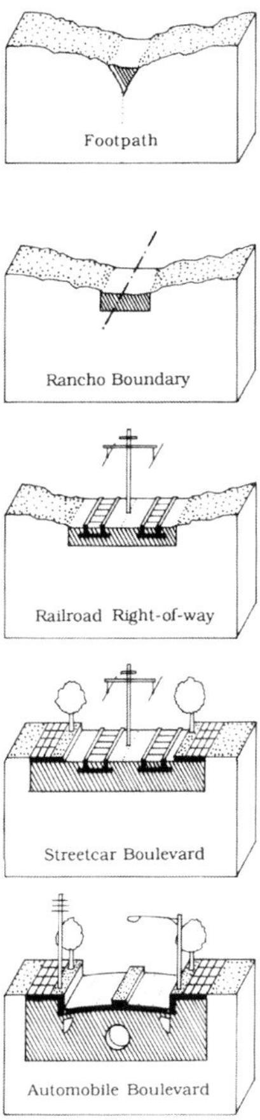

Five stages of the Los Angeles Boulevard

The response of the city and county was to commission a study by a team of three national experts, including Frederick Law Olmstead, Jr. Their report, the 1924 Major Traffic Street Plan, concluded that the causes of the city's traffic problems were the same as in cities across the United States, but for certain historic reasons, the effects were worse in Los Angeles than anywhere else.[7] The principal problem, they observed, was the lack of a well-organized network of thoroughfares. Those which existed (i.e. the boulevards) were too narrow, erratic, and discontinuous to satisfy the traffic flow requirements of a modern city. The report's most emphatic recommendation was therefore an ambitious program of street widening straightening, and extending that would forge the city's haphazard collection of boulevards into a crisp arterial framework.

A key feature of this program was to be the segregation of traffic according to the type of vehicle. Downtown the segregation would occur, as in most older cities, in section: the electric streetcar lines converging on downtown would dive underground at its fringes, to be gathered together in the lower levels of the new Subway Terminal Building in the heart of the commercial district; cars and trucks would continue to use surface streets.

Pacific Electric streetcar entering tunnel to the new downtown Subway Terminal Building, completed in 1925

On the major thoroughfares outside of downtown, the segregation was to be horizontal, by street; imagine today private cars on, say, Wilshire Boulevard, electric streetcars on Santa Monica, buses on Olympic, trucks on Pico, and so on. The designation of "boulevard" itself was to be strictly reserved for those streets which carried private cars. They would generally be lined with private residences and extensively planted. Of the boulevards, Wilshire was to be widened to an extraordinary 200 feet, endowing it with the same unassailable dimensions and prestige as Paris's Avenue Foch.

In essence, the Plan went far but not far enough, for its authors could not yet conceive of a city where the periphery would not only compete with the traditional downtown, but actually overwhelm it. The authors did mention, in a footnote, the possibility of more drastic solutions in the form of elevated roadways for private cars, but were not prepared to put this idea forward as a formal recommendation. By extension, they could barely conceive of the regional boulevards as anything more than thoroughfares leading into downtown, although they acknowledged the need for more lateral roadways to connect the various suburbs to each other. There was little discussion of the actual character—social, architectural, urbanistic—of the old boulevards once they were transformed into modern arterials; of the mass and surface of the architecture that would line them; of the impact of off-street parking on sidewalk activity. It was assumed that if travel into the center could be facilitated, and congestion within the center eased, then the whole civic apparatus of department stores, symphony halls, law courts, public parks, museums, and so on would take care of itself as it always had, along the edges of the traditional downtown street. This plan failed to establish a social or aesthetic vision of the grid of long-distance boulevards as the ultimate framework of the city's civic, commercial, and neighborhood life.

Nevertheless, just prior to the voter referendum (which would overwhelmingly approve the Plan), the Los Angeles Times urges the support of "every voter who is proud of Los Angeles and wants to see it become the world's most beautiful metropolis".[8] This was at best a faint-hearted echo of the City Beautiful movement, which was by then little more than a distant memory from before the First World War. A more sanguine endorsement was offered by the president of the Traffic Commission, who observed that "millions must be spent to convert our streets into a balanced roadbed capable of handling the enormous and mounting traffic of this modern era."[9] It was precisely this determination to create the "balanced roadbed" which overshadowed any concern with the "beautiful metropolis".

The public's enthusiasm for the 1924 Plan only deepened the general disappointment when, by the early 30's, it became apparent that ever increasing decentralization and automobile use had already rendered the plan obsolete. This failure, along with the defeat of proposals in 1925 and 1935 for a comprehensive mass-transit system, simply removed any remaining resistance to the construction of the city's first limited-access roadway. The Automobile Club issued the first published proposal for a freeway system in 1937; the Arroyo Seco Parkway was begun in 1938 and completed in 1940. Within five years, the entire electric streetcar system, in decline for two decades, would be virtually dismantled, to be substituted by a system of bus lines. Decentralizing industries also accelerated the shift from train to truck transport of goods. The new form of the city was crystallizing. The boulevards, envisioned in the 1924 plan as the main channels for all metropolitan movement, would soon be demoted to mere "surface streets" in the hierarchy of regional automotive transport. As increasing sums of money, attention and energy went into the creation of the world's most extensive urban freeway system, the changing role of the boulevards in the public life of the city—beyond their arterial function—was barely discussed.

The unspoken effect of these developments was a gradual shift in the very terms of the whole urban metaphor, from the stable, almost classicizing idiom of train and streetcar engineering to the new and liquid language of the automobile. The power of the combustion engine and the agility of rubber tires meant that steep grades, quick stops and starts, short turning radiuses, and all of the other limitations on rail transport were almost magically swept away, leaving in front of the engineer's dazzled eyes a vision not of great bridges but of great rivers, flowing swift and smooth and unchallenged across every conceivable terrain. Rail transport—with its monumental terminals, steel truss bridges and sky-lit sheds, passenger cars like small basilicas and compartments like Victorian salons—had always had a powerful affinity with architecture. But the new engineering allied with everything architecture resisted and was not: velocity, seamlessness, and a tendency towards environmental exclusion. Rail transport had reinforced, both in its designers and its passengers, an architectural consciousness; the automobile substituted an entirely new one which, in a few short years, managed to reverse the millennial primacy of architecture over movement. Firmness gave way to flow.

7

Pathogen

Signs and Symptoms on the Boulevard

Sickness sensitizes man for observation, like a photographic plate.

—E. AND J. DE GONCOURT

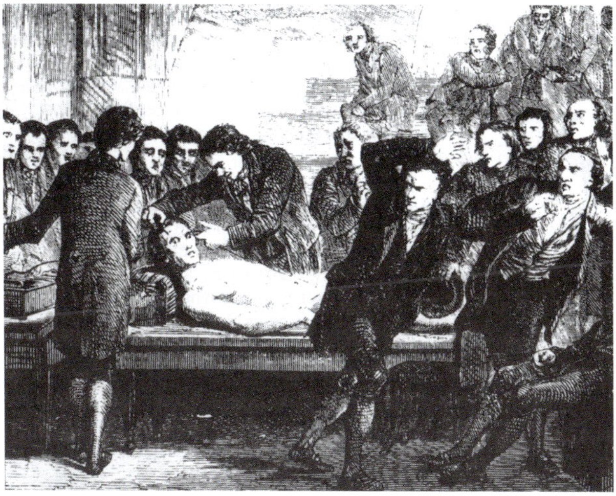

Soon after the development of the automobile, it became clear that higher speeds would eventually require new forms of communication, for at speeds ten times faster than walking, the signs and symbols of the old pedestrian environment were lost in a blur. Victor Hugo had predicted in the previous century that the proliferation of the printed word would kill architecture's communicative role, but he could hardly have anticipated that words and pictures—enlarged by commerce to architectural scale—might threaten architecture's very existence.

Commercial signage had already covered much of the architectural surface of American downtowns as early as the 1850's, but his was still an essentially pedestrian-directed semiology, typically intended to be read at slow speeds from a sidewalk across the street.[1] The arrival of the various track-riding transports by the turn of the century led to somewhat larger, more conspicuous signs for reading at 10-15 mph; but the combination of the automobile and improved road conditions, which accelerated movement up to 30 mph and beyond, precipitated a more dramatic development. While on rural roads the side elevations of barns provided ready made canvases for the advertiser's art, in those urban areas between downtown and the farm a new architectural form was needed to carry the message. Horizontally disposed, vertically cantilevered, wafer thin, and uninhabited, billboards combined the three-dimensional brawn of warehouses with the two-dimensional flimsiness of stage sets. They were arranged in response to a new perceptual condition. Previously passengers on trains were only able to catch lateral glimpses of the landscape, whether in the city or country; but automobile passengers enjoyed the same commanding forward views as train conductors. The drama of distant sighting and anticipation—and the privileged position once reserved for city walls and the spires of cathedrals—could now be usurped by roadside signage.

By 1921, the undeveloped middle segments of Wilshire Boulevards were lined with billboards at close intervals, paired in wedge shaped formations which faced traffic from both directions.[2] Here was a case in which the signage preceded the architecture, and more importantly, provided an unforgettable precedent for the eventual detachment of building and sign. This sequence of huge planar images fused by speed and light must have evoked at least unconscious associations with the then emerging cinema, and made the boulevards seem excitingly modern, even in the open landscape. The contemporaneous development along Wilshire and Pico of some of the earliest drive-in theaters—whose screens were essentially large white billboards—further intensified the experience, for moving images could now also be seen while moving. Compared to such novel kinesthetic pleasures, architecture's allure may have understandably begun to look faded.

There soon appeared, however, some promising indications of an architectonic language revitalized by the unprecedented challenges of the motor age. The specific problem was how to reconfigure the mass of those buildings which, by virtue of their commercial or civic functions, required a strong phenomenal presence on boulevards which were no longer dominated by streetcar and pedestrian. One of the earliest attempted solutions was the 1922 plan for Westwood Boulevard, the main avenue of an eponymous village-like development at the base of the western hills, adjacent to

Wilshire Boulevard, 85% of those who came to Westwood arrived by car, a situation which was apparently anticipated—even encouraged—by the developers.

While the transport conditions for this experiment were new, its pictorial source was not. In the colonial cities of Mexico, such double-scaled townscapes had been perfected for nearly four hundred years. The belltowers and domes of the cathedrals and monasteries—the big-scale elements—had been used to proclaim the domination of a new civil and ecclesiastic authority across great distances, while a gracious and more intimate pattern of plazas and porticos served the walking residents. In Westwood, the dome of the colonial church was transferred to a bank, the bell tower to a gas station; both of them perfect functional correspondents of a new kind of middle-class colonialism. At the same time, these architectural forms were on the way to becoming pure signs. While the dome on the bank actually covered an interior space (now a clothing boutique), the bell tower had no interior space and no bells. Furthermore, a belt-and-suspenders strategy led

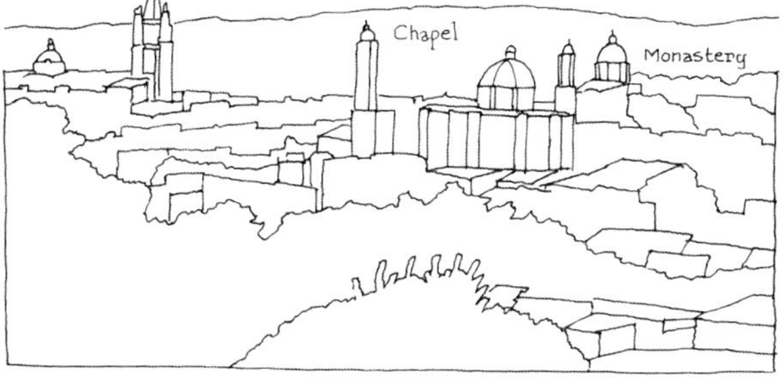

Comparative views of Westwood Boulevard in the 1930's (above) and the town of San Miguel de Allende in Mexico founded in 1555 (below)

to the reinforcement of these "archi-signs" with illuminated word-signs reading "Standard Oil" and "Bank of America". Could there have been a better advertisement for the imperial status of America in the 20's, or a more ironic reminder of Mexico's 1921 nationalization of the American oil companies? The unconscious cultural source of such fusions in both word and image may have been the Cubist collages of the previous decade.

The next phase in the accommodation of the automobile began with the 1928 construction of the Bullocks Wilshire department store on an inner suburban segment of Wilshire Boulevard. With the exception of the museums at Exposition Park, Bullocks was the first major commercial or civic institution to relocate outside of downtown, beyond the pueblo boundary. Its famous (because almost unprecedented) provision of a large parking lot and elaborate porte-cochère entrance at the back of the building was an impressive demonstration of the influence of the automobile on architectural programming, while the store's location at the very starting line of the westward suburban sprint signaled the accelerating trend towards decentralization. Of even greater significance for architectural design was the further refinement of the Westwood model. The massing was again organized into low and high pieces, but of considerably greater bulk: a 10-story tower set along the middle edge of a 5-story base. The contrast of the two volumes resulted in both a striking silhouette and the integration of the two scales, neither of which would have been achieved in a single, one-height block of equivalent cubic footage.

Just as significant were the store's departures from the Westwood model, for now the imagery was based not on a historic model, but on the new machine-based abstractions launched at the 1925 Exposition des Arts Decoratifs in Paris. Also gone was the super-scaled exterior signage; instead the tower was fitted with elaborate equipment for nocturnal illumination, unusual in a building of primarily daytime use. The Bullocks model—tower and base, abstract imagery, double scale—was duplicated again and again throughout the 1930's along Wilshire Boulevard, in buildings like the Wiltern and Desmonds in the Miracle Mile shopping district. In the latter, a further stylistic refinement was demonstrated: the chunky, repetitive, piston-like forms of Art Deco gave way to the unbroken streamlining of the Moderne. This entire package was eventually applied even to low rise buildings like drive-in restaurants and supermarkets...it was as if, for one historic moment, equipped with an innovative form-type, architecture had regained its self-confidence within the frantically changing landscape of lights, signs and speed.

This bright moment, however, turned out to be a mere holding operation against the deluge that was to follow the Second World War. After a hiatus during which the country's productive energies were directed towards the war effort, the city's population—both human and automotive—surged upwards even faster. As land prices rose and ever larger ratios of parking-to-building were required, the Bullock's model proved

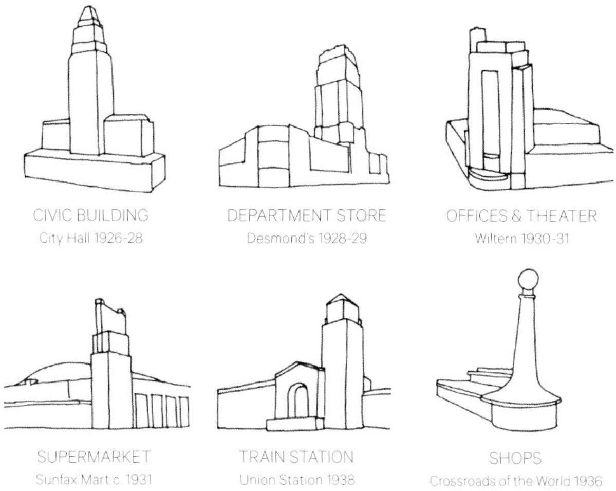

Comparative examples of the base-and-tower type, 1925-38.

to be an insufficiently dense type of tower and an overly expensive kind of sign. It was thus split into two new types of the 1950's: the vertical office tower box and the horizontal shopping box. The tower's footprint covered the maximum allowable area of the site, bore no memorable profile, and failed to develop anything resembling a double urban scale; in most cases large letters were attached to its surfaces as a means of identification. The shopping box developed along the same lines, except that it was generally assigned to a much larger property and set well back from the street, its heraldic responsibilities conceded to a large, freestanding sign.

The increasingly prominent role of retail and advertising signs along the boulevards was intensified in the 1960's and 70's by the rapid development of a freeway system which, for reasons of safety rather than taste, put almost all non-essential signage out of sight. The thwarting on the freeways of the compulsions to hurl commercial prose at people in automobiles had the effect of shunting the whole windstorm of retail capitalism down the aisles of the boulevards. In a virtual parody of Hugo's prediction, billboards were attached to the sides of buildings, bolted to their roofs, or thrust up free standing from single steel posts anchored in parking lots. Retail shops grew electric logos bigger than their display windows, while entire buildings were painted bright colors or actually shaped like the products sold within. Busses were equipped with signs front and back, as were taxis, vans and trucks. Bus shelters

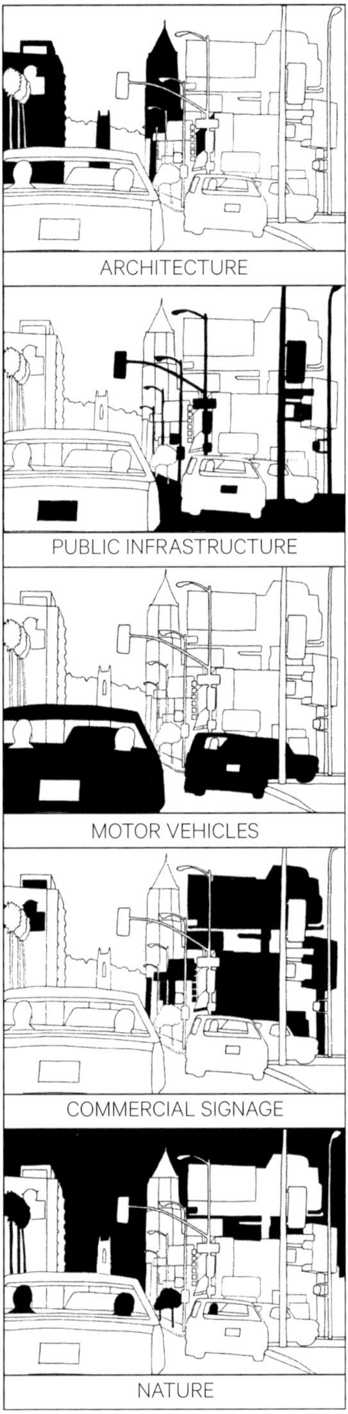

Visual elements of a typical boulevard; the amount of the frame's area occupied by each element increases slightly from top to bottom and even bus benches were treated as convenient surfaces for communication. Deciduous trees with sign-obscuring foliage were clipped or cut down altogether, to be replaced on occasion with slender, non-obstructing palm trees. Equally slender utility poles carrying the very veins of the system were accepted because they were both transparent and economical, as were the parking lots and service docks on which the entire operation depended. In every sense, the technical, economic, and cultural forces of free-market capitalism were displayed without pretense or discrimination.

This "victory of symbols-in-space over forms-in-space", as Venturi labeled it in *Learning from Las Vegas*, led to environments like Lincoln Boulevard, which is U.S. Highway 1 passing through Venice. The width of the road, the vitiated architectural typology, the spatial vastness of the parking lots, the uncontrolled riot of signage, and the presence of unadorned utility poles and wires all combine to make Lincoln one of the city's most intense "strip" environments. The use of the word strip itself has interesting connotations, for while it used to suggest something that was merely linear, like a narrow piece of fabric, the word now echoes with both violent and erotic associations: to strip-mine, to strip paint with a razor, to strip down to the flesh, to strip away someone's dignity; when we speak of "strip development", such harsh images linger beneath the cool suggestion of mere linearity. For critics in the 60's like Peter Blake, the implication was the stripping away of architecture's (and indeed civilization's) defenses against a pathogenic urban form, whose pure commercial determinism was denounced as both vulgar and dangerous.[3] Even those who purported to sympathize with it resorted to similarly distorted or exaggerated interpretations. Many words and pictures were devoted to the sideshow deformities of the boulevard's Pop architecture, with an enthusiasm bordering on camp. Even the astute and lively *Learning from Las Vegas* was slyly condescending, for it focused on the most particular, most artificial and arguably the most vulgar of all boulevards.

Beyond Las Vegas and the Sunset Strip, there was a downside to all the Warholian fun, for the boulevards just as emphatically displayed pathologies that were social rather than physical. The 1965 riots in Watts, which shattered any illusions of a city without poverty or racial strife, took place primarily not on freeways, beaches or residential streets, but on the commercial boulevards. Photographs of the wreckage of buildings and signage along the area's principal boulevard, 103rd Street, became virtual ciphers for an intolerable situation. The boulevards, in a kind of compulsive public service, continue to arbor sobering displays of drug addiction, homelessness, and other collective and individual failures of our society.

But the boulevards can convey social vigor as well and often through the degraded medium of signage. The jostling of Spanish-language theater marquees, awnings, posters, banners, and shop-window displays along downtown's Broadway announce not only the health of retail trade but the vitality of the community which supports it and which is in turn represented by it. In the same way, the growth of the city's Korean and Iranian populations is announced by a profusion of Korean and Persian signs along certain stretches of Olympic and Westwood Boulevards. The virtue of such signs in other languages, and especially in the intriguing calligraphy of different alphabets, is to briefly render the familiar foreign. We are reminded by these momentary cultural displacements that there is not—and never has been—a single reality to the city, only singular myths. Those who have tried, for example, to force the conversion of all such signage into English can only see the boulevards as unhealthy threats to the myths they already cherish rather than as invitations to new ones. But as Los Angeles couples unprecedented growth with unprecedented diversity, it is no longer very productive to treat the boulevards as fabulous invalids. More than ever they are essential lines of urban exchange, identifying boundaries for the residential neighborhoods which they grid, and mirrors of our social and physical condition. In sickness and in health, they are the closest things we have to a truly public realm.

8 Fuselage

Cross-Sections of the Public Realm

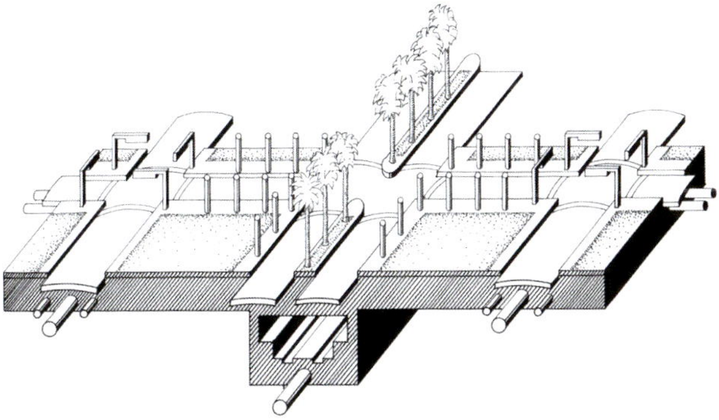

Cross-section of a typical boulevard intersection

In the Introduction to this pamphlet, I suggested the pitfalls of treating the boulevards like airplanes, on which economic and technical requirements overwhelm all other considerations. The aeronautic metaphor is still a very useful one, however, for two reasons. The first is the necessity, in aircraft construction, of integrating all aspects of design. If the boulevard were thought of as a land craft, all those involved in its construction would have to coordinate their efforts, like aviation subcontractors. The second is that in the terms of the metaphor, the zone we usually think of as the boulevard—the roadbed, sidewalks, and edges of buildings—would correspond not to the entire aircraft, but only to its fuselage. For the boulevard to function, we would have to take into account the wings and engines as well. In architectural terms, this means that the boulevard—or for that matter any modern street—has to be treated integrally across its entire cross-section, which includes not only the surfaces of the street channel, but all underground development, rear and side elevations, alleys, parking areas, and adjacent neighborhoods. The co-coordinated operation of all these elements together is what powers the fuselage of the boulevard. In this interpretation, attempts to redesign a boulevard primarily on the basis of its roadbed and street-wall would be the equivalent of restyling the passenger cabin of a 747. This approach is inadequate, for our boulevards (like our aging fleet of jets) require structural rather than merely cosmetic attention.[1]

As a graphic tool for such investigations, the street cross-section, and its variants like the section perspective and section oblique, were developed in the mid-nineteenth century when the traditional "U"-shaped enclosure of the street was rent apart by increasingly sophisticated technologies. The solid ground of the traditional street dissolved into a thin plane spanning generous channels for utilities and transport below; the solid street walls of traditional architecture become more and more transparent as structural bays grew wider and glass plate larger. In response, cross-sectional views of streets began to shift the ground plane from the bottom of the page to the middle, and laterally to extend deeper and deeper into adjacent buildings. A brief history of the street cross-section would have to include 19th century views of the streets, sewers and subways of Paris and New York; Soria y Mata's 1895 boulevard section for the Linear City; Hénard's various proposals for streets and traffic in Paris after 1900; Harvey Wiley Corbett's multi-level street proposals of the 1930's to relieve traffic congestion in New York; and Diego Rivera's contemporaneous use of section perspective in his paintings in order to depict class conflict and injustice. These sectional drawings both reveal hidden structures of urban reality, and invite their transformation.

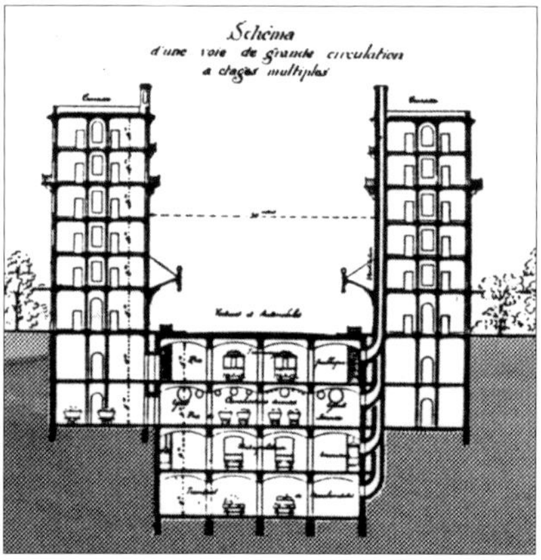

Henard's 1910 proposal for a multi-level street.

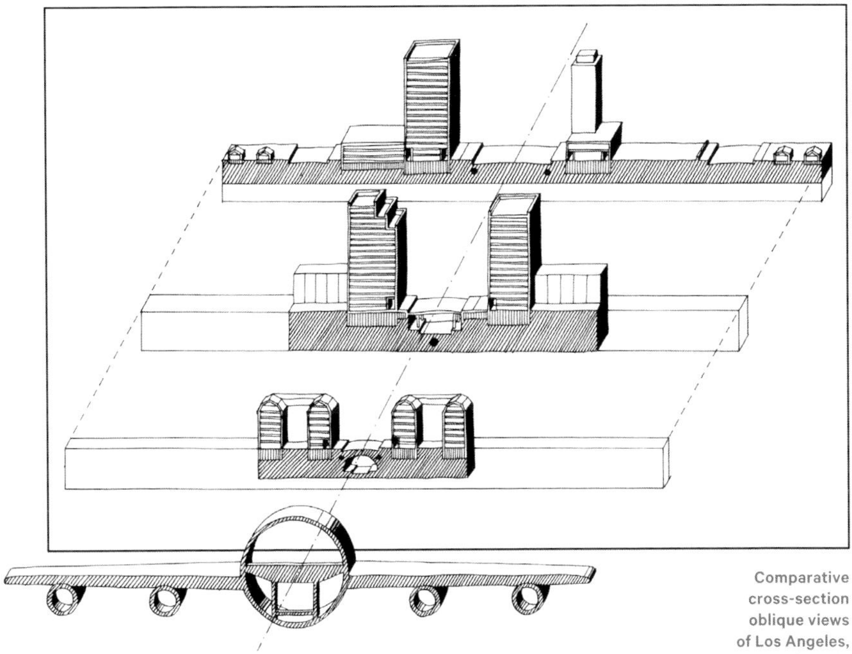

Comparative cross-section oblique views of Los Angeles, New York, Paris boulevards and a 747 fuselage

It is through the section drawing of the boulevard, rather than the plan, that we can best begin to relate urban form to urban experience, particularly with respect to the elusive transitions from public to private space. One measure of a city is the variety and richness of experiences which it fosters, and any attempt to rationalize a concept as multifarious as "urban experience" may seem hopelessly academic. But there are certain structural relationships which are endlessly repeated in the modern American city and which subtly color our interaction with it. Of these, it may be useful to simply identify two which have a particular influence on the interaction of architecture and urban space: the zone of arrival and the zone of entry.

Despite Venturi's claim that "in the brutal automobile landscape of great distances and high speed... the subtleties of pure architectural space can no longer be savored," [2] it is probably safe to say that even on the boulevards, the subtle distinction between arriving and entering still exists. The word arrive derives from the Latin *arripare*. Since a *ripa* is a shore or riverbank, the idea of arrival originally described a nautical experience; the transitional movement from boat to land… to "go ashore" is a pretty close parallel. By contrast, enter comes from the Latin *intrare*, whose root is *intra*, meaning "within". The concept of interiority and exteriority are thus embedded in the term, which implies the existence of a boundary between inside and out. So arrival can be thought of as emphasizing the transition from one mode or quality (water to land, country to city, obscurity to fame) while entry places more emphasis on the transition from one bounded space to another (outside to in, porch to foyer). Arriving implies the definitive end of one condition and the beginning of another, whereas entering puts all the emphasis on the beginning of something new—in physical terms, arrival glows with the memory of the journey just made, while entry is full of spatial anticipation.

If we try to apply these two terms to daily experience in the city, the most basic form of arrival occurs at the moment of transition between different modes of movement, usually from some kind of vehicle to walking on foot. We used to arrive in cities grandly and centrally when we detrained, disembarked, or dismounted; we now arrive functionally and regionally when we deplane (any efforts to promote the use of other terms of modern arrival like debus and decar have not been a conspicuous success). Wherever these transitions occur defines a zone of arrival. We then proceed to the zone of entry, which is situated within that first constructed layer—gate, portico, doorway—of our destination. In architectural terms, the arrival zone usually occurs somewhere within the site plan, the entry zone within the building plan.

These perhaps all too obvious relationships help us to identify a key feature of traditional urbanity. If we construct a line between a person's transitional point of arrival and his transitional point of entry, we have mapped an "experiential path." On the traditional street, regardless of whether the eventual destination was on private or public property, this path almost always began in or passed through the public realm (a term which I use here not in the metaphysical sense of Hannah Arendt and others[3], but in the very straightforward American sense of public property). Public space was kind of switchboard which connected arrival and entry, and unambiguously established the thresholds of private property. The spontaneous presence of many people arriving in the public realm and entering – usually on foot – into bounded spaces, whether public or private, created a vital cross-ventilation of purpose which Stanford Anderson has called urban sympatry, a biological condition in which the same zone or region is peacefully shared by many different species.[4]

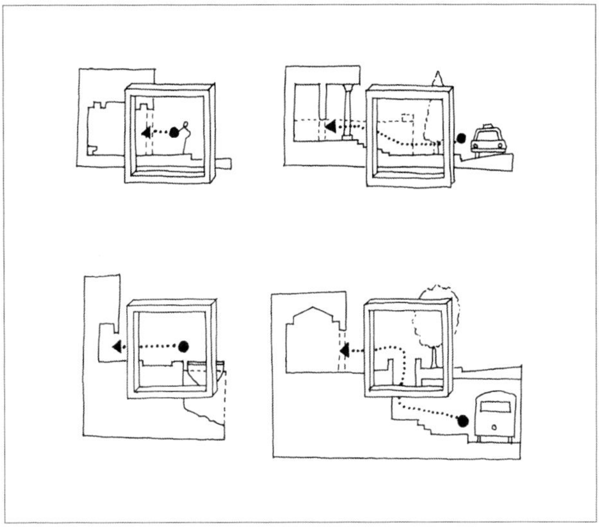

The traditional street: relationship of the public realm to the experiential path between arrival and entry.

This arrangement had always seemed so self-perpetuating—indeed, so organic—that it required hardly any attention. But the street's relatively stable ecology was thrown into turmoil in the 1920's by a revolution that was half technological and half social. The development of combustion of steam propelled land vehicles did not in itself represent a threat. Indeed, when first introduced, automobiles were actually hailed as potential saviours of the street, because they appeared to be smaller, quieter, and cleaner than the horse and carriage. Only when the fact of the automobile was combined with the unprecedented mass ownership of private vehicles had a truly revolutionary force been created.

The proliferation of the car had two faces. One was on the street itself, where increased traffic congestion made life worse for drivers, but may actually have made the street somewhat more hospitable for pedestrians by reducing speeds. The other face was less conspicuous, but constituted (and still does) the real challenge for the architects, as opposed to the engineers, of the street. This was the need to store the car whenever it had to be temporarily abandoned by its driver, that is to say whenever the driver approached the zone of destination. This awkward situation was called "parking", a term whose pleasant Arcadian ring provided a kind of taxonomic fig leaf. The condition as we now know it is as much behavioral

as physical, which would be apparent if Los Angeles imposed a regulation that every car be driven by a chauffer who never parks it; there would be an overnight revolution in the architectural form of the city. For the foreseeable future, however, the beginning of most urban experiences will usually be marked by the obligation to temporarily warehouse a very large machine.

The most radical effect of this condition on the structure of the boulevards was to remove the zone of arrival from the public realm. The construction of parking lots and garages, particularly those underneath buildings, behind buildings, and on top of buildings, not only placed the arrival zone on private property, but also tended to capture the "experiential path" entirely within that private property by providing direct connection to the zone of entry. The result was a subtle vitiation of sidewalk activity in particular and public life in general. Such structural strategies were and still are justified in the persuasive name of efficiency, but just as often—for example in the Music Center downtown—they are consciously intended to bypass a public realm which most suburbanites are presumed to fear. The irony is that while democracy fundamentally depends on the existence of a healthy public realm, majoritarian principles are often used to justify its neglect.

The privatization of the "experiential path" through contained parking has not yet completely destroyed all traces of public life on the boulevards. A number of instructive exceptions include, surprisingly, the main roadway at Los Angeles International Airport (which is actually an extension of Century Boulevard). Because the parking structures are always across the street from the terminals, the public realm stands between the zone of arrival and the zone of entry. This condition, combined with the exceptionally heavy use of passenger vans, buses and taxis, creates one of the liveliest public sidewalk scenes in the city, despite the banality of

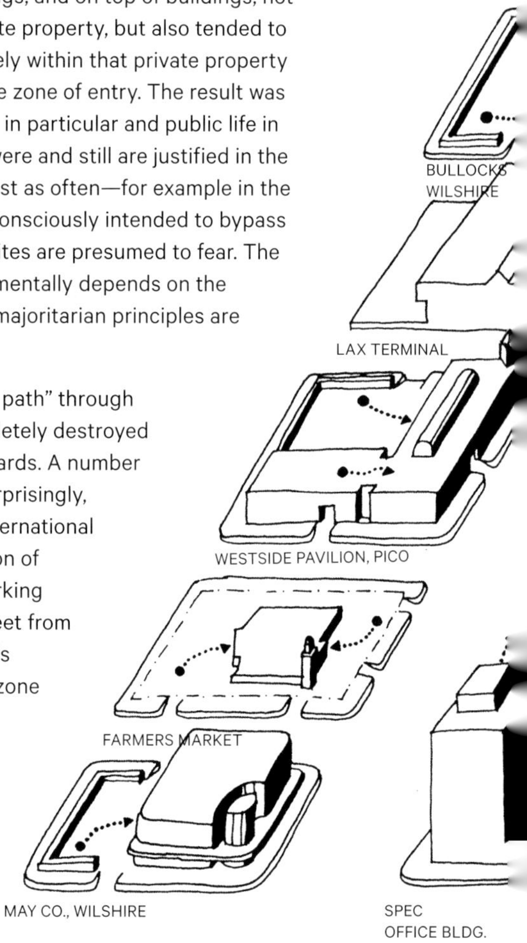

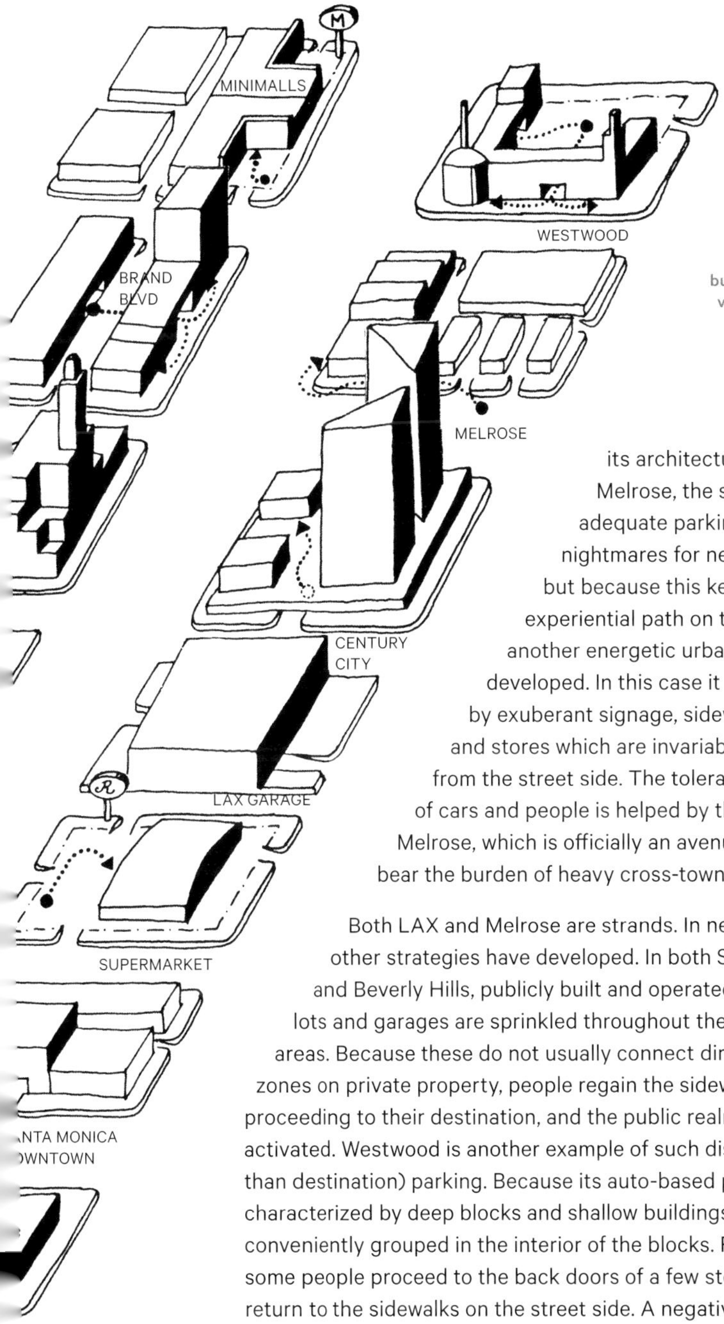

Relationship of parking arrival to building entrance for various key building and block types in Los Angeles

its architectural frame. On Melrose, the simple lack of adequate parking has created nightmares for nearby residents, but because this keeps the experiential path on the sidewalk, another energetic urban scene has developed. In this case it is reinforced by exuberant signage, sidewalk cafes, and stores which are invariably entered from the street side. The tolerable balance of cars and people is helped by the fact that Melrose, which is officially an avenue, does not bear the burden of heavy cross-town traffic.

Both LAX and Melrose are strands. In net areas, other strategies have developed. In both Santa Monica and Beverly Hills, publicly built and operated parking lots and garages are sprinkled throughout the downtown areas. Because these do not usually connect directly to entry zones on private property, people regain the sidewalk before proceeding to their destination, and the public realm is thereby activated. Westwood is another example of such district (rather than destination) parking. Because its auto-based pattern is characterized by deep blocks and shallow buildings, parking is conveniently grouped in the interior of the blocks. From there, some people proceed to the back doors of a few stores, but most return to the sidewalks on the street side. A negative illustration can be seen at Century City, which is laid out in strict accordance with modernist anti-urban principles, despite its name. There are generally no sidewalks on the public boulevards and parking is usually located under a podium level which connects the whole project. The tens of thousands of people who make up its daily working population are thus shepherded into private plazas, courts, and bridges, patrolled by a private army of security guards. To the corollary of the Los Angeles riddle—can a "City" that generally looks like a city actually be a suburban mall with towers—Century City provides a definitive answer.

On the basis of these and other examples, I propose that, in the schools of architecture, engineering, planning, and landscape architecture, we reconsider the form of the boulevard. The impulse to design buildings in context, now degraded into bloodless formulas of matching cornice lines and skin-deep historicism, is given a transfusion when the boulevard itself is treated as architecture. Design studios which posit the boulevard as both site and program can navigate the exhilarating waters between megastructural oppression on one hand and a killing chaos on the other. William MacDonald has described the long, twisting high streets of the late Roman colonies as "loosed but palpable unities"—this may be the most succinct characterization yet of the boulevards of Los Angeles. For investigations into the possibilities of such unity, the categories and recommendations in the accompanying chart may serve as useful points of departure.

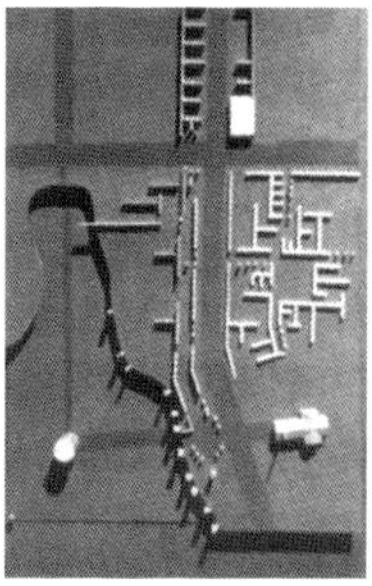

Student project: boulevards as a vibrant subject for integrated urban, landscape, and architectural studios

Block Pattern

- Strands: transition from commercial to high-density residential to low-density
- Nets: large blocks, thin buildings allow parking at the block interior
- Small blocks increase on-street parking

Parking

- Small district parking structures with retail at sidewalk
- Discouragement of private connections from parking to building, especially given the benign climate
- Parking as public utility
- Asymmetrical street: parking one side, destinations other.
- Parking under street.
- Monthly parkers on upper floor, groundfloor for short-term.
- Parking fees reduced on higher floors.
- Some monthly parking on each floor, with varying prices.

Movement

- Jitneys
- Slow lanes seperated by planted median
- One-way streets create rhythmic flow, predictability, safety.
- Two-way streets create greater variety, interest, less freeway-like.
- Median achieves best of both: parking, activities, planting.
- Balanced concern arterial function and qualities as a place.
- Diagonal pedestrian crossings.

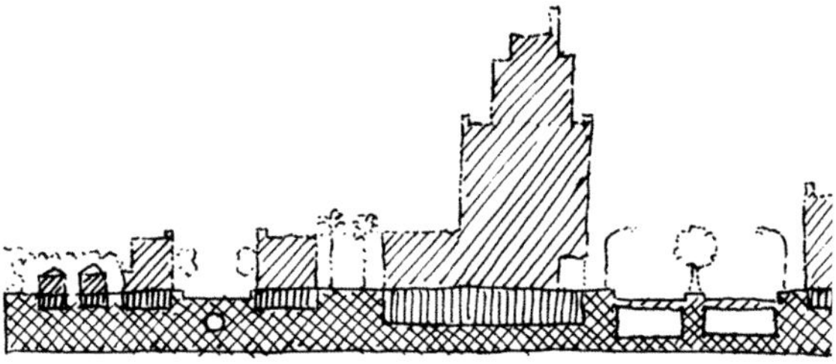

New Types Which Weave the Section Together.

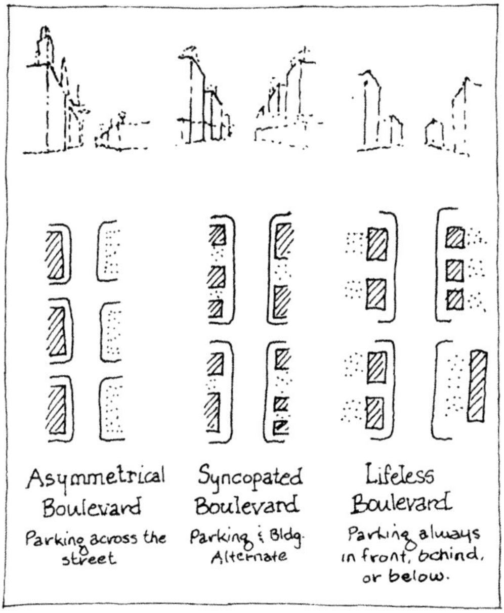

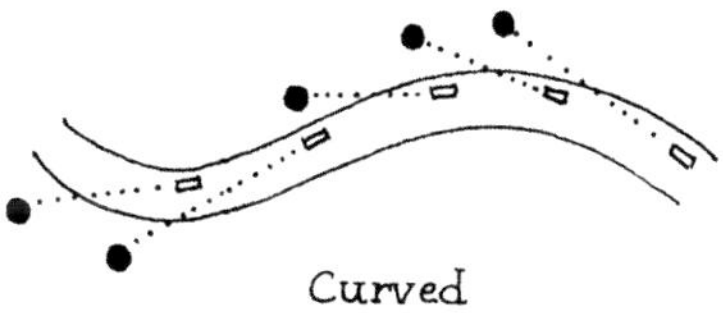

Curved Boulevard: Sequential Focus on Alternating Sides

Public Infrastructure

• Coordination (rather than concealment) of the street lighting, telephone/power poles, traffic signage

• Review of materials for sidewalks, curbs, pedestrian crossings

Architecture

• "Two-storyness" (per William Whyte)

• Double- or triple- scale

• Lively signage

• Architectural integration of car and pedestrian

• Front-back arcades or passages

• Finer grain, texture, materials at street scale

• Asymmetry reflects sun conditions

• Asymmetry encourages cross-axial readings

• Sidewalk activities: cafes and restaurants, vendors

Landscaping

• Used to reinforce, not cover up, basic structure

• Used to improve microclimate, especially reduction of wind, dust, heat, pollutants

• Asymmetrical treatment to reflect sun conditions

ASYMMETRIC · BOULEVARD

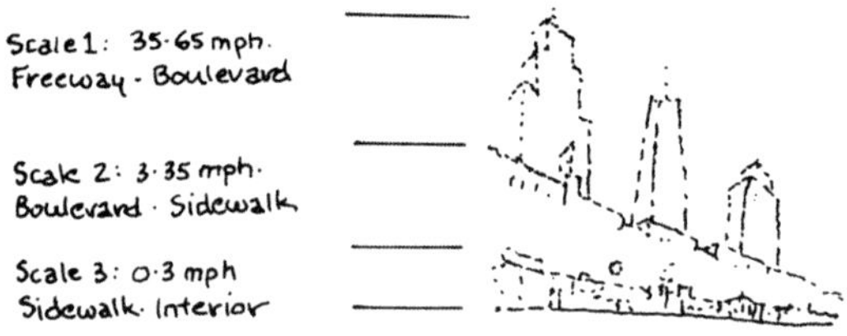

TRIPLE - SCALE ARCHITECTURE

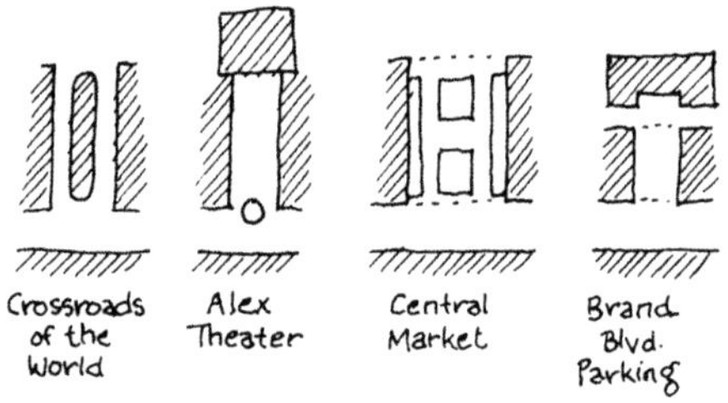

Perpendicular Space Reinforces the Boulevard.

The rationale for these proposals is apparent all around us. When the city was young and lightly populated with respect to its area, it could well afford to perpetuate the myth of a private pastoral sanctuary for every family; but as the city races to become the nation's largest, the signs of increasing density are everywhere, and the old myths must disappear from the rhetoric as surely as they have already disappeared form the scene. The blunt instrument of a recent proposition which simply chopped in half all commercial development along most of the boulevards does not even begin to address the question of how Los Angeles will evolve into a new kind of city. Obstructionist groups with names like "Not Yet New York" fail to recognize that Los Angeles is not yet Los Angeles, and that our urban prototypes must continue to adapt and change. Unfortunately what the voters have generally reacted to is a deterioration of their neighborhoods with respect, more than anything else, to traffic and parking. They are taking the shortsighted view (Americans are famous for this) and have failed to see the interconnection of traffic, parking, architecture, and the future shape of the city.

The architecture of the boulevards should not, and in any case probably could not, aspire to the kind of monumentality which springs from cultural consensus and stability. But nor should architecture conspire to eradicate the vitality from the public space of the boulevards on falsely deterministic grounds. If the zoning regulations or building codes are to blame, then let us try to change them. If parking is the problem then let us reconsider it. If the habits and misconceptions of city officials or residents put public space at risk, then let us at least try to point this out. Such efforts would perhaps not be justified on worn out machines, but the boulevards survive as vital bodies. They have been around for one hundred and two years, and there is no reason to think that in their second century, they will prove any less essential—or challenging—to our daily life in Los Angeles, or our highest visions of the American city.

Notes

Introduction

1 Reyner Banham "Los Angeles: the Architecture of Four Ecologies" (NewYork: Penguin 1971). Banham ends his classic book with a vigorous admonition against the use of conventional planning concepts and strategies for Los Angeles.
2 "Standard Street Dimensions", Department of Public Works, Bureau of Engi neering, City of Los Angeles; adopted March 27, 1969 by the City Planning Commission.
3 "Street Naming Policy" adopted in April 1967 by the Los Angeles County Street Naming Committee.
4 For discussions of the public realm see: Sennett, Richard, The Fall of Public Man (New York: Knopf 1977); Arendt, Hanna, "The Public Realm: The Common" in Blazer, Nathan; and Lilla, Mark, Eds., "The Public Face of Architecture" (New York: The Free Press 1987).

1 – Suture
The Pueblo/Rancho Landscars

1 For the best general discussion of the Laws of the Indies and their influence on Los Angeles, see: Crouch, Dora; Mundigo, Axcl; and Garr, Daniel, "Spanish Town Planning in North America" (Cambridge; MIT 1982). Also see: Reps, John, "Cities of the American West: A History of Frontier Planning" (Princeton 1979).
2 Crouch, et.al.
3 Ibid.
4 Robinson, W.W., Land in California (Berkeley: University of California 1948).
5 Based on a map of the ranchos in Palmer Conner, "The Romance of the Ranchos" (Los Angeles: Title Insurance and Trust Company, 1939).
6 Venturi, Robert; Brown, Denise Scott; and Izenour, Steven, "Learning From Las Vegas" (Cambridge: MIT 1977).

2 – Umbilical
The Spawning of Sunset Boulevards

1 Leonard Pitt, "The Midewesternization of a Cowtown", in California history, Spring 1981. For a pictorial source on this and other periods of Sunset Boulevard, see: Kennelley, Joe; and Hankey, Roy, "Sunset Boulevard: America's Dream Street" (Burbank: Darwin 1981).
2 Reps, John, "Cities of the American West". Provides both a history and maps of many of the paper towns.
3 Harlow, Neal, "Maps and Surveys of the Pueblo Lands of Los Angeles" (Los Angeles: Dawson's Bookshop 1976).
4 Sources: "Oxford English Dictionary"; Lavedan, Pierre, "Histoire d'Urbanisme de Paris"; and Girouard, Mark, "Cities and People" (New Haven: Yale 1985).
5 This building first came to my attention as a detail in a photograph of downtown Los Angeles reproduced in Bruce Henstell's Los Angeles: An Illustrated History (New York: Knopf 1980).
6 Ralph Hyde, "Gilded Scenes and Shining Prospects: Panoramic Views of British Towns 1575-1900" (New Haven: Yale Center for British Art 1985).
7 It was Bill Mason of the Los Angeles County Natural History Museum who suggested that the word "Paris", just visible on the panorama's exterior, probably referred to a portrayal of the Battle of Paris rather than of Paris generally.
8 The existence and influence of a sizeable French community was brought to my attention by Bruce Henstell.

3 – Spine
Piecemeal Grandeur on Wilshire

1 Arturo Soria y Mata, "La Cité Linéaire: Nouvelle Architecture de Villes" (Paris: C.E.R.A. 1979).
2 Ibid. From introduction by Carlos Sambricio.
3 Reps, "Cities of the American West", map p.259
4 Ralph Hancock, "Fabulous Boulevard" (New York: Funk & Wagnalls 1949).
5 Minutes, Los Angeles City Council, Volume 44, p.717, November 11, 1895.
6 Ibid. Volume 46, February 10, 1896.
7 Hancock, "Fabulous Boulevard".
8 Ibid.
9 Ibid.
10 In 1925, J.F. Sartori, President of the Subway Terminal Corporation, said, "The Subway Terminal Building means stabilization of the present central business district. The status of that district has remained uncertain because of the tremendous growth of the city... Experience in large Eastern

cities has shown that nothing is more damaging than a constantly shifting business center." Quoted in Laurance Hill, "La Reina: Los Angeles in Three Centuries" (Los Angeles: Security First National Bank, 1929).

11 Banham, Los Angeles.

4 - Girdle
The Studios Face the Boulevards

1 Robert Anderson, "The Motion Picture Patents Company A Reevaluation", in Tino Balio, ed., The American Film Industry (Madison: University of Wisconsin, 1976).

2 Bruce Torrence, "Hollywood: The First Hundred Years" (New York: New York Zeotrope 1982).

3 For a pictorial source on the studios (film, radio, and television) see: Heimann, Jim, Hooray for Hollywood (San Francisco: Chronicle 1983).

4 Ibid.

5 - Phosphor
Day or Night on Hollywood Boulevard

For pictorial sources see Heimann, "Hooray for Hollywood"; Torrence, Hollywood and Picture Palaces, Washington: National Trust for Historic Preservation, 1988.

6 - Torrent
The Boulevards Accelerate

1 Hill, La Reina, 70.

2 Clay Mcshane, "Transforming the Use of Urban Space: A look at the Revolution in Street Pavements, 1880-1924", Journal of Urban History, Vol. 5, No. 3, May 1979.

3 For general histories of transport see: Boulton, W.H., "The Pageant of Transport Through the Ages" (London: Benjamin Blom 1969); Kidner, R.W., "A Short History of Mechanical Traction and Travel, Vol. I, Road" (Kent: Oakwood 1947); or Miller, John Anderson, "Fares, Please!: From Horse-Cars to Streamliners" (New York: Appleton-Century 1941). For a good summary of the history of transport systems in Los Angeles see: Brodsly, David, "L.A. Freeway: An Appreciative Essay" (Berkeley: University of California 1981).

4 Hill, "La Reina".

5 Quoted in Scott Bottles, "Los Angeles and the automobile: The Making of the Modern City" (Berkeley: Univ. of California 1987) p.112. This is the most authoritative work on the subject.

6 Le Corbusier, "The City of Tomorrow and Its Planning" (Cambridge: M.I.T.).

7 Bottles, "Los Angeles and the Automobile".

8 Ibid.

9 Ibid.

7 - Pathogen
Signs and Symptoms on the Boulevards

1 The subject of architecture, signage and roads in the United States has been given the most thorough treatment in Chester H. Liebs, "Main Street to Miracle Mile: American Roadside Architecture" (Boston: Little Brown 1985). Venturi, Scott Brown and Izenour's Learning From Las Vegas in 1965 was among the earliest works to treat popular and commercial architecture as if it mattered. For Los Angeles specifically, David Gebhart and Harriette von Breton's "L.A. In the 30's" is an invaluable source.

2 Hancock, "Fabulous Boulevard", 310. Hancock indicates that by 1949, there were 311 billboards along the sixteen miles of Wilshire. 133 of these were landscaped. Lots along Wilshire leased out for billboards could earn as much as $50,000 per year.

3 Peter Blake, "God's Own Junkyard: The Planned Deterioration of America's Landscape" (New York: Holt, Rinehart & Winston, 1979).

8 - Fuselage
Cross-Section of the Public Realm

1 The 1988 competition for Olympic Boulevard, for example, did not specifically preclude such structural investigations, but in its program requirements and tone tended to encourage cosmetic solutions.

2 Venturi et.al., "Learning From Las Vegas".

3 See Arendt, "The Public Realm: The Common".

4 Anderson, Stanford, "People in the Physical Environment: The Urban Ecology of Streets", in Anderson, Stanford, ed., On Streets (Cambridge: MIT 1986).

Twenty-Five Years Later:
Boulevards in Practice

1

Episodic and Symbolic Boulevards

Atlanta: Peachtree Street and Auburn Avenue

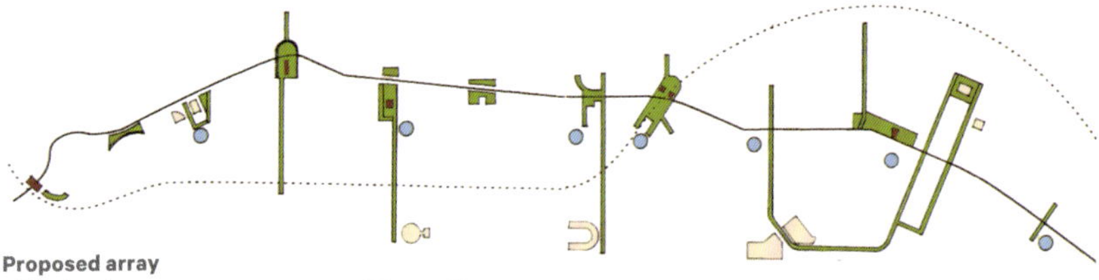

Proposed array of "Lateral Gardens" along Peachtree Street

When *Los Angeles Boulevard* was published in 1989, the design literature on streets was limited, and the prospects for actually designing a street were almost non-existent. Then, in 1990, a civic and business coalition in Atlanta decided to sponsor an open national competition to redesign two miles of Peachtree Street, the city's most prominent civic and commercial boulevard.

For me, the competition was an irresistible opportunity—and a taunt. At the time I was teaching design at U.C. Berkeley's school of architecture, and my featured seminar was called "The City Street." When the competition was announced, I felt there was no way I could not enter, given my claim to some degree of expertise on streets, especially long boulevards. And with its unusually generous prize purse of $120,000 (and promise of a contract to build for the winner), the competition seemed like a high-stakes challenge to test the ideas in *Los Angeles Boulevard* in the real world.

Based on earlier visits to Atlanta, I saw Peachtree Street as Atlanta's version of an L.A. boulevard in general, and of Wilshire Boulevard in particular, even though it is only a fraction of Wilshire's length. The competition offered the exciting prospect of grappling with a fundamental question: how to approach the redesign of an extended public street. How was a street different from other linear spatial forms, such as a long arcaded walkway through a college campus, or the nave of a cathedral—singular elements in a unified setting or building? How, in other words, was urban design different from architectural design?

I was haunted by Jane Jacobs' warning that architects could not really be trusted to design cities, since they approached problems seeking the "order of art," whereas cities were all about the "order of life." Could you have both art and life in the form of cities? Could a boulevard be both alive and beautiful? And in a more vexing vein, could such a thing happen in a city which, like so many in America, had largely capitulated to the spatial demands of the automobile?

Peachtree Street was not a Champs Elysée or a Michigan Avenue. It was a former country road that gradually evolved into an urban avenue. Its southern terminus was anchored in the street grid of downtown Atlanta, from which it began to twist and turn as it widened into an avenue through the neighborhoods of Midtown, before finally crossing two highways to arrive in the affluent northside suburbs as a broad automobile boulevard. As its width and character changed repeatedly so did the jarring variety of architectural scales and styles along its edges. Peachtree had a kind of on again-off again urbanity. Even the major subway line which ran under Peachtree sometimes shifted over to a parallel street, putting key stations a block or more away.

And yet Peachtree was important to Atlantans for a number of reasons: its historic associations with Atlanta and Georgia (the Peachtree State, after all), its prestige and associated land values as an address, and its unmatched aggregation of important buildings and civic institutions. Peachtree had symbolic power, bolstered by economic interest, and it seemed to embody Atlanta in almost every respect.

Except at least one. For many black Atlantans, a populous and often prosperous minority in the Southern city that liked to boast it was "too busy to hate," there was another street with even more resonance. Auburn Avenue, or "Sweet Auburn," was the spine of the historic African-American neighborhood where Dr. Martin Luther King had preached, and where much of Civil Rights movement's history had been written. Auburn terminated right at Peachtree in the heart of downtown. So after the initial announcement of the Peachtree competition, there was pushback about the omission of Auburn from the design brief. As a result, the organizers added Auburn to the competition as a second street to be designed. It would have the same jury, but separate prizes. Even before the competition began, I was seeing that city streets were, as I had suspected, deeply important to many people, but often for different and even conflicting reasons.

Our approach to Peachtree was to emphasize its episodic character. We highlighted the many destinations which were not directly on Peachtree but which, as a group, seemed to straddle it at distances ranging from a block to a mile. We concluded that Peachtree was not so much Atlanta's spine—fastening everything to it—as its common thread, giving linear form to a dispersed array of sites. So our design focused not on the continuous line of the street, but on its major intersections, which we referred to these as "episodes" in the linear narrative of Peachtree Street. At each intersection, we proposed "lateral gardens"—perpendicular green links of varying lengths and scales which would connect to the nearby destinations. Between the intersections, rather than suggesting rigid design guidelines, we proposed letting the street evolve organically, much in the way it had for the previous one hundred years.

This was a kind of anti-monumental approach, the antithesis of the regularized and aesthetically controlled boulevards of Paris or avenues of Washington D.C. And it reflected a phrase I read much later, and loved, which William MacDonald used to describe the stunning extended main streets that the Romans built in their colonial cities: "loose but palpable entities." In retrospect, I also see now that the strong emphasis on the lateral streets to create an integrated landscape was a small-scale rehearsal for the Arc project in Palestine more than a decade later, when we emphasized lateral transit boulevards perpendicular to a curved rail and infrastructure line.

The first round of the competition drew 110 entries from thirteen countries. Five finalists were selected for the second round. We were among them. In the end, we won second prize for both Peachtree Street and Auburn Avenue. For a young design practice just getting started, this was perhaps the ideal outcome, since it provided a welcome double-dose of recognition (and renumeration) without committing us to move towards construction, for which we were clearly not ready. The project was published in Harvard Architecture Review in 1997, and has since served as a touchstone for the office in terms of the comprehensiveness of the analysis, the clarity of the strategy, and the detailed elegance of the drawings.

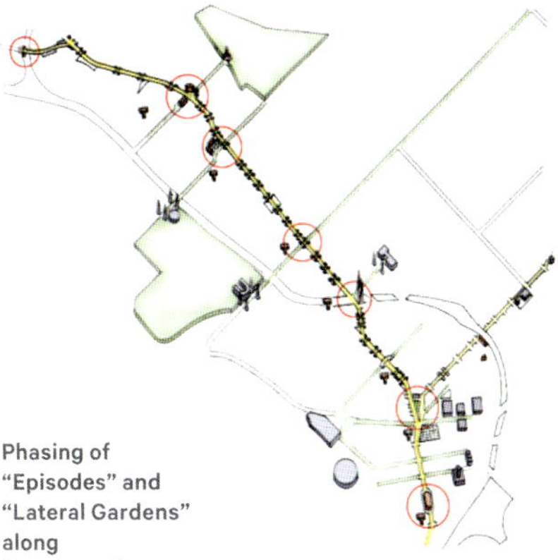

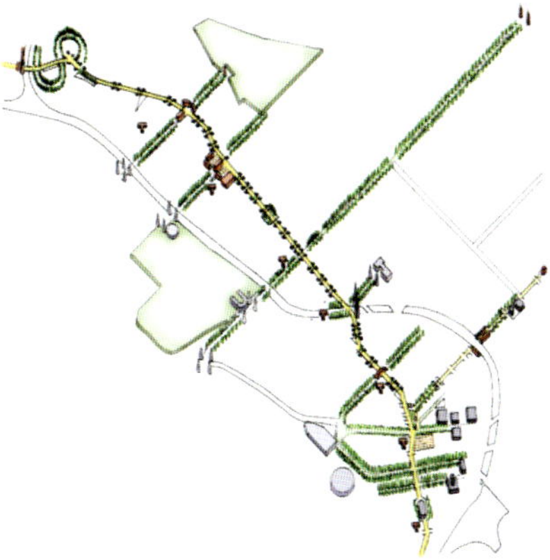

Phasing of "Episodes" and "Lateral Gardens" along Peachtree Street and Auburn Avenue

FIVE YEAR PLAN

TWENTY-FIVE YEAR PLAN

Two "lateral gardens" along Peachtree Street, from above and at eye level

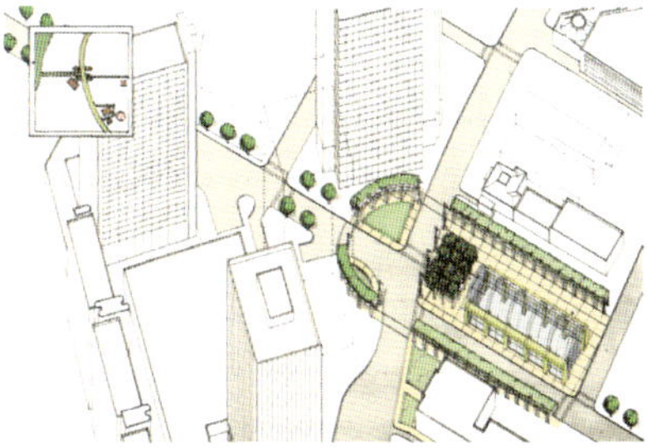

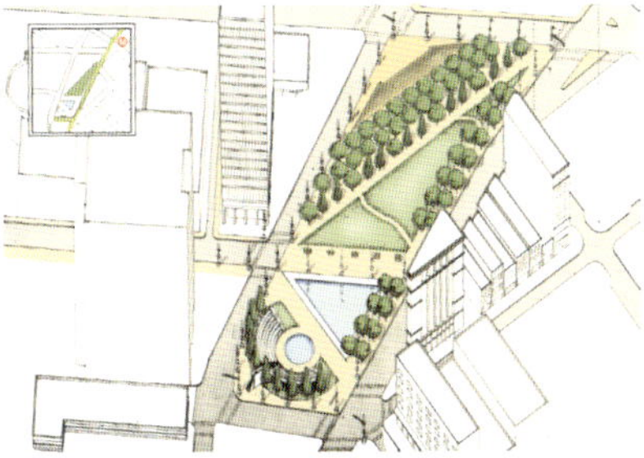

2 Electric Boulevards

Los Angeles: Electric Trolleybus System

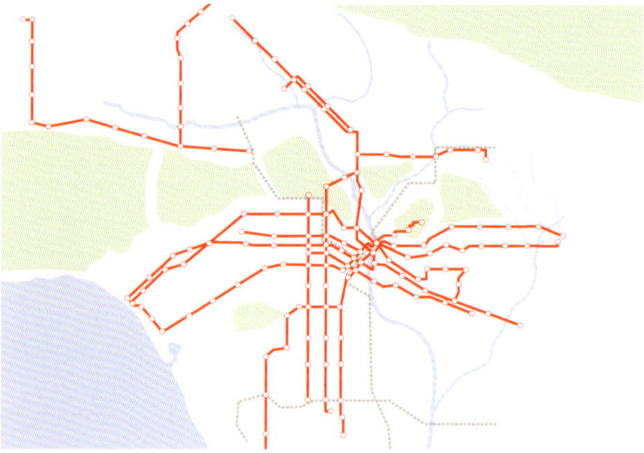

200 miles of proposed Electric Trolleybus routes throughout Los Angeles County

After returning to Los Angeles in 1991, I sent a proposal to Nick Patsaouras, president of L.A. County's transit agency, to develop some ideas on the design of the boulevards and their relation to public transit. I was hoping for an opportunity to look at a block or two of boulevard. He came back with a somewhat shocking counter-proposal: help the agency design 200 miles of boulevards for a planned conversion from buses to electric trolleybuses (ETB's). Be careful what you wish for.

The Electric Trolley Bus project provided an extraordinary opportunity to look at not just a singular boulevard but at all of the region's boulevards together as a system. This was an enormous jump in scale from the detailed street corner designs for Peachtree Street. It required a typological approach. Over the course of many months, we surveyed the existing boulevard system and identified nine distinct types of boulevards - or rather boulevard segments, since no boulevard remained consistently one type along its length. We gave names to each segment type, such as Downtown Avenue, Neighborhood Main Street, Residential Parkway, Viaduct, etc. From these, we developed a kind of overlay for a new type: the Electric Trolley Boulevard, which would have to thread its way—overhead power lines and all—across miles of urban landscape.

The design of the Electric Trolley Boulevard required a detailed examination and understanding of how electric trolleybuses operate in the street, and of the electric infrastructure—catenary wires, hardware, and support poles—needed to propel them. As some Southern Californians knew from visits to San Francisco, which has an extensive ETB system, the poles and wires needed for ETB's can be visually intrusive, creating silhouetted webs above the street. This caused some public concern, so a great deal of attention was focused on understanding and minimizing the visual impact of the wires on the typical boulevard vista.

The sheer breadth of the system meant that it would traverse hundreds of different neighborhoods and communities, raising the question of district identity and character: should this regional system pass unchanging through all areas for clarity and economy, or should it change its appearance according to its setting? In the end, we developed a system we called the flexipole, a kit of pole types and interchangeable attachments which satisfied all the basic engineering and operational requirements for transit, but could be modified—in bases, colors, luminaires, signs—to reflect community character.

The project also exposed us to the complicated issues related to different forms of transit—how bus service differs from urban rail, how different vehicle types shape perceptions of transit, how speed, reliability, safety, and comfort affect the performance and acceptance of transit projects. The ETB project unfolded before the city of Curitiba, Brazil's now-famous Bus Rapid Transit (BRT) system became widely known, but the ETB project anticipated many of the same issues and debates about BRT versus LRT (Light Rail) today.

After several years of design and engineering, the project was eventually brought to a halt. This was in part due to lingering doubts about the electric trolleybus itself as a transit technology. Though ETB had the enormous advantage of being emissions free, in a region desperately trying to improve its air quality, there was concern that newer, better transport technologies—such as fuel cells or natural gas—were just around the corner, and would render the ETB investment obsolete.

The project also suffered ultimately from an atmosphere of social upheaval and racial tension; the Rodney King riots took place during the middle of our efforts. This was reflected in

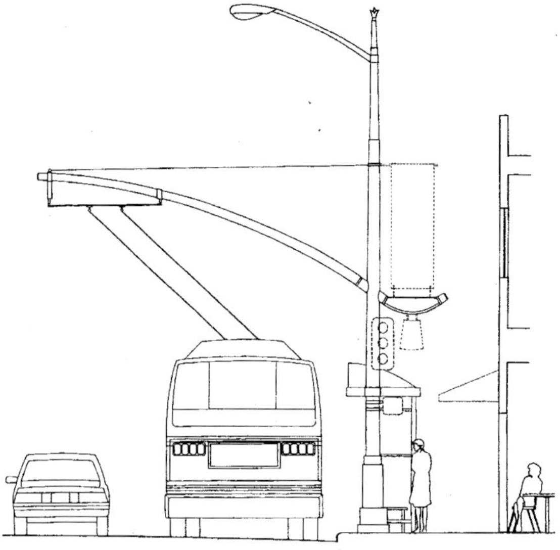

Integrated street elements of the Electric Trolleybus Boulevard

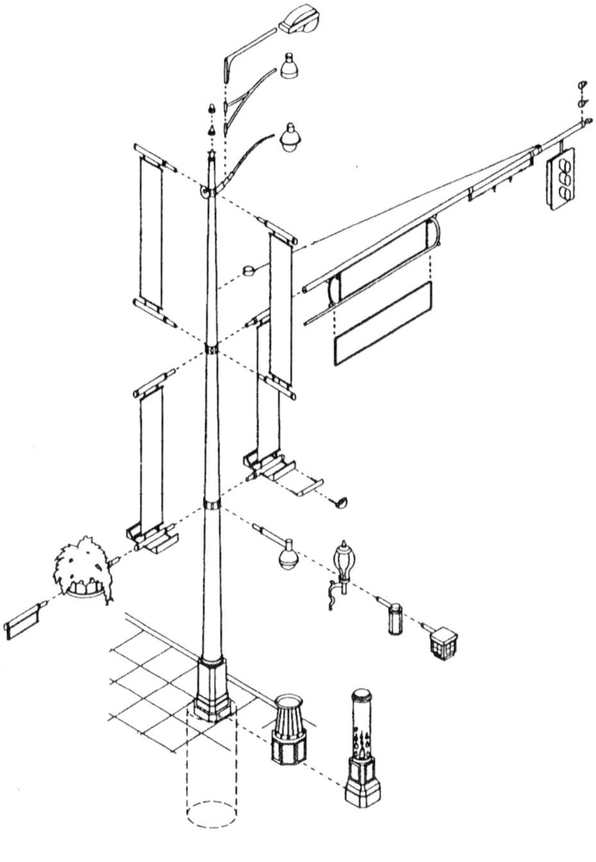

The Flexipole: engineered core with adjustable attachments to reflect different district character along the routes

the concerns of different communities affected by the ETB project, who felt they were competing for scarce resources, transit and otherwise, and were suspicious of large-scale projects, no matter how well intentioned.

Despite the project's demise, I was able to experience first hand what I had anticipated in *Los Angeles Boulevard*—the underlying economic and political forces that shape public streets and public space. In our outreach efforts, I was able to visit neighborhoods across Los Angeles County to participate in community meetings and workshops. This experience drove home the point that large regional systems have direct and strong impacts on very local conditions and individual lives, whether a single block, a storefront, or the pedestrian crossing in front of a school. In thinking about and designing cities, that balancing of concerns at multiple scales is perhaps the most difficult, and important, aspect of our work.

Four examples of the Electric Trolleybus Boulevard typology

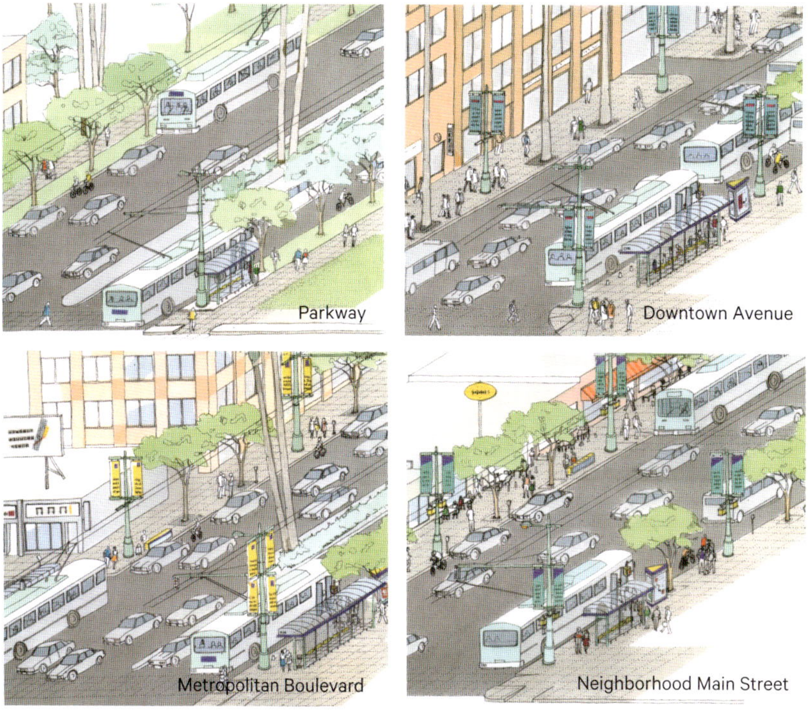

3 Metro Boulevard

Los Angeles: Hill Street

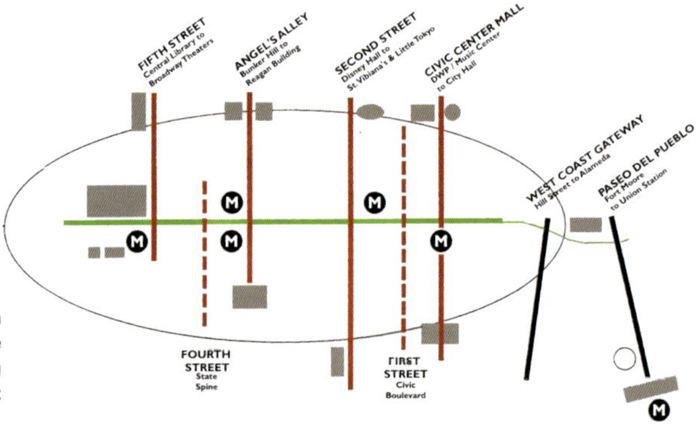

Key lateral pedestrian linkages from the subway portals along Hill Street

Following the ETB project, transit agency officials asked us to continue working with them on another project. This time, instead of a regional network of boulevards, the focus was on a single street: the five-block segment of Hill Street, in the heart of L.A.'s historic downtown, that carried the Red Line subway below its surface. This meant designing a street that was part of a dense grid of urban streets and blocks, as opposed to the freestanding urban linearity—straddled by residential neighborhoods on either side—of a typical Los Angeles boulevard. And like wooden Russian dolls fitting one inside the next, the project contained two smaller projects within the five blocks: the complete design for a single block, and the design and construction of a small public space in the middle of that block. The smaller scale of the project offered the chance to put into practice some of our more detailed ideas from the Peachtree Street competition.

This multiplicity of scales reflected downtown's rich layers of history. Though L.A. has an undeserved reputation as a city either missing a past or indifferent to it, downtown has been continuously settled and expanded for more than 230 years, since its founding in 1781. The traces of successive layers of habitation and construction are visible—some easily, others requiring a more discerning eye. Downtown rewards those who enjoy the presentness of the past.

In historic cities, that past includes architecture, streets, plazas, and public spaces, threaded together by the movement systems that animate them. In reviewing the evolution of transport in downtown, you begin with walking (the first non-indigenous settlers arrived from northern Mexico on foot) and then over time add horses, horse-drawn carriages, horse-drawn streetcars, stream locomotives, cable cars, bicycles, electric trolleys, elevators, funiculars, automobiles, trucks, escalators, subway trains, buses, and electric buses. Each subsequent mode of transport has had to incorporate the previous ones, which in turn usually had to adjust their way of operating. When designing in historic city centers, it's important to master the historic record so as to be capable of reconstructing in your mind's eye this time-lapse urban ballet.

The project's five blocks linked two of the Red Line's stations, Pershing Square and Civic Center. Transit and walking are connected—transit users usually become pedestrians at some point in their journey. We conducted a fine-grained examination of the street's "pedestrian infrastructure"—its sidewalks, alleys, crosswalks, steps, doorways, and general sense of safety, amenity, and walkability. Hill Street runs along the foot of Bunker Hill, whose unusual steepness for a downtown area allowed us to document the ways that topography influences pedestrian activity—both spurring it (vistas, shortcuts, exercise, etc.) and inhibiting it (long climbs, inhospitable walls, barriers for the elderly and disabled, etc.).

Lateral link: Angels Flight Railway connecting Hill Street to the top of Bunker Hill

Our plan called for extensive shade trees and sidewalk lighting to improve the experience of walking on Hill Street, the introduction of new mid-block crosswalks to provide more choices of route, and the conversion of the roadway from an intimidating one-way "arterial" into a calmer, two-way avenue with occasional landscaped medians. All of this was accomplished, and as Hill Street became more walkable and livable, significant new residential and mixed-use projects have begun to fill in. This change drove home the point that while economics is still the final determinant of what gets built in cities, creating a hospitable public setting for redevelopment is a critical part of the effort. The interaction of the public sector and private markets is dynamic and unpredictable, but in democratic societies, this is the horse you must ride if you want to reshape a city. Public space and private property are the yin and yang of urban life.

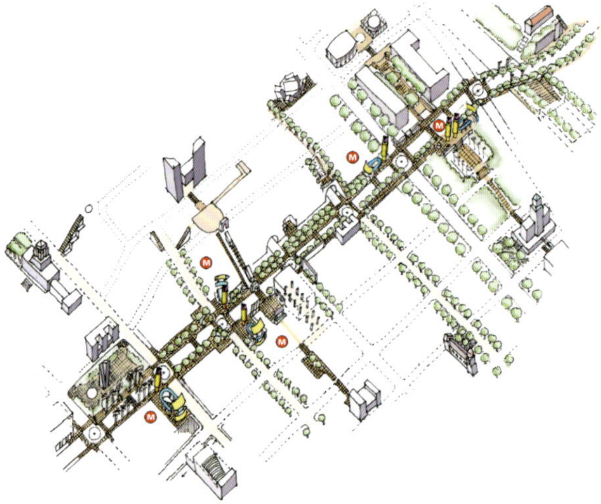

Aerial view of the five blocks of Hill Street and the lateral pedestrian connections to key downtown destinations

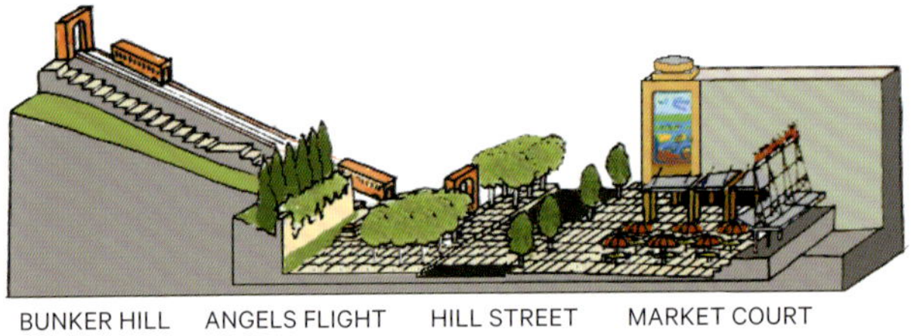

Conceptual section through Bunker Hill: Angels Flight Railway and Market Court

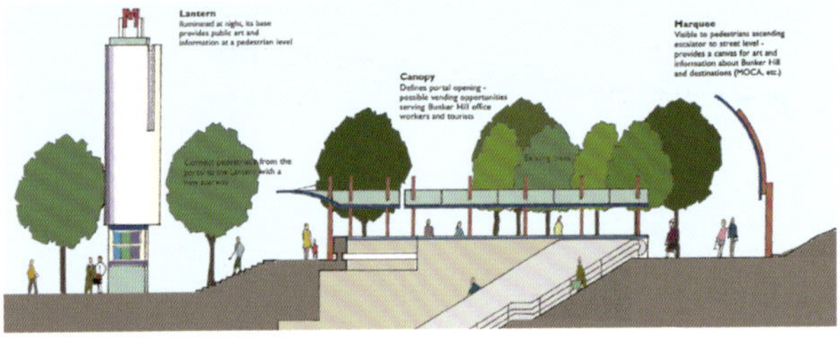

Streetscape at 4th and Hill Metro Station: new canopies, landscape, and iconic lanterns at each portal

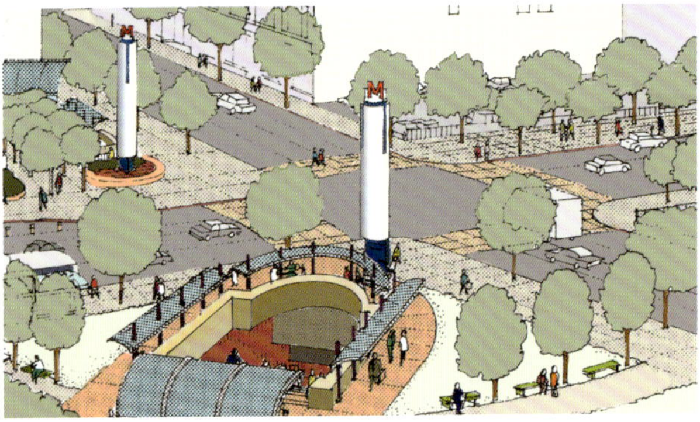

The single block requiring special attention ran from the Red Line subway entrance at the corner of 4th and Hill north to Grand Central Market. The market is an important historic and architectural landmark and a beloved indoor crossroads of fruit stalls and eateries; its preservation is a testament to the dogged efforts of committed individuals and the redevelopment agency. Our design work included large numbers of new street trees on Hill, and the creation of a new hillside park called Angels Knoll, which became the leafy centerpiece of the film "500 Days of Summer." The work anticipated the renewed importance of parks and green space in revitalizing city centers. Parks had been declining because of reduced municipal budgets for maintenance and fears of gang activity; but the subsequent success of parks Millennium in Chicago, and Bryant and High Line in New York has shown parks to be powerful tools for rethinking our cities.

The project's smallest feature involved the transformation of the Market's parking lot and loading dock into a vibrant public space. The site lies directly across the street from the lower station of another beloved landmark and transit facility, Angels Flight Railway. We created a theater-like arrangement that opened its arms to pedestrians coming down from Bunker Hill, and in reverse, created a two-tiered terrace with panoramic views up the hill. Passersby pause on the big curved bench at the sidewalk; market visitors bring their lunch outside and eat in the shade of tipu trees and bougainvillea screens. Behind the stage, the trucks continue to deliver fruit and vegetables to the market, as they have for almost a hundred years. The project is modest; in an age of iconic overkill, its gentle liveliness still seems like a small victory for public space.

Market Court terrace at the Hill Street entrance to Grand Central Market

4 Civic and Cultural Boulevards

Los Angeles Civic Center: Grand, First, Spring and Main

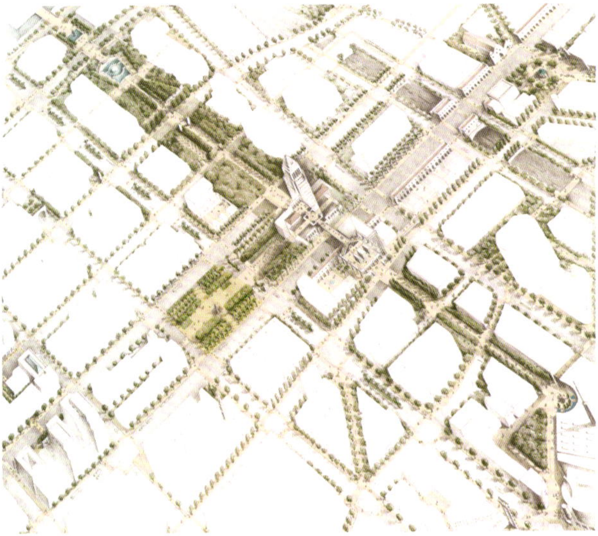

Aerial view of the "Ten-Minute Diamond" for the Los Angeles Civic Center

The successful work on Hill Street and at Market Court set the stage for more than a decade of work on the streets of downtown Los Angeles. The official client varied, and over time included the Civic Center Authority, the Community Redevelopment Agency, the city's Department of Transportation, the county's Metropolitan Transportation Authority, and the non-profit Project Restore. But in all cases, the historic, civic, and cultural importance of the streets in question meant that larger groups of stakeholders were involved in the design process.

Civic Center Master Plan

The Los Angeles Civic Center is the largest government complex outside of Washington, D.C., employing more than 30,000 workers in the northern end of downtown. We were asked to help improve the physical organization and efficiency of the area by guiding its future development. For this effort, no

HISTORIC BIRDSEYE

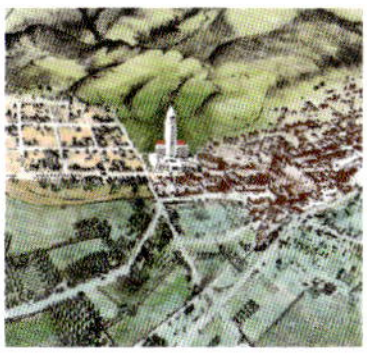

FOUR TOPOGRAPHIES

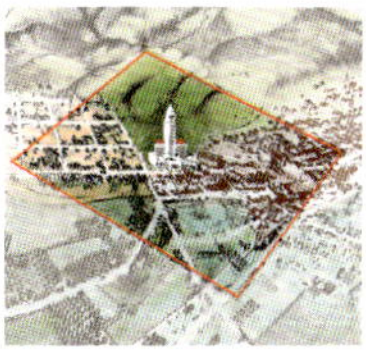

TEN-MINUTE DIAMOND

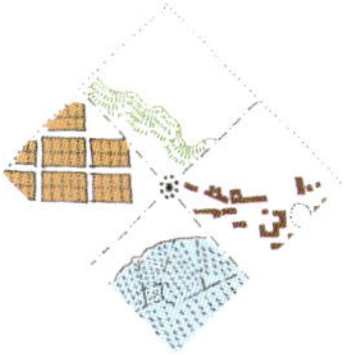

URBAN QUARTERS

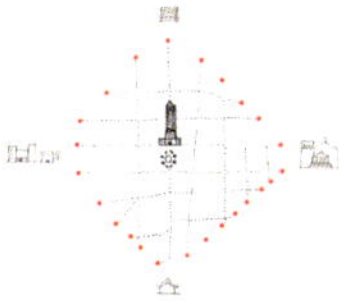

CULTURAL ANCHORS

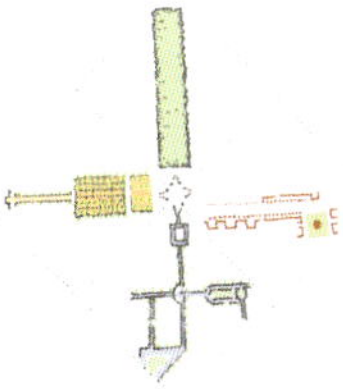

GREEN PUBLIC SPACE

fewer than five levels of government were represented, along with various independent agencies. Our job on the multi-firm team was to focus on the streets and public space, enhancing both transit and pedestrian linkages for the Civic Center. The site and the design questions were complex. Should government buildings operate on a discrete campus, or blend in with their urban surroundings? Can civic and cultural uses happily co-exist? How do you avoid a government ghetto, empty on nights and weekends, when cultural uses are most active? And given the growing demand for downtown housing, how could you integrate residential uses and neighborhood character into a setting that was at best monumental, and at worst forbidding?

The sheer expanse of the Civic Center's dispersed collection of government buildings begged the question of scale, and we began measuring walking distance in minutes—using a standard 3 miles per hour. Planners typically draw a circle around a site for such measurements, but when we plotted actual routes on the street grid, using the rotunda of City Hall as our center point, we found that a ten-minute walk in any direction produced a zone with the shape of a diamond. The Ten-Minute Diamond, a simple conceptual framework based on time and walking, captured people's imaginations, which gave it staying power.

Tantalizingly, the four points of the diamond captured key cultural destinations: the Los Angles Music Center, the historic Bradbury Building and Grand Central Market, The Geffen Contemporary Museum, and La Plaza and Olvera Street. When overlaid on historic plans of downtown, the diamond also captured four distinct historical/topographic zones: the original 18th Century Spanish/Mexican settlement of El Pueblo, the slopes of Bunker Hill, the 19th Century American grid, and the low-lying river plain of Little Tokyo. We divided the diamond in Quarters and named them accordingly. Each quarter had a new or enhanced public space or garden that linked up, like a pinwheel, around City Hall.

So streets and public spaces, far from mere utilitarian leftovers, became the urban framework for development. Potential sites were identified for new buildings of various uses. The economic premise, as we had seen in Atlanta and on Hill Street, was that the public sector could prepare fertile ground for directed public-private investment. The plan was adopted by the City Council in 1997 and continues to influence thinking and development in the Civic Center.

Grand Avenue

Grand Avenue, which runs along the ridge of Bunker Hill, could be considered the Frankenstein monster of downtown Los Angeles: an experimental mechanical street, constructed in the wake of the massive demolition of buildings and the destruction of natural topography of Bunker Hill. The Bunker Hill project, dating from the 1950's, was one of the nation's first examples of "redevelopment", a legal process in which a long-standing neighborhood is deemed blighted, then destroyed in part or in whole, than rebuilt with money raised on the expected increase in value from the new development (a funding mechanism known as tax-increment financing, which Haussmann used to rebuild Paris). This street story has been unfolding for more than 50 years, and it is still not done.

The name is right. The street has conjured up grand schemes, grand ambitions, grand egos. To the extent that cities, both the streets which define them and the buildings which line the streets, are expressions of power and prestige, Grand Avenue

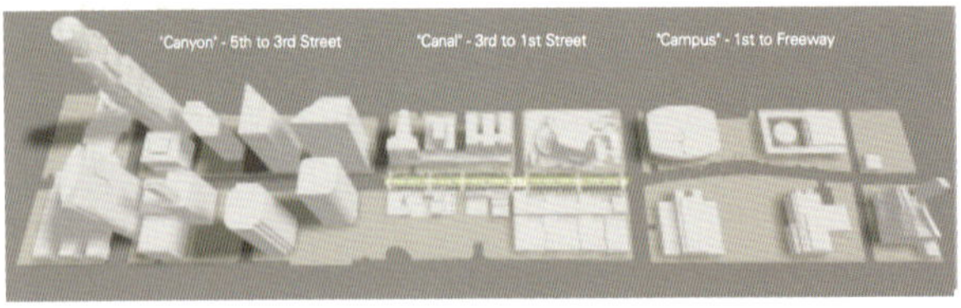

Proposed "Canyon", "Canal" and "Campus" segments for Grand Avenue

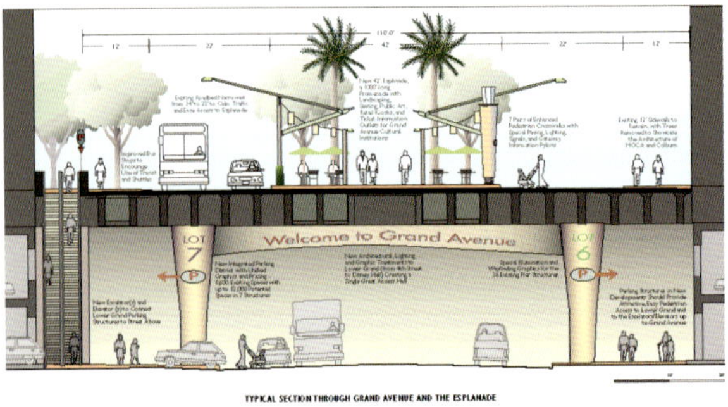

Cross-section showing enhanced pedestrian connections from the parking on Lower Grand to the destinations on Upper Grand, including the proposed Esplanade in the center of the street

provides L.A.'s most obvious case study.

At the northern end, in the 1970's the prominent Chandler family led the construction of the Music Center as a cultural acropolis (and not incidentally as Los Angeles's answer to Lincoln Center). It set the tone of high-minded and high-stakes competitiveness. At the southern end in the 1980's, a much publicized and controversial developer-led design competition added sleek corporate high-rises and bland high-end condominiums to the mix, all centered on an overwrought commercial plaza with a gobsmacking water feature. Like a buried jewel, the project's much disputed cultural totem was the newly created Museum of Contemporary Art, whose architect, the renowned Arata Isosaki, had to contend with a site that was mainly off the street and underground, surrounded by parking structures. The museum, while technically on Grand, seemed to live in a world of its own.

The 90's brought renewed attempts to fill in the avenue's gaping holes: huge lots still empty (except for parked cars) four decades after the initial demolitions. This resulted—again after much publicity and bitter public disputes—in the triumph of Disney Hall and the quiet but urbane presence of the Colburn School of Music. Even these could not alleviate the impression of a street that was more of an artificial concourse of urban trophies than a vibrant public space. Too much of the life of the place was hidden within or behind the buildings and below the street, where Lower Grand provided invisible access to nearly 10,000 parking spaces.

When in 1998 we had our chance, as so many architects before and since, to influence the design of the street, we used our previous Civic Center work to diagnose the apparent lifelessness of the street, and concluded that the problem—and opportunity—lay in the street's cross-section, both in width and height. We found that the roadbed's highway-like dimensions could be sufficiently reduced to permit the introduction of a leafy, active median along its length. Inspired by Barcelona's Ramblas but shaped to reflect downtown Los Angeles, this "esplanade" would have palm trees, gardens, kiosks, cafes, information pavilions, and water features, and would provide pedestrians with privileged center-street views of the architectural parade. New escalators up from Lower Grand's parking structures would mean that those arriving by car, instead of being shunted directly into corporate lobbies, would be brought directly up to the avenue's sidewalks, adding to their vibrancy.

The plan had both fans and detractors. Some saw an opportunity at last to realize Grand Avenue as a lively, walkable place. Others seemed to feel that L.A. was still a car town and needed a wide avenue of headlights rather than a Euro-paseo. What became clear to me during the process was the alluring but problematic role of the street as an outdoor gallery for personal prestige. At one point, I found myself standing in a large board room, presenting the design to a mayor, a cardinal, powerful real estate developers and property owners, the heads of key city departments, and the leaders of downtown's major cultural institutions. While the reception was positive, it felt more like a Shakespearean conclave of competing dukes than a public process for a shared vision. Ironically, our own efforts were finally ended not by community consensus or substantive critique, but by the objections of one architect (and his public relations agent at the *Los Angeles Times*) who did not wish views of his building to be obstructed by trees and kiosks in the middle of the street. The occasionally outsized and capricious influence of certain individuals is part of the politics of urban design, and it was an important if somewhat painful lesson.

First Street

Fortunately, in 2004 we were asked to continue our efforts on a key street perpendicular to Grand: the two miles of First Street starting at Bunker Hill's office buildings and cultural temples, passing through the Civic Center and Little Tokyo, crossing the Los Angeles River, and ending up at the important Latino neighborhood of Boyle Heights. After previous projects on behalf of government agencies and then public-private consortiums, we now had an opportunity to design with a non-profit organization as our client, which we found an excellent match for the office's values and approach. In the years that followed, non-profit civic and cultural organizations have become some our most constant and beloved clients for working on boulevards, streets, and public spaces. Project Restore, ably led by Ed Avila, had successfully shepherded the restoration of L.A.'s marvel of a city hall and now aimed to better connect the massive building to its surroundings. In many ways, this was a continuation of our Civic Center work, but with a still broader scope, across the full span of the river valley of Los Angeles.

First Street demanded attention not just because of its historic and civic importance, but also because of more than $1 billion of planned investments along its edges and down its center, among them a new light rail line and stations, a new high school, a new police headquarters, and a spate of mixed-use developments. This provided a valuable case study for streets where confirmed investment on adjacent property is the stimulus for enhancement of public space, rather than the other way around. And because many of the projects were already under way—in design and engineering or even under construction—we learned that in a period of economic growth, urban designers must work in dynamic circumstances, responding to projects that are already taking shape before you start.

Our plan, nicknamed Mozart to Mariachi because of its anchors at Bunker Hill's Disney Hall on the west and Mariachi Plaza on the east, emerged from a detailed study of the historic relationship of the river valley and the city's development. This large-scale topographic framework, which we dubbed "The First Valley," recognized that the original pueblo was located entirely in relationship to the river (close enough for water access, not so close as to risk flooding), and that the river's first crossing point and first bridges were at First Street. While detailed plans were developed for the full two miles, special loving attention was paid to the First Street

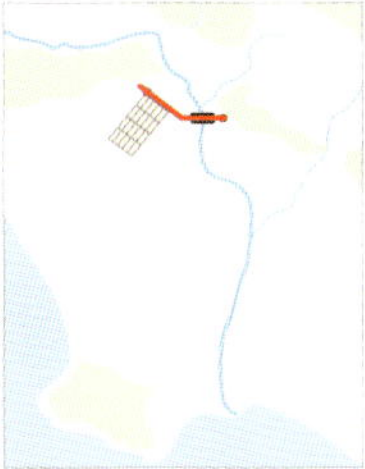

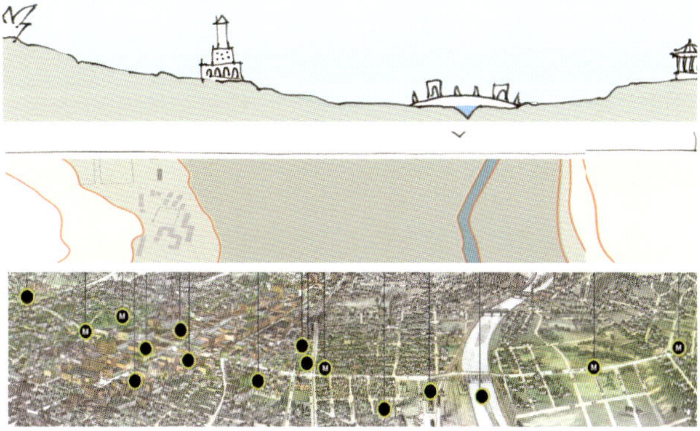

Conceptual cross-section and plan of the "First Valley" from Bunker Hill to Boyle Heights

Proposed shops and community facilities under the First Street Bridge

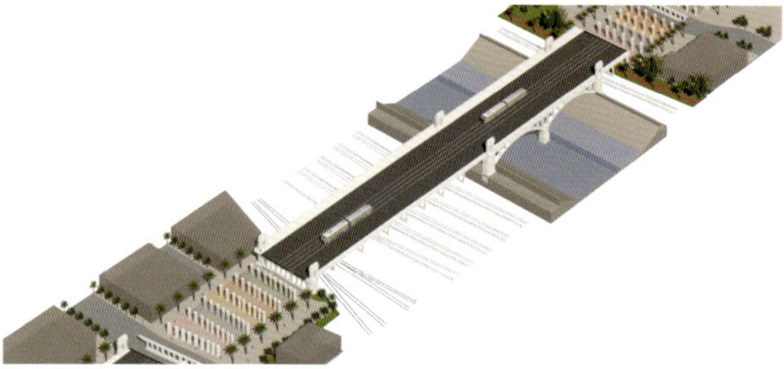

"Peel-away" birds-eye view of the proposal for community facilities beneath the First Street Bridge

Proposed public space along the Los Angeles River at First Street Bridge

Bridge. We discovered it had enormous potential in the poorly used spaces beneath it, and in its capacity to contribute to the revitalization of the Los Angeles River, whose heroic advocates were gaining considerable strength in their efforts.

Spring and Main / La Plaza

After the First Street plan was completed in 2006, Project Restore asked us to pivot 90 degrees and develop a plan for the two north-south streets—Spring and Main—which bracket City Hall and connect it to the most historically sensitive site in the city. Los Angeles is more than 200 years old, and its origins, though sometimes deluged by sprawl, are deeply rooted in Spanish and Mexican urban history, a subject of enduring interest for me. In the years during and after graduate architecture school, I had spent much time traveling in Mexico and

Peru to study the cities of Latin America created according to the rules of the astonishing 16th century documents known as the Laws of the Indies. The Laws generated the basic urban form of more than 300 new cities in the Spanish New World and have been called the most influential urban planning documents of all time.

But other than providing case studies of cities with grid patterns and plazas at their centers, I had not expected these laws to re-emerge so centrally in our design work. Now we would have an opportunity to take a really profound look at El Pueblo, the original Los Angeles settlement, which is in fact a direct if imperfect product of the Laws of the Indies. We had visited some of this terrain during the Ten-Minute Diamond project, but now we could plunge deeply into the subject and resolve some unanswered questions. In particular, we wanted to document the development "thrusts" of the pueblo and downtown: the ways in which the challenging terrain (not at all flat, like that

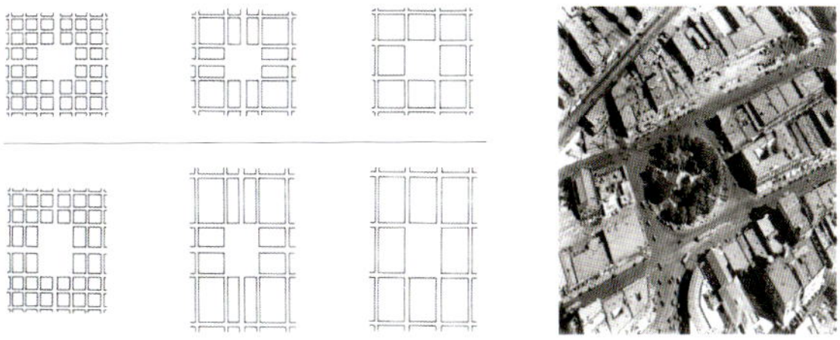

Research: diagrams of Mexican plazas derived from the Laws of the Indies, with aerial view of the original Los Angeles Plaza at far right

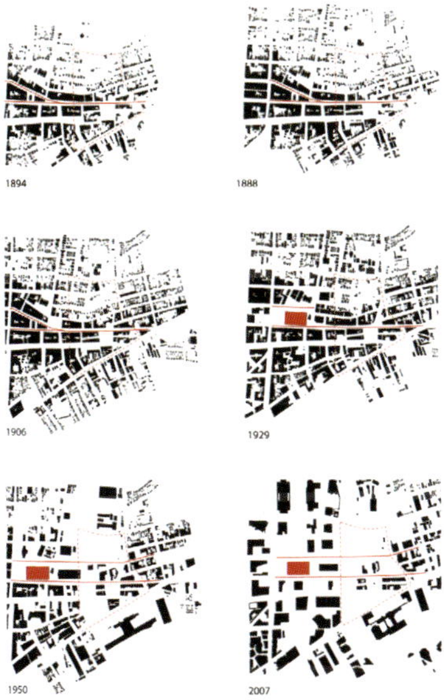

Research: detailed plan studies of the historic growth and then demolition of the Los Angeles pueblo

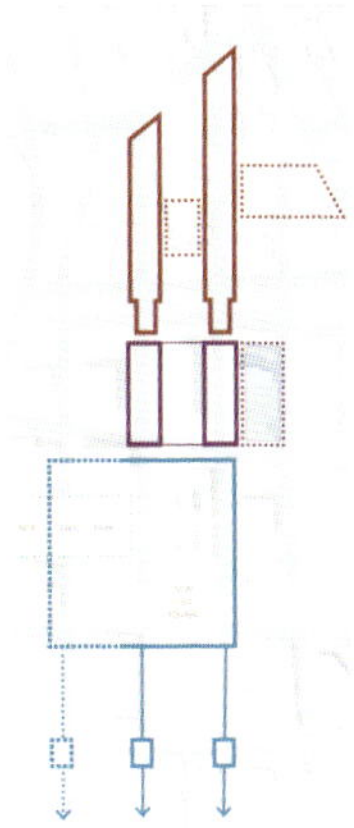

Conceptual plan diagram for Spring and Main, from the Civic Center (blue) across the freeway (purple) to the Pueblo (red)

GREEN SPACE NETWORK

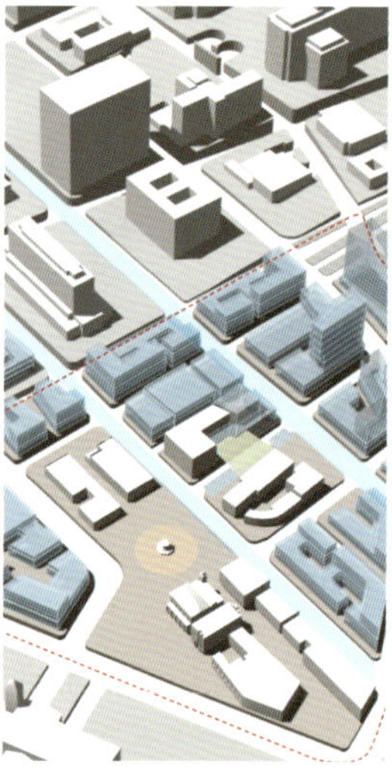

NEW DEVELOPMENT

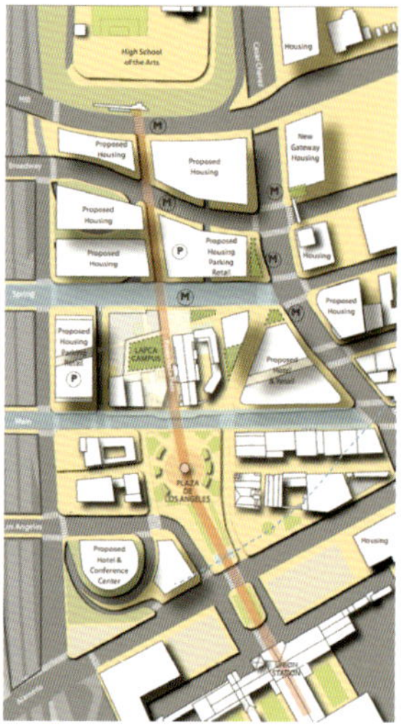

COMPOSITE

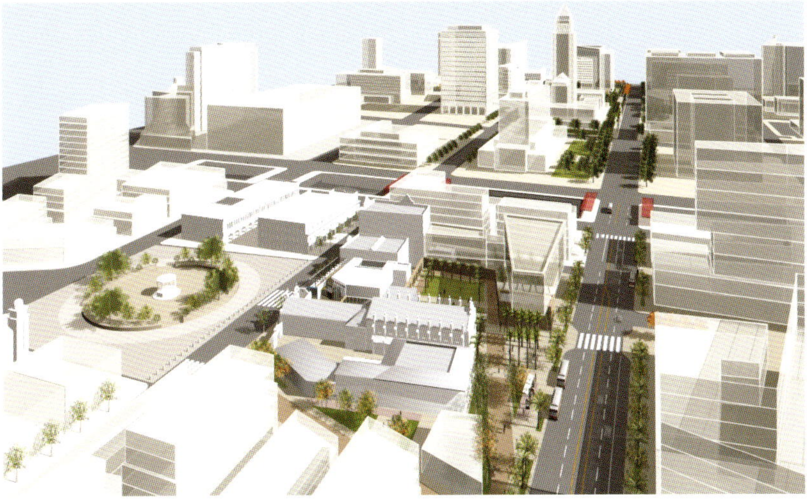

Plans and aerial views (left and above) of the proposal for Spring Street, El Pueblo, the original plaza, and La Plaza de Cultura y Artes

of so many American grid cities) forced a series of sometimes confusing reorientations in the direction of downtown's urban development. And dealing with a parallel pair of streets ratified my earlier observations in Mexico that a strong central plaza tends to elevate pairs of streets to great importance, as opposed to the singular Main Streets of many American cities.

The timing was felicitous because at that moment, County Supervisor Gloria Molina was realizing her longstanding dream of developing a cultural center, La Plaza de Cultura y Artes, at the heart of the pueblo. As our work on Spring and Main progressed, we were asked to develop a detailed master plan for the cultural center, next to La Placita, the pueblo's original church. You could not ask for a more richly loaded or meaningful site, and in many ways the project captures that rare combination of history, topography, urban form, landscape, street life, architecture, and cultural expression which is at the heart of our practice.

Aerial view of the proposed campus for La Plaza de Cultura y Artes

We were enormously proud of the results. But the clouds of the Great Recession, gathering mass as we neared completion, fully broke in 2008, and the project—like so many others—had to be dramatically scaled back. Urban design and public life swim in the sea of economics, a lesson driven home once again, this time in the fragile eco-system of non-profit cultural institutions. But La Plaza de Cultura y Artes did open in 2011 with some exceptional exhibits on L.A.'s urban history. And the overall work on Spring and Main, called "Civic Crossroads," was designed to withstand short-term economic conditions and may yet influence development going forward.

Proposed new entrance to La Plaza de Cultura y Artes on Main Street, next to the plaza church

5

Rapid Boulevards

Los Angeles: Wilshire, Ventura, Lankershim

The fully built Los Angeles Metro Rapid bus network

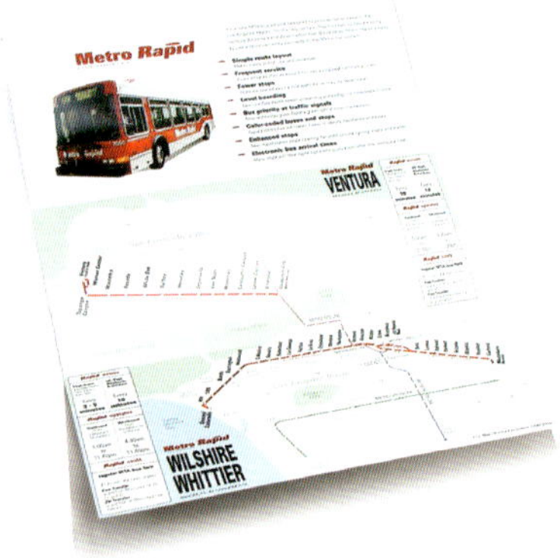

The two pilot routes opened in 2000 along Wilshire and Ventura Boulevards

Metro Rapid

Seven years after the electric trolley bus project ended, we came back to a major bus project. In *Los Angeles Boulevard*, I had discussed rail transit, but had not focused much attention on the humble but ubiquitous buses that rumbled along the boulevards by the thousands. The region had more than a million bus boardings a day, second only to New York, and the buses went almost everywhere. But often the trips were slow, since unlike trains the buses did not have their own tunnel, or track, or even separate lane, and got stuck in traffic like every other vehicle on the road. In L.A., buses were *public* transit, but they weren't *rapid* transit.

The Electric Trolley Bus project had focused on a cleaner model of the same system but would not necessarily have improved speeds. Now, new studies by city and county transit officials showed that a large part of bus delays were not due to traffic congestion but to "dwell time," the precious seconds and minutes spent not moving at the bus stop and at red lights. First, the stops were too close together. And second, much time was wasted as people scrambled for the door, fumbled for coins, asked the driver for information, and so on. If the stops could be separated by up to half a mile (similar to light rail stations), if boarding could be speeded up through better design at the stops, and if sophisticated new traffic signal technology could give each bus a green light most of the time, a new service of truly rapid buses could be developed at very low cost. In 1999, we were asked to develop prototypes for both the stop and the buses that would serve them, a combination of site layout, station design, graphics, and branding. We recommended calling the system Metro Rapid.

Metro Rapid unfolded at a time when cities around the world were taking a fresh look at bus systems, which had not really changed for more than 60 years. Inspired by the revolutionary new bus system in Curitiba, Brazil, known as Bus Rapid Transit or "BRT," Los Angeles architect Martha Welborne escorted a mayoral delegation to Curitiba and succeeded in winning political support for BRT in Los Angeles. So Metro Rapid developed at just the right moment to serve as the region's first demonstration project for BRT. Instead of selecting a quiet route for the experiment, the MTA boldly selected 22 miles along the Wilshire/Whittier Boulevard corridor, the busiest bus boulevard in the system and one of most heavily used transit routes in the country, and 17 miles of Ventura Boulevard, the east-west bus spine for the San Fernando Valley.

We were encouraged to be innovative. The project incorporated new vehicle design, new operational design, and new on-board technology, including real-time tracking of each bus and traffic signal "pre-emption." Branding was a design imperative, to announce the new service and change entrenched perceptions of bus transit. This required a strong and consistent image for the service as a whole, but a physically variable prototype for the station stops, since each sidewalk setting was dramatically different and often constrained, with space sometimes as narrow as six feet in width.

Proposed extended Rapid stop with three "umbrella gates" at Wilshire / Vermont

Completed Rapid stop at Wilshire and Normandie: "flagpole" sign, "umbrella gate", leanbars, map kiosk, and special paving

Inspired by Curitiba's strong and simple color-coded buses, we began with a study of the vehicles themselves. The drab existing buses seemed to telegraph poor service. We saw each bus as a potential moving icon to convey the merits of the new service, and settled on a simple red with bold white graphics—we were also able to persuade the MTA to forego advertising on the buses. And we felt that bus and stop should match, so that when a bus came to the stop, it felt visually anchored with related colors and graphics.

On the 200 miles of ETB routes, we hadn't been able to spend much time on the hundreds of individual stops. Now, along the 40 miles of the Metro Rapid demonstration routes, we were able to study with great care each of the forty-eight proposed stops. The designs came down to the inch—we minimized obstructions and used the carefully spaced columns of the translucent canopies to create "boarding gates" for reduced dwell time.

Though the design and materials were economical, the result was a new level of visual quality and comfort at bus stops. Upgraded from the typically punitive bus stop with broken sidewalk and a grudging advertising bench, the new stops for Metro Rapid lent dignity to the experience of taking the bus and shaved significant time off of almost every trip. Follow-up studies showed as much as a 30% reduction in travel time; initial ridership increased by up to 40 percent, with one third of that ridership increase from new riders who had never used public transit. The demonstration projects had succeeded, and today there are nearly 400 miles of Metro Rapid routes throughout Los Angeles County.

Rapid stop elements: map kiosk, "flapole" sign, "umbrella gate," and coordinated bus livery

Proposed North Hollywood Station mixed-use complex along Lankershim Boulevard, at the intersection of the Red Line subway and the Orange Line BRT

Station view from Lankershim Boulevard

Great hall within the station

Lankershim Boulevard

In 2006 we participated in a master plan competition for an extraordinary site in North Hollywood along Lankershim Boulevard. The project would integrate the existing subway station (the terminus of the Red Line), a new BRT line on its own right-of-way (the Orange Line), a Metro Rapid line, and a host of local and express buses. Combined with the usual private vehicles, pedestrians, and even bicyclists, the master plan needed to interweave multiple forms of movement whose complexity was almost unprecedented for Los Angeles. It went beyond anything I had anticipated in *Los Angeles Boulevard* just seven years earlier. Woven into the movement pattern were major new investments in housing, office, and retail intended to make North Hollywood a dense and dynamic urban crossroads.

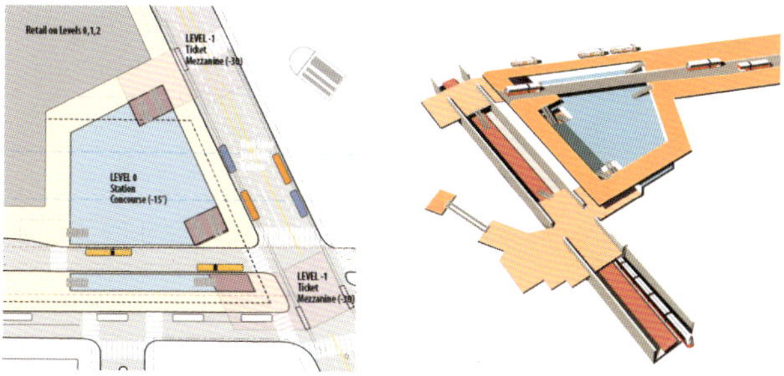

Complex interweaving of subway, BRT, local bus, and pedestrian networks along the boulevard

Our developer-led team was not ultimately selected, but the experience was both positive and encouraging. We learned how to document with great clarity the very complicated spaghetti pattern of crossing transit routes which straddled both sides of the diagonal boulevard. We then shaped these into a single large complex we called North Hollywood Station. We took advantage of the existing subway station to create below-grade connections beneath the boulevard, and then invoked the great tradition of glass-shed train stations to create a striking building and memorable arrival point for the new district. In the end we could see first hand how far Los Angeles had come from the days of Electric Trolley Bus project fifteen years earlier, in the extent of its transit investments and the growing sophistication of its urban development and public space agenda.

6 Business Boulevards

Hollywood: Highland, Santa Monica

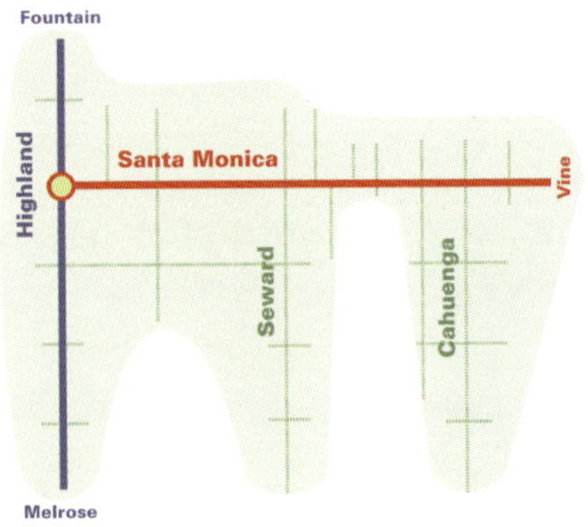

Boundaries of Hollywood Media District along Highland Avenue and Santa Monica Boulevard

For more than a decade, our clients were primarily public agencies, who generally shared our goal of improving the design of the public realm. But in the 1990's, faced with the reduced budgets of many local governments, private businesses and property owners in urban areas recognized the need to create a new kind of partnership to deliver certain key services that cities were struggling to provide. The "Business Improvement District," or BID, was pioneered in New York City and then spread nationwide. Essentially, a group of private interests within a defined district agreed to tax themselves to create a fund for public services such as street cleaning, safety patrols, and, in later stages, enhancements of public space.

We were contacted by the Hollywood Media District BID to help them develop a master plan for their area, arrayed primarily along two boulevards: Highland and Santa Monica. Unlike its counterpart, the Hollywood Entertainment District, which was centered on the tourist district along Hollywood Boulevard, the HMD was primarily a working district, with a long history of film post-production and support services.

The district included a major film studio, dozens of media companies housed in shed-like buildings, scattered restaurants, and a small but active row of live theaters.

In Los Angeles Boulevard I had discussed the economic factors affecting the design and experience of the boulevards, but here was a chance to work firsthand with a group of people whose livelihoods, along with those of several thousand employees, were at least affected by if not dependent on the boulevards. This meant thinking and designing from private property outward to public space instead of the other way around. The members of HMD told us that the district was doing fairly well economically, and their early "clean and safe" efforts had paid off in reducing the litter, graffiti, and crime which had become widespread in Hollywood. But they had determined that in order to attract and retain new employers and employees, they needed to invest in the public environment to spur the opening of more cafes, restaurants, and shops.

Their concerns ranged from the small scale issues of graphics and street furnishings, mid-scale goals for landscaping and lighting, and large-scale ambitions to give the entire area an upgraded look and feel. HMD could use both the planned projects and the finished results for their marketing and development efforts. Their members also ranged in scale, from gas stations, cafes, and non-profit theaters, to medium sized lumber yards and film editing studios, to a major commercial studio with multiple buildings and sound stages, almost a city in itself.

We spent a great deal of time talking with individual business owners, as well as coordinating with public agencies. We recommended beginning with Highland Avenue, where improvements could be made almost immediately, and then developing a longer-term plan for Santa Monica Boulevard, which had more complex issues to address, such as major bus lines, tall utility poles, and the inherent restrictions of a state-owned highway.

As part of our initial work, we developed an overall visual identity and language program—color palette, typography, logo—to help distinguish and unify the district. For Highland Avenue, we focused on a major landscape program to add crosswalks, medians and street trees, along with a signature gateway at Melrose Avenue. We also developed a striking new approach to street lighting. On Santa Monica Boulevard, we

Melrose gateway sign,
medians, and landscaping
(rendering and construction)

Color palette and
logo for the district

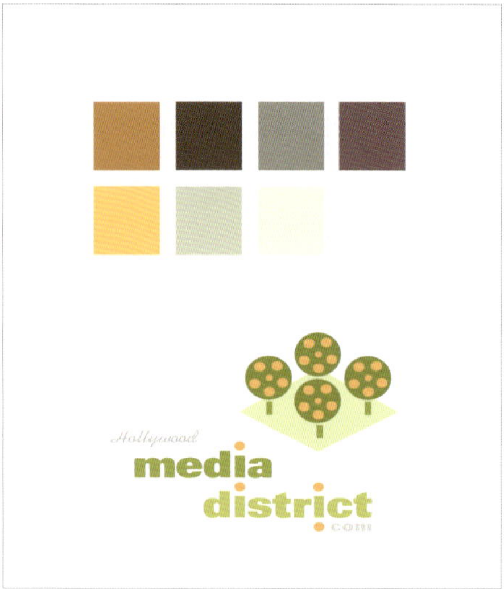

Identity / wayfinding
banners for Theater Row
on Santa Monica Boulevard

emphasized a reconfiguration of the roadway, upgraded bus stops, and a special wayfinding banner program for theater row, using photographs we had taken of actors from all the independent companies. The banners added color and imagery, and they were also numbered to help people find particular theaters.

Much of the work on Highland was implemented, and the boulevard has been transformed, not only in its streetscape, but in the new housing, shops, and restaurants which the improvements have spurred (this gave me particular pleasure since I had used Highland Avenue as the archetypal boulevard in one of *Los Angeles Boulevard's* graphic studies). Santa Monica Boulevard has been upgraded as well, including the addition of a Metro Rapid line, so that we were able to see two elements of our work—transit enhancements and fixed improvements—operating along the same boulevard. More than anything else, the project reinforced in our minds the complex but critical dynamic of private and public interest, and private and public space, that characterizes vibrant urban life. An overly monumental approach to streets can create a sterile public environment; but a purely private approach can create places that feel visually chaotic and excessively commercial. There is an art in cities of balancing and integrating these two forces to create boulevards which are a joy to experience.

Proposed treatment of intersection of Santa Monica Boulevard and Highland Avenue

7

Boulevards as National Infrastructure

Palestine: The Arc for a Palestinian State

The Arc national infrastructure corridor connecting the primary towns and cities of Gaza and the West Bank, to accommodate a doubling of the population to 6 million Palestinians

At the beginning of 2004 an opportunity came our way that would require the consolidation of everything we had learned, after thirteen years of practice, about cities and boulevards. But it did not look that promising at first.

We received a call from a senior analyst at RAND Corporation, the renowned think tank, asking if in six weeks we might be able to develop some initial concepts for housing large numbers of immigrants who would be expected to return to the West Bank and Gaza upon the founding of a Palestinian state. An interested donor had suggested that the best approach might be the creation of a new city for up to three million people. We were offered a small stipend.

The proposition was daunting. Other than a trip to Israel as a teenager some thirty years earlier, I had no first-hand knowledge of the region. Housing was not our particular specialty. RAND itself was somewhat mysterious to me. And six weeks seemed an almost laughable amount of time to address any aspect of one of the world's most intractable political conflicts. With as many caveats and exclusions as I could think of, I said yes.

RAND had been trying, for more than a year, to answer the question of what would be needed for a prospective Palestinian state to succeed. A multidisciplinary team—standard practice for RAND—had developed scenarios for various sectors such as governance, security, economics, justice, health, and education, but was now addressing a critical problem in demographics: an expected doubling of the Palestinian population by 2020, from three million to six million. Where would these new inhabitants live? And how would this affect the overall political and economic framework?

Armed with little more than a large stack of maps (some in Russian, others marked "Central Intelligence Agency") and a few general instructions conveyed by telephone, our office began by mapping multiple aspects of the West Bank and Gaza towns and cities where Palestinians presently lived. We soon rejected the concept of a new city, because it would require too much land, drain resources from other areas, and take too long to develop. We developed recommendations for the strategic enlargement of existing cities, and calculated that if the expanded areas could be developed at moderate densities of around 30,000 people per square mile, there was enough land to accommodate three million additional people.

But it wasn't enough to build housing. People had to be connected to each other and to employment centers in order to create the conditions for economic self-sufficiency. The curved mountain ridge of the West Bank meant that most of the cities were arrayed in an almost linear fashion. In contrast to Los Angeles's expensive problem of having to connect in all directions, the West Bank's line of cities offered the simple and tantalizing prospect of a primary linking corridor equipped with both a highway and an inter-city train. The corridor could also carry much needed infrastructure—telecommunications, electricity, water, natural gas. And the curve could be extended southward across Israel's Negev Desert to connect directly to Gaza, thereby addressing one of the nagging problems for a prospective Palestine: making a single state from two separate territories. The simplicity of the concept would be one of its strengths. The Arc was born.

Concept Plan of the Arc, showing the infrastructure corridor connecting and growing the cities along transit boulevards

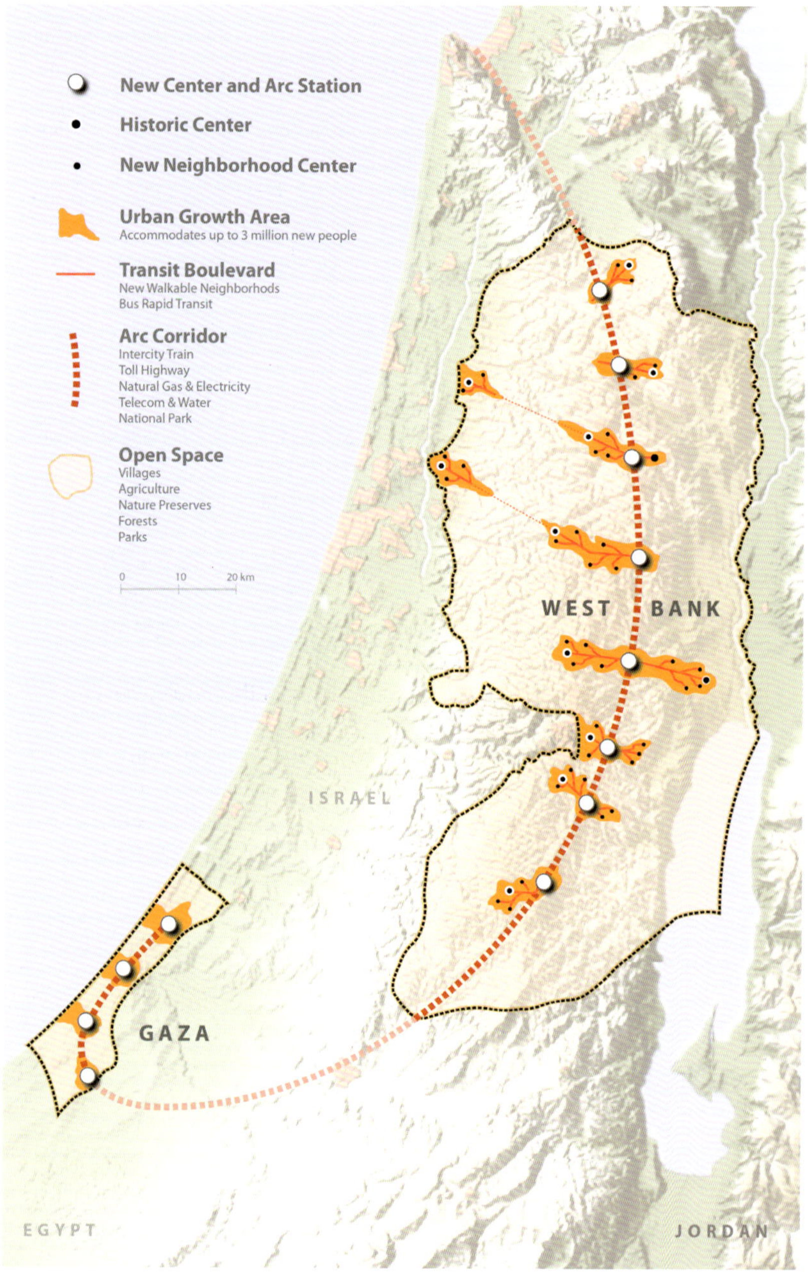

We brought sketches for our initial meetings with the RAND team, and the idea seemed to pass muster with a series of discriminating audiences: the experienced research team, RAND's leadership, the project's main donor, and, eventually, a number of highly credentialed Israelis and Palestinians in Los Angeles and Washington. But the venues for our briefings were all domestic: travel to the region was precluded by the continuing violence of the Second Intifada. Nonetheless, our contract was extended through the summer so that we could develop the Arc concept further with more research, diagrams, and illustrative drawings, now in close collaboration with the RAND Palestine team: demographers, economists, security specialists, water experts, former diplomatic officials, Middle East specialists. It was exciting to see urban design finding its place in this very unexpected company.

In this next iteration, we fleshed out our early premise that the Arc infrastructure corridor should not penetrate the cores of the cities, which were historic and densely populated. Instead, the Arc would pass by the perimeter of each city. The train would stop at a new train station that would serve as the centerpiece of a new station district. That district would in turn be connected laterally to the old city by a new boulevard equipped with bus rapid transit, which could be threaded through historic neighborhoods and—unlike light rail—contend with the hilly terrain. The proposed transit boulevard would also create the conditions for the development of the new residential neighborhoods along its edges. If the Arc was the national infrastructure spine with a train, each city would have a vertebral boulevard with a bus. The resulting urban development would accommodate three million additional Palestinian city dwellers, all within walking distance of an integrated national public transport system.

The Arc project evolved through the fall, but plans to produce a final report for the entire Palestine project became somewhat bogged down. Then, in November of 2004, Yasser Arafat suddenly died, and the entire Israeli-Palestinian equation seemed to change overnight (two months later, veteran negotiator Mahmoud Abbas would become the new president of the Palestinian Authority.) RAND recognized the need to have its research available just when a new diplomatic window was opening. An all-hands-on-deck call went out over the Thanksgiving holiday, kicking off a period of intensive collaborative that produced the galleys for not one but two

Top: The Arc's relationship to the natural landscape

Bottom: Prototypical aerial view of the Arc corridor creating a new district as an extension of the old city

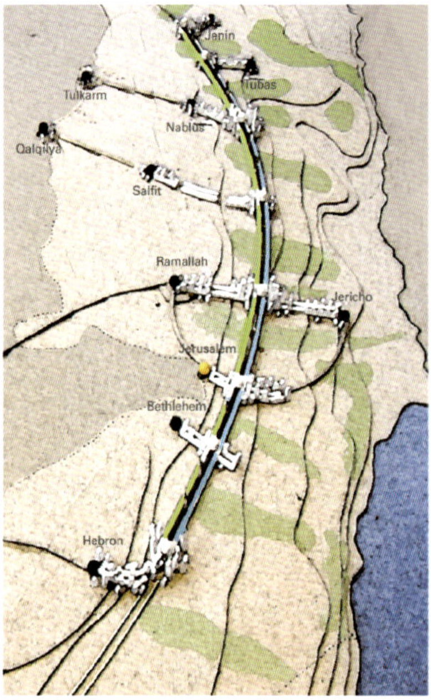

books in just three months. The first, *Building A Successful Palestinian State*, was a 400-page tome covering RAND's extensive research in almost all the major sectors of statehood. The second, *The Arc: A Formal Structure for a Palestinian State*, was 93 pages and heavily illustrated. RAND's team felt it was one of the most visually compelling books the institution had ever published.

By February, the violence in the region had quelled sufficiently to contemplate the team's first full-fledged visit to the region for briefings. But it was unclear whether either the Israelis or Palestinians would be receptive to our team's findings and proposals. To test the waters, four of us headed to London on one-way tickets, unsure whether we would continue on to the Middle East or return in disappointment to the United States. Once there, the signals we received, both in visits to 10 Downing Street and the Foreign Office, as well as through informal contacts in the region by telephone and e-mail, gave RAND's leadership sufficient encouragement to extend our journey. On February 21, we arrived in Jerusalem for what would turn out to be an extraordinary week of briefings, including one with then Finance Minister Salam Fayyad, who would become (and remains as of this writing) the Palestinian Prime Minister.

Sequence showing phased implementation of the transit boulevard, the Arc corridor, and the new district

Encouraged by the initial response, the official publication of the books was launched with an April press conference at Washington's National Press Club. This was followed by the New York Times' extraordinary coverage of the Arc in a 3-page story by veteran Middle East correspondent James Bennet. It appeared on the day of our departure for our second trip the region. The profile of the project was suddenly very high: we met with, among many others, Palestinian President Abbas, who said of the Arc, "This project is very important for my people." Over the next five years, through countless setbacks and restorations, I made more than twenty trips—to Jerusalem, Ramallah, Gaza, Hebron, Nablus, Tel Aviv, Amman, Geneva, London, Brussels, Chicago, Paris, Washington, and New York—all with the hope (much encouraged by many others) that the Arc might in some small way help contribute to diplomatic progress.

During those many extended trips within Israel and the Palestinian Territories, I became quite familiar with the Holy Land's terrain. Visitors have long noted the affinities of California's landscape with those of the western Mediterranean, particularly Spain and North Africa, from which so much of its

Prototypical bus rapid transit station and new neighborhood along the transit boulevard, connecting the Arc train station to the historic city center

Prototypical station integrated with new housing and neighborhood facilities along the transit boulevard

Prototypical station with cistern and photovoltaic panels

vegetation and architecture derives (by way of Latin America). This affinity applies to the far eastern Mediterranean as well, and during my travels in the West Bank and Gaza, and Israel proper, I was often reminded of Southern California's terrain. But it was still something of an irony and even a shock to think that ideas about L.A.'s boulevards might somehow contribute to peace in such an ancient and contested land.

The simplicity and directness of the Arc idea gave it a seemingly remarkable power that had brought it to the attention of the most senior elected and diplomatic officials. But it was based on no more than the search for solutions to perennial, even ordinary urban problems. It seemed a relief to many we spoke with to be thinking about the everyday challenges of getting to work and buying food at the market, rather than engaging in the bitter dialogue of historic blame and retribution. Boulevards, while sometimes glamorous and sometimes banal, can provide the humane framework for living our daily lives with dignity and hope, even where these are in short supply.

As of this writing, the project is on hold. The Obama administration's extraordinary diplomatic initiatives, launched literally on the day of the President's 2009 inauguration with the appointment of George Mitchell as special envoy, created a new sense of optimism, and brought our team to promising meetings with senior officials both at the State Department and the National Security Council. Meanwhile, the Palestinian Authority's Minister of Transport asked us to undertake the development of a National Transportation Master Plan based on the principles of the Arc, and the Prime Minister's office sought funding from the Arab Development Bank and others. In the same period, under the recently elected President Sarkozy, France took a newly active role in the region, and the government invited us to the Elysée Palace and later the Quai d'Orsay, home of the Ministry of Foreign Affairs, for talks with French officials and French transport companies.

But all of these promising currents soon ran full force into political headwinds: Israel's rightward turn in its 2009 elections, the seemingly unbridgeable schism between the Palestinian factions of Fatah and Hamas, and a bitterly divided U.S. Congress. Overshadowing all of these was the enormous hope and turmoil of the Arab Spring, which began in Tunisia in December 2010, spread to the revolt in Egypt, and continues to this day with the horrific violence of Syria's civil strife. Uncertainty prevails, and the fate of the two-state solution—an independent Israel and Palestine living side by side in peace, security, and prosperity—seems as precarious as it has ever been.

And yet in the eight years we have been working on the Arc project, there have been at least five occasions when I confided to my family that the project was surely dead, only to see it revived by unexpected circumstances. Conflicts may be long, but cities last longer. We will continue to wait and see. And continue to hope.

8 Lost Boulevards

Pittsburgh: The Streets of Allegheny City

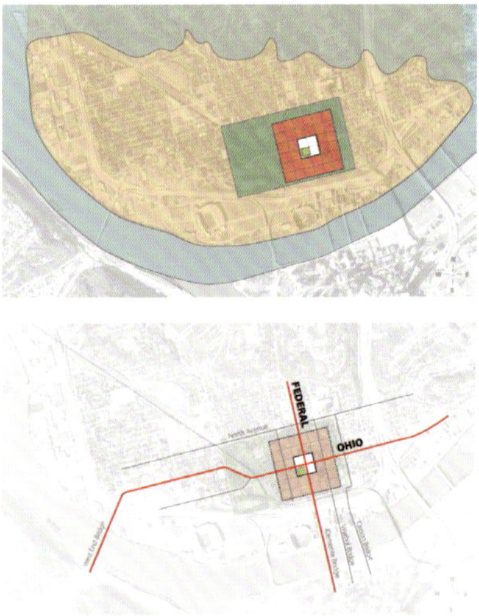

The historic 36 blocks (red) and Commons (green) of downtown Allegheny City, located across the river from downtown Pittsburgh, and bisected by Federal and Ohio

Sometimes boulevards disappear. This turned out to be the case in Pittsburgh, where the city's renowned Children's Museum had asked us to help them strengthen their connection to the surrounding district. The museum is located on the "North Side," a large cluster of neighborhoods directly across the river from downtown Pittsburgh. We were one of four teams working on an initiative the museum dubbed the Charm Bracelet. Its goal was to link the museum to the North Side's numerous places of cultural interest, including the National Aviary, the Mattress Factory arts center, the Warhol Museum, and the Carnegie Science Center. Each team took a slightly different approach to the problem. Ours turned out to be, in the phrase coined by one of my staff, "urban forensics."

Was there a crime to be solved? Well, in a way it turned out there was, but at the beginning we weren't sure. All we knew—having not yet been to Pittsburgh—was that the urban plan of the area around the museum was strikingly odd. The museum seemed to be comprised of a cluster of buildings embedded within a larger group of structures that looked like a fragmented campus or office park surrounded by a square ring roadway, surrounded in turn by dense residential neighborhoods. The pattern was not recognizable.

In our initial investigation, we started peeling back layers to discover an extraordinarily interesting—and dismaying—urban history. The North Side, it turned out, had once been a thriving city of its own, Allegheny City, and a cross-river rival of Pittsburgh's. The citizens of Pittsburgh had been eyeing Allegheny City enviously for some time and on several occasions sought to annex it, through complex legal maneuvers and questionable ballot measures. In 1907 Pittsburgh succeeded, and Allegheny City was swallowed whole. Its municipal apparatus was dismantled (for example, the old city hall was torn down) and its political unity destroyed by fragmenting its neighborhoods into several wards of Pittsburgh. Though no blood was shed, to this day North Siders are aware of the forced annexation, some with residual bitterness. It was not Palestine, but it reminded me of the powerful attachment of people to land no matter what the setting or scale.

And yet the worst was yet to come. Initially, Allegheny City remained physically intact. It had been laid out in 1784 by John Redick in a plan of stunning simplicity and clarity: a square doughnut comprised of thirty-six square blocks, with the four central blocks removed for a capacious public square. The thirty-six blocks were in turn surrounded on all four sides by a one-hundred acre commons, so that the perfectly square city floated in a sea of green pasture—an almost unprecedented urban vision. The provision of the square and the commons led John Reps, the eminent American urban historian, to praise the original plan both for its careful design and "extremely generous" allocation of public space. The Children's Museum, it turned out, occupied two of the historic landmark buildings facing the central public square of downtown Allegheny City.

But you couldn't tell from looking. Allegheny City's urban structure and public space, carefully nurtured and grown by its citizens for over 175 years, was practically wiped out in the 1960's, when Robert Moses came to town for a visit and inspired local officials and executives to "redevelop" the North Side by tearing down more than 500 buildings, including the beloved Market Hall next to the public square. The pretext given was urban blight. The substitute offered was a mediocre suburban mall and office complex, which subsumed nearly half of the thirty-six blocks. An intimidating black office tower was built directly within the old public square, whose remaining area was converted into a charmless concrete plaza with the requisite concrete fountain. Four of the original streets were widened and linked to create the ring road, further isolating the center from its surroundings. And perhaps most egregiously, a massive new four-block parking structure created a Berlin-like wall that cut Allegheny City off from the river and the bridges into downtown Pittsburgh. No wonder that, on my first visit to Pittsburgh, the taxi driver had difficulty finding his way to the Children's Museum.

Much of our work on the project involved energetic, even passionate research. We used every tool at our disposal, including relatively new online

Reddick's orginal 36 blocks in 1784; the destruction of the 1970's; and the proposed reconstruction of downtown Allegheny City

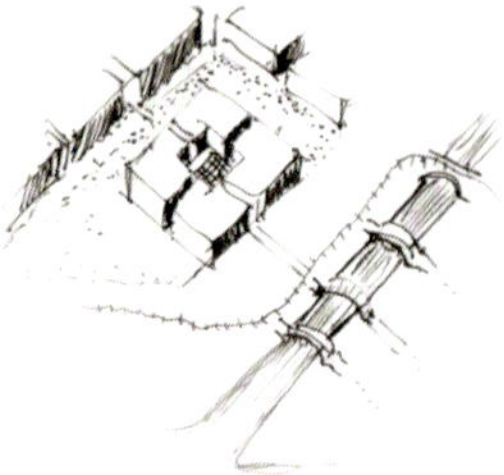

Allegheny City has lots of "local color", figuratively and literally

An Allegheny City color palette can help strengthen civic identity

The historic character and color of Allegheny City

The four-block "Diamond", or public square, at the heart of Allegheny City, being renovated in phases by the Children's Museum of Pittsburgh

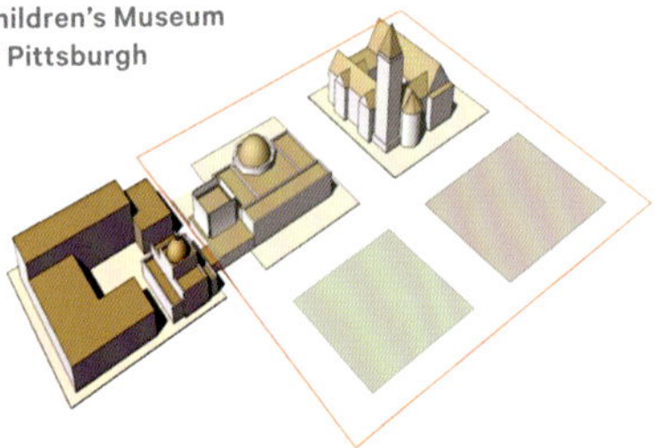

"Where is Allegheny City?" board game

digital archives, to gather historic maps, photographs, documents, newspaper articles, and personal testimonies in order to reconstruct what had happened to Allegheny City. It turned out almost everyone knew something about it, but no one had ever seen the story whole. We presented the physical history in a kind of time-lapse slideshow and video that left people gasping and, in some cases, in tears. We felt a great deal of sorrow ourselves as we discovered what had been lost or, more accurately, wantonly destroyed.

And yet there was hope, and it came in many forms. First, some of the best historic buildings had been saved, thanks to the efforts of Pittsburgh's first preservationists, who went on to form the now-powerful Pittsburgh Preservation Trust. Second, under the extraordinary leadership of its director Jane Werner, the Children's Museum renovated the old post office, acquired the old planetarium, erected an award-winning modernist structure between them, renovated the nearby Carnegie theater, replaced the forlorn concrete plaza with a new and verdant central square, and now has its eye on the adjacent, and empty, Carnegie Library. Third, citizens groups have zealously protected the surrounding Commons, which survive as a wonderful park, surrounded in turn by historic neighborhoods that also survived, just barely, the redevelopment onslaught to become vibrant communities.

And finally, enough traces and structures remained of Alleghency City's square form—its 14 streets and 36 blocks—that we were able, in our design proposal, to show how this extraordinary urban ensemble could be brought back to life. With a judicious reconstruction of the street grid, redesign of the streets as beautiful boulevards, limited demolition, and energetic infill construction of carefully sited new buildings with sustainable design and creative uses, Allegheny City's historic downtown could revive in a new and vigorous form. With the center reconstructed, links outward became plausible, both to the North Side's exceptional cultural assets and to the river, the bridges, and downtown Pittsburgh. Allegheny City could become a vibrant, sustainable, dense, mixed-use, livable, walkable, transit-accessible district—a model for all of Pittsburgh.

Almost 225 years after Allegheny City's founding, 100 years after its forced annexation, 40 years after the destructive remaking of its core, Allegheny City seems to be opening a new chapter, written by its citizens and leaders, full of hope and possibility. The sad story may turn out to be a tale of inspiration after all. It inspired us with a fresh reminder of the importance of streets and boulevards in structuring both the land and the lives of the people who occupy it.

9 New District, New Boulevard

Copenhagen: The Docklands of Nordhavnen

Copenhagen 1898, with Nordhavnen circled

Proposed master plan for the reorganization and extension of the Nordhavnen docklands, organized along a primary boulevard and surrounded by parkland

Sometimes you have to design from afar, as if in a dream. In Pittsburgh, our work began without ever having been to the city, but was followed by several visits during which, unsurprisingly, the powerful materiality of place affected our understanding and approach. Our competition entry for Copenhagen's Nordhavnen district, however, was necessarily started and finished without ever having set foot on the site or in the city. This is not an unusual condition for international competitions, but it was unusual for us, since so much of our work depends on a very close reading and first hand sensory experience of the place, whether a building, a block, a street, a district, a downtown, or a city. In this case, we had to dream of Copenhagen, and even more, to dream within the dream of streets, boulevards and buildings on sites where in many cases there was currently no land, only the cold salty splashing of the Oresund.

The city controlled Nordhavnen, an enormous zone of docklands directly northeast and within walking distance of the historic core. Perhaps inspired by the transformation of similar docklands in Malmo, its Swedish neighbor across the Oresund, Copenhangen launched an international design competition to completely reshape and extend (with landfill) the Nordhavnen docklands into a green, livable, sustainable district for living, working, and playing. The competition

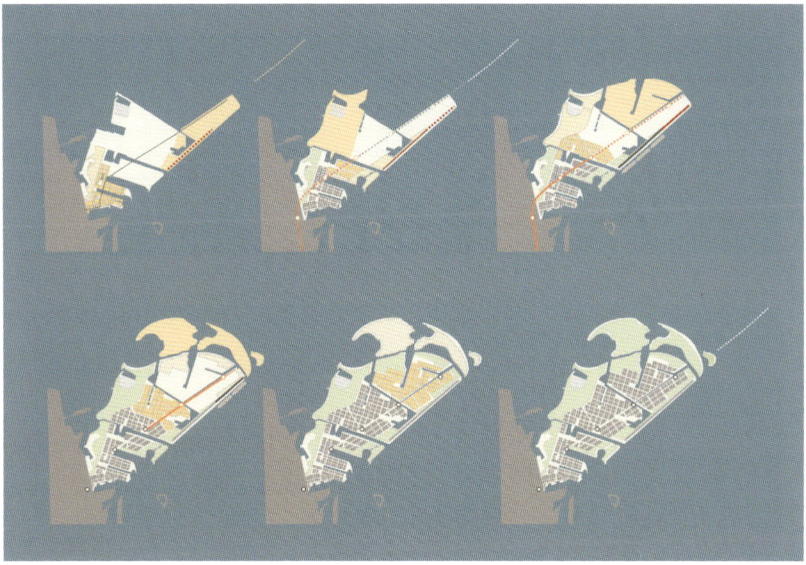

Proposed 10-year phasing for implementation of the plan

appealed to us for its perfect range of scales—from individual buildings, streets, and squares up to an entire district—and because of our admiration from afar of the work of Jan Gehl, the Danish architect and urban designer who has been so instrumental in making Copenhagen a model city for walking and biking.

The whole long district was a kind of fragmented peninsula—nearly an island, with only one congested zone of connection with the mainland. We took Manhattan as something of an inspiration, in that we bundled the density towards the middle, organized along a major boulevard, equipped with an extension of the city's subway system. It was paralleled by a seaside boulevard and promenade that accommodated a long row of berths for massive cruise ships. Multiple neighborhoods, laid out on a flexible and shifting grid, were each interlaced with canals organized around a central harbor and green

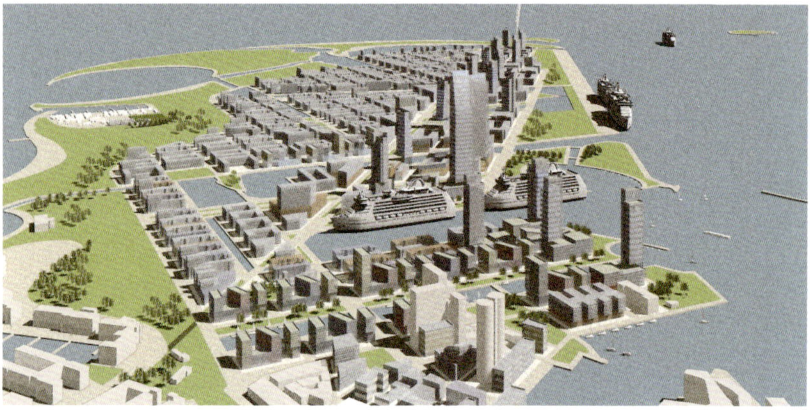

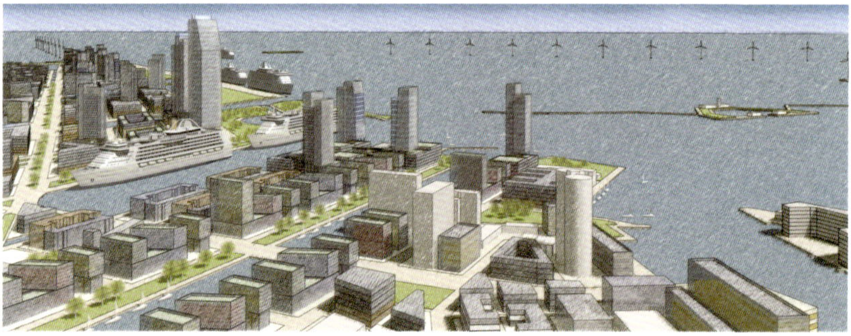

space. The whole district was surrounded with continuous parkland and recreation areas on landfill along the water edges, creating a continuous walkway and bikeway around the district and linking it to the rest of Copenhagen.

Aerial view of the full build-out of the proposal, with Nordhavnen Boulevard forming the central spine

Three views showing the mix of tall and low buildings, water and green space, streets and bridges

Our approach turned out to be antithetical to the winning schemes. By coincidence, I was able to visit Copenhagen shortly after the competition deadline and was able to go to Nordhavnen to see all 700 (!) competition entries displayed in an enormous warehouse on one of the docks. It was fascinating to see the results of that many minds thinking about the same spatial and social issues for the same physical place. I felt our scheme held up well with the rest, and I picked out one or two that I thought were the most likely winners.

When the results were announced some time later, neither those schemes nor ours were premiated, even with honorable mentions. Almost all of the winning firms (anonymous during selection) turned out to be Danish or Scandinavian, suggesting either a real cultural difference in sensibility and approach, the importance of actually knowing and visiting the site firsthand, or both. The winning schemes were generally much more small-scale and fragmented, with built and green spaces broken into very small, almost mosaic-like pieces. They did not have the clear hierarchy we had sought to create, but instead suggested more of a continuous mat or carpet pattern.

This may reflect the flattened social hierarchies of those very successful societies, and their resistance to hierarchical planning which might suggest overly centralized authority and power. In fact, even though the jury selected first, second and third place winners, the authorities later asked all three of the winning teams to work together to develop the final plan, which is now being implemented. This was an impressive demonstration of Denmark's collaborative ethos. It will be interesting to watch Nordhavnen evolve in the coming decades. In any case we were very proud of our submission, which represented perhaps the most detailed plan over the largest area we had ever developed, and which pushed our graphic efforts to a new level.

10 My Downtown Streets, Revived

Hartford: The iQuilt Plan

Pedestrians and cars on Pratt Street in downtown Hartford, 1964

In the mid 1960's, when I was 10, I began taking the Albany Avenue bus from my home in the suburbs into downtown Hartford. In those days, downtown was where the department store was, and the symphony, and the dentist, and the barber. Up till that point, I had always been driven into downtown by an adult. Once I got nervously off the bus, it became instantly clear that when you walk by yourself through a city center, without any particular destination or appointment, you discover it with new eyes. Years later I came upon a quotation from renowned architect Louis Kahn, who felt similarly about his own childhood in Philadelphia: "A city is the place of availabilities. It is the place where a small boy, as he walks through it, may see something that will tell him what he wants to do his whole life." He seemed to be speaking for me, since wandering through cities, discovering them, loving them, studying them, learning to really see them, and eventually even reshaping them, is in many ways what I have done my whole life. It began in downtown Hartford. I did not expect it to circle back there more than 35 years later.

Perhaps I should have. I learned to love landscape painting at the Wadsworth Atheneum and Brahms at the Bushnell Memorial. I purchased coveted sheet music at the city's only real music store, housed in the gorgeous terra cotta-clad Goodwin Building. My first major paper for Yale's renowned architectural historian Vincent Scully was a study of Bushnell Park and its surrounding buildings. My senior thesis was a design for the adaptive reuse of H.H. Richardson's magnificent brownstone palace, the Cheney Building on Hartford's Main Street. I worked on my first political campaign as the driver and factotum for a Hartford mayoral candidate (my uncle, as it happens). And my first job in architecture was for Tyler Smith at the Hartford Architecture Conservancy, the pioneering preservation group that went on to save and renovate countless valuable buildings.

But that was later. As a young boy, those bus rides opened my eyes. I got my first joltingly close-up view of disability, in the form of a well-known young street vendor whose limbs involuntarily spasmed as he sold newspapers and candy from his wheelchair near the Old State House; my first experience of petty crime, when three boys confronted me outside the Empire Bakery (whose jelly donuts I loved) and relieved me of my pocket change—no donut that day; and my first encounters with poverty, as my return bus to West Hartford passed through the ghetto of the North End, where glimpses of wet laundry dripping on fire escapes, sidewalk trash at the door of a corner bar, and the angry countenance of a man yelling at his children revealed aspects of the city I knew little about. It was an early education in the endless complexity, fascination, and challenges of urban form and urban life.

The compact and irregular street plan of Hartford, dating from 1636, provided the inspiration for the iQuilt Plan

I left Hartford in my teens, and went on to live, at least for short periods, in many other cities: Boston, Washington, New Haven, Paris, New York, Rome, Minneapolis, and San Francisco, finally settling for good in Los Angeles. But Hartford—where my great-grandfather arrived from Russia in 1895 and where, more than a century later, much of my family still lives—has remained, if not my home, then my home town. So it was an intriguing surprise when, in 2008, I received a call from Ronna Reynolds, Vice-President of the Bushnell Center for the Performing Arts, to see if I could help her board rethink the Bushnell's connection to its urban neighborhood. She had selected our firm because of our work on the Arc project; she did not know I was from Hartford but was delighted to learn I

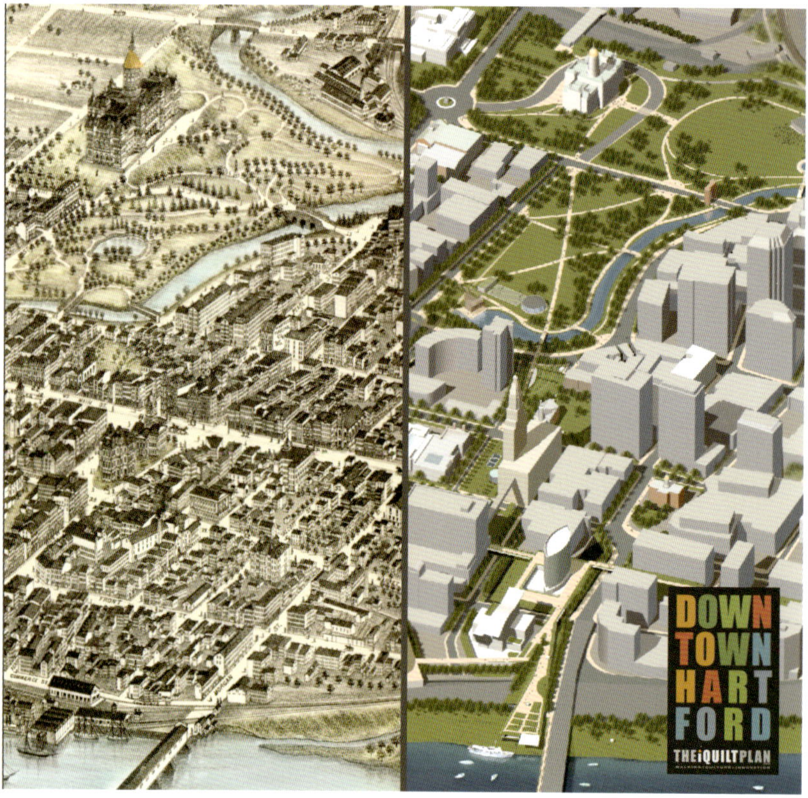

Two Parks

Existing Spaces

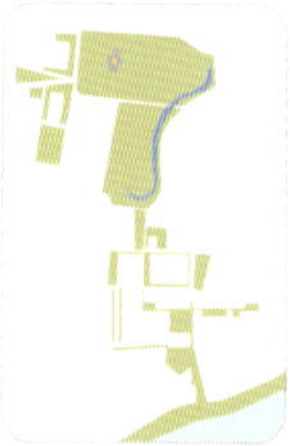

GreenWalk

Cultural Assets

iQuilt

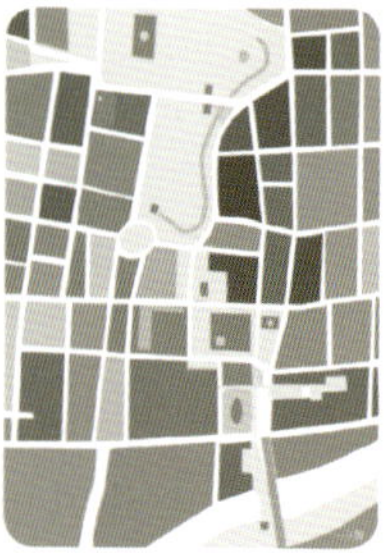

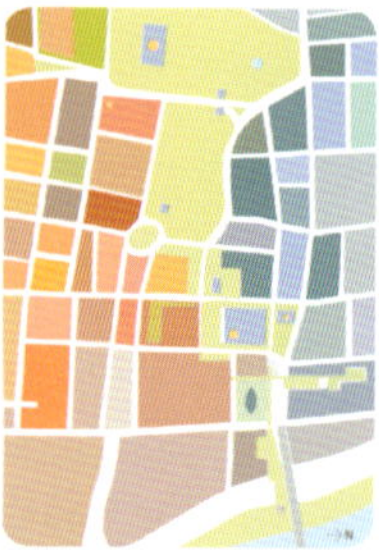

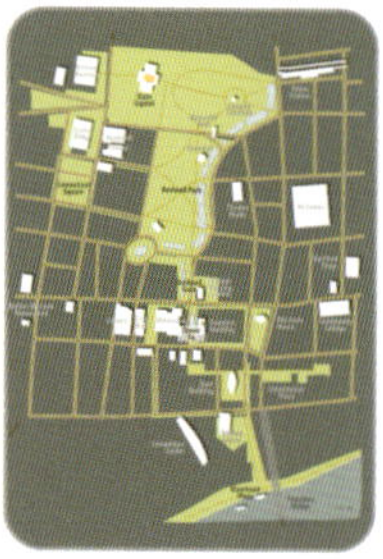

was a native. Apparently, it was time for me to go home. As of this writing, I have spent much of the last five years traveling back to Hartford every few months to continue our work on what has become known, simply, as the iQuilt.

The project began at the Bushnell, which is an exceptionally successful cultural institution, but which is somewhat isolated from the rest of downtown. Its leaders wondered how they could make the surroundings—now dominated by surface parking lots and state government buildings—more lively. They were interested in improving the experience of their visitors before and after performances by enhancing the surrounding pedestrian pathways, with an emphasis on cultural information, amenities, and physical linkages. Hartford, once a very wealthy city and still a wealthy metropolitan region, has outsized cultural assets. It is usually ranked in the top 20 American cities for arts and culture, and downtown alone has more than 45 sites and venues of historic and cultural interest.

An 1877 birdseye view of downtown Hartford, next to an aerial of the iQuilt Plan and its centerpiece, the GreenWalk, connecting the state capitol at the top to the Connecticut River waterfront at the bottom.

The iQuilt Plan integrates Hartford's extensive cultural assets with linked green spaces to create a walkable cultural district

But downtown had long suffered the same depopulation as other American cities and had become primarily a 9-5 workplace for suburban commuters. Its streets were dominated by cars, its blocks by parking lots. This was beginning to change, with significant new public investments (convention center, science center, and bridge to the riverfront), a growing and active residential community (including a 45-story apartment building and numerous converted commercial structures) and an expanding web of pedestrian amenities (enhanced sidewalks, crosswalks, and lighting). We encouraged the Bushnell, which has a long history of civic leadership, to expand the project beyond their immediate neighborhood to include downtown as a whole: how could all of these assets be pulled together to make downtown a vibrant, integrated cultural district?

One of downtown's strongest assets was its compactness—it can still be crossed on foot in any direction in less than 20 minutes. And its two great natural features, historic Bushnell Park and the newly upgraded riverfront of the Connecticut River, were tantalizingly close, but still disconnected. In fact everything was close—the park, river, state capitol, and cultural assets—but most everything needed to be better connected for pedestrians. The disconnection was due in part to fragmentation from the demands of the automobile, but also to a somewhat complicated and confusing street

Proposed Bushnell Gardens visitors center and teaching gardens

Proposed Heublein Cafe and Terrace in Bushnell Gardens

Proposed Park House in Bushnell Gardens

Bushnell Park, with restored flowing water, connected by proposed Bushnell Gardens to Main Street

Far left: Plan of the GreenWalk

plan. The plan dates back to Hartford's founding in 1636 (I like to point out that's just 21 years after Shakespeare died). We observed that, unlike a typical American urban grid, this early Colonial plan is charmingly irregular, with streets which follow the terrain and so curve, bend, come to an end without warning, and change names without explanation. It was less like a perfect checkerboard than an irregular handmade quilt.

Another asset was the city and region's long history of innovation, of inventiveness and ingenuity, from shipping to insurance to rifles to jet engines and helicopters. The city's economic hopes, its leaders agree, depend on attracting and retaining creative and innovative people, not just highlighting cultural assets. So the plan took the "i" for innovation, and the quilt of the street plan, and became The iQuilt Plan. Some people like the name, some don't, but it has stuck, and now has considerable brand equity. My own view is that iQuilt is just another name for downtown Hartford and is really a means to an end: framing a new way of seeing downtown in order to create the economic and urban vibrancy that the city needs and deserves.

The heart of the iQuilt plan is the GreenWalk, a continuous one-mile chain of parks, plazas, and green streets that connects the State Capitol, with its magnificent gold dome, to the waterfront of the Connecticut River. Most of the pieces of the chain are in place; some need enhancement; other pieces need to be filled in. But when completed, the GreenWalk would be a unique urban asset, combining park space, green infrastructure, a walkable spine, and a cultural framework, with almost all of downtown's cultural assets either on the GreenWalk or within a five-minute walk.

And the centerpiece, the emerald jewel of the GreenWalk, is Bushnell Park, which was created as America's first publicly funded park, and which showcased the Park River that wound along its edges. The river flooded twice in the 1930's, and was subsequently put underground in a conduit. The park has never quite recovered. The iQuilt plan includes a comprehensive park restoration that returns flowing water to the park after an absence of more than 70 years.

Other features include the installation, now under way, of a downtown-wide pedestrian wayfinding system, including directional signs and walking maps; the installation of cultural and historic markers; the enhancement of several corporate

Proposed cafe and entrance marquee along Capitol Avenue for the Bushnell Center for the Performing Arts

Graphic variations on the iQuilt themes of walking, culture, and innovation

iQuilt Wayfinding signs (showing destinations in minutes on foot) mounted to the back of pedestrian signals

An integrated visual language of typography, color, street signs, cultural markers, information, and pedestrian amenities

plazas with new cafes, landscaping, green roofs, lighting, cultural markers, and other amenities; the reconfiguration of several streets and traffic circles with "road diets" and new designs as complete streets for walking and biking, with green infrastructure to store and clean stormwater runoff; the transformation of a large state parking lot into a green, mixed-use public space; and a comprehensive master plan for Main Street that restructures the bus transit system to better integrate it with downtown destinations. All of these efforts are keyed to ongoing discussions with property owners, developers, and state and city officials aimed at kickstarting the construction of as many as 3,000 new housing units, to be added to the current stock of around 2,000. The plan has many different elements, large and small, costly and economical, short-term and long term. They will unfold over time at different paces. But the emerging result should be an increasingly connected, integrated, sustainable, green, walkable, livable, culturally and economically vibrant district.

Twenty-five years separate my childhood experiences of Hartford's streets to the first writing on Los Angeles boulevards, and another 25 years have passed as I return to the point of origin. This half century gives me just half the perspective of my grandmother, who lived in Hartford until her death this year at the age of 107, and who remembered when the trolley cars along Main Street were pulled by horses. In our many talks about the project, which she yearned to see realized, she could see the city not just in years, but in rolling decades, and maybe even in passing centuries. We know that cities are shaped in space, but it's easy to forget they are also shaped in time. What we build now matters now, but so do our memories of the past and our dreams for the future. Today's work will affect the lives to be lived and the recollections to be gathered for the generations that follow. Recognizing this sharply inclines me towards humility. To have a hand in the shaping of streets and cities is a great pleasure, but also a privilege and responsibility. I try to walk and dream our boulevards with great love, but also with great care.

Illustrations

All illustrations not listed above are by Doug Suisman / Suisman Urban Design

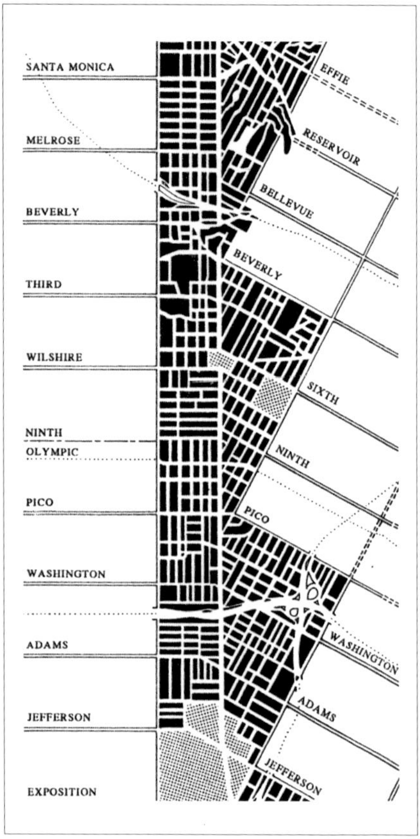

EXPLORING CAREERS AS A CARPENTER

By

Marilyn Jones

The Rosen Publishing Group
New York

Published in 1985 by The Rosen Publishing Group
29 East 21st Street, New York, NY 10010

First Edition

Library of Congress Cataloging in Publication Data

Jones, Marilyn.
Exploring careers as a carpenter.

Summary: Discusses the variety of jobs available to a carpenter, the advantages and disadvantages of the work, and where and how to get the necessary training.
1. Carpentry—Vocational guidance. [1. Carpentry—Vocational guidance. 2. Vocational guidance] I. Title.
TH5608.7.J66 1984 694′.023′73 84-8239
ISBN 0-8239-0624-8

Manufactured in the United States of America

Contents

The author wishes to thank the following people for their invaluable help in preparing this book for writing: Austin Abell, Mike Andres, Dale Burchett, James Erhart, George Franke, Mike Garrison, Thomas Haile, Robert Hardley, Clyde Huber, Jackie June, Parvin Lambertus, Gottfried Reck, Robert Silliman, and David Wilding.

Dedication

To Carol Warehime, my good friend

Chapter 1

Wood and the Carpenter

A truck loaded high with logs plies its steady course along Highway 61 in central Kentucky, causing traffic behind it to adjust to its speed on the hills where one blind curve follows another. The trapped drivers curse their luck for having had the poor timing to fall in the retinue trailing the truck up and down hills where no passing zones last for as much as half a mile. Then the truck pulls into a lumber mill on the outskirts of Elizabethtown, "E-town," as it's called, and the other drivers breathe a sigh of relief, pick up speed, and travel quickly past the mounds of logs stacked in the lumberyard.

The logs may be oak, poplar, walnut, birch, or ash. They will be quartered, sliced, or sent on to veneer plants for slicing there. They will be seasoned, probably by kiln drying, but some may be stacked for air drying for a period of many months. They will be sent, as cut lumber, to mills across Kentucky and the United States.

Millworkers will fashion window sashes, door jambs, doors, and packing crates out of this lumber. Cabinetmakers will build tables, chairs, bookcases, and cabinets from it. Veneer artists will laminate pieces cut from flitches of veneer to other woods to create strong and beautiful woods for furniture. And carpenters will use some of this wood in building frames.

Trees have provided work and homes for Americans from the beginning of the country. These same Kentucky hills were traveled over by Daniel Boone. Eleven miles from Elizabethtown is Hodgenville and the log cabin where Lincoln was born. The Indians were here first, cutting what timber they needed for their homes, their river craft, their firewood.

Trees provide shelter and protection to travelers. People build tree houses to be closer to nature, to be away from the world. We get sap from maple trees in the spring. Hammocks can be slung from tree to tree to swing in on hot summer days. We put birdhouses in trees. In the winter we put bird feeders in the trees and feed our bird populations daily. Trees add to the value of property. Farmhouses are usually surrounded by trees for insulation from the summer heat. Some farmhouses have "husband and wife" trees in the yard, two nearly identical trees flanking the front of the house. Picnics are held under trees. Swings are hung from tree branches. We watch mother birds push their young out of nests and watch for hours as they teach the youngsters to "fly/hop" from branch to branch. We get apples from trees, and peaches, and pears and persimmons. We jog or ride our bikes through city parks early on summer mornings so we can hear woodpeckers in the trees and see the squirrels darting from one tree to another. Dogs use trees to mark their own scent. We carve our initials in trees. Trees absorb some of the pollution in our atmosphere. We climb trees and help our cats climb down from them. Trees are good for swinging from the branches and jumping off into creeks and lakes. Driving along on a day when the heat is unbearable, we feel immediate relief when we come to a stretch of road that is cut through woods, completely shaded by thick tree growth on either side. Trees are good for hiding behind in hide and go seek. We roast marshmallows with green twigs from trees. We live where there are trees. We line our avenues with trees and plant trees in our yards, knowing that something of beauty and value will outlive us. We build picture windows where we can look at trees. Sometimes we think of what tree we would like to be. We bring trees into our homes in midwinter for Christmas celebrations. We hunt pinecones and acorns and fashion arty little objects for ourselves or for others. We put branches on our doors. We buy pictures of trees to look at when we're very tired. We use tree designs in our wallpaper. We lean against trees and contemplate the world. The barks and leaves from some trees make medicine. We drink sassafras tea.

Our major folk heroes had something to do with lumber. Paul Bunyan was a lumberman. John Henry worked for the railroad, driving nails into railway ties. Johnny Appleseed planted apple trees in Ohio. Our pioneers crossed the country in wooden wagons and built log rafts to cross the rivers. Our early bridges were made of wood. We now treasure those early pieces of furniture that were built by expert craftsmen and have withstood the test of time to become "antiques." The First and Second Continental Congresses were held in Carpenter's Hall in Philadelphia.

In more recent times, the tree industry helped to save this nation. In 1933 President Franklin Delano Roosevelt introduced the Civilian Conservation Corps as a means of protecting our natural resources in the forests and also as a means of providing work for hundreds of thousands of youth. These young men mostly came from cities, from homes that were locked in a terrifying Depression. They had no job prospects once they finished school. The CCC gave them the chance to get out of the cities, to get employment, and to build up their strength. Truckloads of young men came to the Adirondack Mountains of New York State, to the Carolinas, and to the forests of the far West. They received their board and some spending money, but most of what they earned was sent home to their folks. By 1941, when Japan attacked Pearl Harbor, we had a corps of strong young men who were able, then, to defend their country. And they planted trees that are over fifty years old now; they put out some forest fires; they learned a love for their environment.

Many other materials have replaced wood as building materials. We use brick or aluminum siding. Some synthetics have taken the place of wood. Plastic furniture is cheap, and a plastic table top can even be made to look like wood. What consumers want is real wood. So a photograph is taken of a large piece of real wood, and that photograph is put on the formica or the plastic for the table top. The result is a table that looks astonishingly like something that was cut from log.

We build atriums for lunchrooms or for teahouses, rooms where we can feel as if we are actually sitting outdoors, surrounded by trees. We bring in logs for cozy fires in the winter, so that we can enjoy the sound and smell of burning wood and, perhaps, feel more closely bound to our ancestors, for whom a log fire was a way of life. We put wood paneling in our homes. Even if it's artificial, we like it. It reminds us of wood, and we like the look and feel of wood. We fill our homes, bars, and restaurants with ferns and potted plants.

Carpenters have been hard hit during the last several years, during the "mini-depression." They have been among the hardest hit of all workers. Many carpenters have been out of work for long periods of time. People make do with what they have when the economy is bad. They postpone the new home or the addition to the house. They may even become amateur repairmen themselves, doing as best they can things that in normal times they would have had done by a carpenter.

Even so, the need for carpenters and good cabinetmakers remains. There is an increasing appreciation for wood and for quality woodwork. There is an increased appreciation for the good things of "the old days," and strong, lovely buildings and good wooden furniture are among those items. There is a deeper reverence for the environment among an ever-growing segment of the population, and respect for trees and the uses of wood is high on the list of environmentalists. There is a move to urge Congress to pass another Civilian Conservation Corps act.

If you're good at it, you can make a decent living out of carpentry. There is a lot of competition, not only within the field of carpentry itself, but from the artisans who work in other related areas: the bricklayers, the plastics workers, the aluminum siding people. But Americans have a love affair with lumber. Americans love wood, and if you become a real craftsman, you can be successful as a carpenter. It is really those logs of birch and ash, of walnut, oak, and poplar that Americans long to have in their homes in quality products.

Hardwood floors polished to a high gloss have become an enviable possession in this country. There is a market for log cabins and log-cabin kits. People hang baskets in their kitchens and all over their homes. Wicker is a very fashionable furniture material. Wood and wood products are popular. People will travel far to find "authentic" wood craft objects that are part of

Americana. We even have a former President who is a cabinetmaker, although most of us never realized that when he was in office. President Carter worked on his furniture-making hobby even while he occupied the White House, it is said. He has been making furniture since he was a young man.

"I owe my success to God and to Phyllis George Brown," one Kentucky craftsman was heard to say at a crafts convention in Louisville. Phyllis George Brown is a former Miss America and the wife of Kentucky's governor. She has single-handedly promoted Kentucky crafts, the crafts of Appalachian people and others in Kentucky whose work is special and worthy of recognition. Such work can now be found in such cities as Washington, D.C. and New York, in stores such as Bloomingdale's and Niemann Marcus. The artisan speaking was a woodworker, a cabinetmaker.

Veneers are another specialty of wood. There is hardly a piece of furniture in a furniture store that does not have a veneer laminated to another wood surface. Veneers come from woods from all over the world: sapele from Africa, pine, oak, elm, aspen, avodere from Africa, eucalyptus, rosewood from Honduras, benge from Africa, Hawaiian koa, tigerwood, zebrawood, butternut, wormy chestnut, Douglas fir, makore, acacia. There are rare jungle woods and woods from the forests of the Adirondacks or Oregon.

People like the look and feel of wood. It is true that carpenters use other materials than wood nowadays. They also use brick, and they use aluminum siding. Carpenters also lay carpet and put in acoustical tile. But when we think of carpentry, we think of wood. Carpenters are builders, and building was among the first crafts of man. It will be around for a long time.

Chapter **II**

The Tools

Hammers are probably the oldest tools, going back as far as primitive man in the Stone Age. Early hammers were really hammering stones, being little more than hand-held stones for pounding. When our ancestors put a handle on the stone, they had a stone hammer. This ancient stone hammer was probably secured to the stone by skins, much like the Eskimo hammer that has sealskin strips securing stone and handle together. Early man used his hammering stone to help him obtain food. He pounded nuts and shells with it. By the time of the Bronze Age he had fashioned a bronze hammer with an eye into which the handle could fit. It was the Romans, however, who developed such a sophisticated hammer that it was not improved upon until modern times. The Romans made a claw hammer, which is what we use, a hammer that also has claws for the removal of nails. In America the handle for this hammer was always made of hickory. In the early days most construction was done with mortise and tenon joints, so the claw hammer didn't get too much work in nail removal. Gradually, however, many more nails were used in construction, and the old Roman hammer often came apart at the handle, or the handle broke from the strain, so an improvement was needed. In 1840 David

Maydole, a blacksmith in Norwich, New York, invented the adz-eye hammer. This hammer was fashioned after an adz, which is something like an axe and a chisel, in that it had an eye that was elongated to embrace more of the handle. This worked perfectly, strengthening the handle so that both hammering and nail removal could be done efficiently. No changes have been made in the hammer since then.

It takes a lot of practice to strike a hammer accurately. Sometimes only the hand and wrist need to be engaged in the action; sometimes, hand, wrist, arm, and shoulder are all needed. Most carpenters develop arthritis in their hammering arm and shoulder. Their shoulder problem is often called bursitis. There is no real cure for this affliction. Carpenters learn to live with the pain as just one of the things they have to put up with in their work. In a full arm swing of the hammer, the hammer often comes within an inch or less of the eye. Much skill is needed in learning to control a hammer, not only for the beauty of the workmanship, but for one's own safety.

Axes and hatchets are tools of the carpenter's trade. They were probably preceded in Stone Age times by the stone celt, a hand tool that primitive man made by chipping a stone into a sharp-edged instrument. With this he could cut and clean the animals and fish he caught and scrape hides clean for wearing. When he put a handle on this instrument, he had an ax. The Romans developed the ax further by making it of iron and putting an eye for a handle in it. The Roman ax was also double-headed. It was very successful as a battle-ax in war, but it became a bit unwieldy when used to cut wood. The American pioneers gave up on the double-bit ax and made a felling ax with just about perfect balance. This ax had a shorter, broader blade than the Roman one and had an eye for the poll on the opposite side of the blade. The American lumberman could work very quickly, very efficiently with this ax, and the rest of the world soon copied it. Its designer is unknown. The Americans used this ax until the middle of the nineteenth century, when demand for lumber was so great that they developed their own version of the double-bit ax, which has been in use ever since.

The ax is an example of a wedge, and so is the adz. The adz was razor-sharp and was kept in pioneer homes to smooth logs, to do a sort of finish work on them. It was used like an ax, but it did the work of a chisel. The user put his foot on a stump to be cut and swung hard from over his head. Chances were that he might cut off his toes, the blade was so thin, so sharp. The adz "chiseled" the wood to a certain smoothness. Boards in the floors and ceilings have been adzed smooth.

The chisel is also a wedge. It dates from what is known as the Polished Stone Age. Gouges also come from this period, and both do similar jobs for the craftsman. Chisels and gouges are virtually the same today as they were in antiquity. The materials have changed, going through all the evolutions from stone to steel, but the chisel and gouge are wedges, very sharp, some with almost paper-thin blades. Chisels are used for carving. They are used for paring wood. They can be used with a mallet in framing work. They are used to clean out mortise holes for mortise and tenon joints. Tom Haile, one of the master violin-makers living at this time, makes most of his own chisels. He carves around the edges of his violin tops with a chisel to ensure a more perfect wedding of sides and top. He carves out all his chin rests with a finely honed chisel, usually one of his own fabrication.

Saws are important to a carpenter; they allow the carpenter to cut through something, usually wood. There are hand saws and machine saws. Of the hand variety, the two basic ones are the crosscut saw and the ripsaw. We know there were saws at least as early as Egyptian times, for there are pictures of Egyptians using saws in their work. We even have some saws from Egyptian tombs. Egyptian saws date back to 4500 B.C.

The crosscut saw operates like a series of small knives, and its cutting action is more in the pushing motion than in the backswing. The ripsaw functions like a set of chisels in a row. It gouges out tiny scoops of fiber along the cutting edge.

Where there was waterpower, the Americans devised a sash saw to cut logs into lengths of board for building. Then the circular saw was developed, and millwork began to be done at mills, not by individual carpenters. This was probably regarded as a great boon by the carpenters, but it was the beginning of industrialization and the end of some of the finest handwork.

The earliest plane may have been a piece of stone wedged into a block of wood. It seems likely that the Phoenicians used planes to smooth their fine ships. There is no evidence, however, that the Egyptians had planes among their tools. Of course, the Romans used planes. The Romans fashioned an iron plane with an iron crossbar. As with most of the Romans' inventions, the plane dropped out of sight during the Dark Ages and wasn't seen again until the Middle Ages. There is a picture of a plane in a painting by Albrecht Dürer, *Melancholia*. Planes then emerged with forward horns for easier handling. These forward horns became quite decorative and may be a reflection of man's need to express himself artistically as well as in a functional way in his tools.

The plane is basically a chisel set in a block of some other material. At one time that material was wood, but planes in the United States now are made of steel. Modern planes are also outfitted with knobs rather than the decorative forward horns. Several refinements in the plane have been made over the years: an adjustable frog screw allows the workman to control the width of the shaving throat, mouth adjustments allow woods to be cleaned to a finer finish, and blades may be used in various positions.

Knives are another form of hand tool that some craftsmen make for themselves. Robert Silliman, who does inlaid work on cabinets and who makes classical guitars, makes most of his own knives. Tom Haile has fashioned many of his knives. The first knife was probably also fashioned by someone who knew just what he wanted and knew how to make this cutting instrument according to his skills. Knives are different from chisels in that their cutting edge is along the side and is two-beveled. Knives are used for carving as well as for cutting.

The carpenter also needs a variety of clamps, and some workmen, such as Haile and Silliman, make their own. According to Silliman, "I may never use the same clamp or chisel for the same thing again, so I'm prepared to make a new one each time I go to work." There are also bench clamps to secure a piece of wood to the workbench.

The good carpenter accumulates a good supply of hand tools over the years. In addition, he may have some machine tools in his shop. The tools mentioned here are only a few of those in most of the groups.

There are hewing hatchets, claw hatchets, and half-hatchets. There are shingling hatchets and carpenter's adzes. In the saw family, there are band saws, coping saws, hacksaws, dovetail saws, and compression saws. There are gang saws, tension saws, pushing saws, and pulling saws. Chisels aren't just chisels, either. There are carving chisels, cold chisels, corner chisels, and firmer chisels. There are round-nosed chisels, skew chisels, and turning chisels.

Besides the tools already mentioned there are boring tools. In this category, we find the awls. The brad awl, which looks like a chisel on a long, thin steel rod, is probably the oldest boring tool. The brad awl is rotated back and forth in the material it is meant to bore. Perhaps that is exactly how primitive man worked his fishbone through material to form holes, back and forth, back and forth.

An auger is another boring tool. The auger has a handle with an eye to receive a bit. The handle is rotated in a clockwise direction, and the bit does the work of boring out the hole. There are different bits to scoop out different types of holes: spoon bits, shell bits, pod bits, center bits, and twist bits. The Scotch bit is one of the most popular bits; it is fashioned like a screw with a cutting tool on one end. The gimlet goes back to ancient times and was used extensively by carpenters until power tools virtually replaced it after World War II. The gimlet's cutting edge is on the side of the tool, rather than on the end as in other boring tools. The Archimedean drill is another tool that dates back to antiquity and was much in use until power tools became popular. It is a sort of push drill and is used to make small holes.

Besides these tools, there are measuring instruments and layout tools. There are compasses, squares, levels, and gauges. There are transits and levels for surveying.

The Archimedean drill made holes for wooden screws. Screws also go back to Roman times, possibly even to the Greeks. For years wooden screws were cut on a screw tap, a box or hole with threads of metal for carving screws. Many times wooden screws were carved by hand. Wooden screws were beautiful and were also very efficient. They were made in the shop by early American cabinetmakers and could be found in spinning wheels, on workbenches, and in linen presses.

Most of our tools can be traced back to primitive man. Saws, hammers, axes, and hatchets were used in some form by Stone Age people. Chisels, planes, and awls also date back to early man. The Egyptians, Phoenicians, and Greeks developed building tools still further, but it was the Romans who made tools so sophisticated that they were not improved upon until recent times.

Some tools that are fairly modern in origin are screwdrivers and nail sets. Everybody uses screwdrivers now, but they only came into existence with the development of the metal screw in the latter half of the nineteenth century. As wire nails were uncommon before that time, there was no need for nail sets that could be used to drive the heads of nails below the surface of the wood. The turning lathe was used in the Middle Ages, but it is not certain how much older than that it is. The turning lathe is one of the most useful pieces of equipment for the cabinetmaker. With it the cabinetmaker can fashion beautifully turned chair legs, bedposts, candlesticks, and cabinet posts. Violin-makers and guitar builders use lathes in their shops. Millworkers use lathes.

Spokeshaves are common carving tools that came into

being fairly recently. The name spokeshave suggests that it may have been the result of some wheelwright's work in his shop. Just as the Maydole hammer, also known as the adz-eye hammer, and the American felling ax were developed by blacksmiths who were confronted with practical problems, so the spokeshave may have come into existence to solve a particular problem. The spokeshave is essential to a good cabinetmaker. It is a precision cutting tool which, like the plane, can be adjusted in the width of its cuttings. It can cut along an arc. It can be used to make concave carvings and is often used to carve designs for chair backs or on cabinets.

Chapter **III**

Joints

The carpenter's union is called The United Brotherhood of Carpenters and Joiners. Joinery, or the art of joining two pieces of wood together, ranks with importance enough to merit its own classification in the union. Essential to carpentry skills is the ability to make good joints.

When you go to buy furniture, look at the workmanship of the joints. Particularly if you are purchasing what goes by the name of "antique" furniture, look at the joints carefully. Early American craftsmen made the joints of their furniture so tight that they are still tight, and the chairs, tables, and cabinets are quite durable. Authentic pieces of early cabinetmaking show much better joining techniques than are seen in assembly-line furniture.

Examine some old barns for the joinery used. Sometimes the carpenter put square pegs in round holes for a tighter fit, or he would notch the pegs so that they would catch in the hole and stay in. Some pegs were made larger than the holes they were going into, and a mallet or pin maul was used to hammer them in solidly. Using green wood for pegs ensured a tight fit. Pegs might have a wedge hammered into the ends to hold them in place.

Even today, when it is so much easier, faster, and

cheaper to buy mass-produced nails and screws, some joints are still put together by shaping one board to receive the other. The old joints hold better and resist wear and tear better for some purposes. The joinery may be done at a mill and sent on to the builder or consumer. In that sense it is also a product of mass production. The finish workers, as they are called—or millworkers—do the joining. Window sashes are stronger with mortise and tenon joints. Door jambs can stand up to repeated slammings better with rabbet joints than if they were nailed together. Stairs bear the weight of many people and are more durable if they are made with tongue and groove joints than if they are nailed or screwed together. Good cabinets are still made with drawers having dovetailed joints.

Mitered joints are often used on molding. Crown molding, for example, goes around the top of the wall, where the wall meets the ceiling. The molding has to go around corners, and mitered joints serve this function well. In mitered joining, two boards are beveled at an angle, usually a 45-degree angle, and then joined to each other, either by gluing along the length of their joined surface or by nailing together. They may also be joined with a spline, a form of tongue and groove construction in which a strip from one board fits into a groove on the other board. Triangular splines may also be inserted in a groove in the mitered corner. As molding is usually of thin wood and is used for decorative purposes, nailing mitered joints is the least desirable practice. It is almost impossible to hide the nail heads, particularly because molding is not often painted, but is stained, varnished, and polished.

Stairs, transoms, and windows often have molding as finishing touches. A miter box can help you get the accurate angle you want to cut. A saw is guided through the grooves in the miter box to cut precisely the measured angle.

Dovetail joints are so called because, when viewed from one perspective, they resemble tails. Sometimes these joints are simply referred to as "tails." When people talk about dovetail joints, they invariably interlock the fingers of their hands to illustrate what occurs in dovetailing. These joints are a variation of the mortise and tenon joint, having both projections, or pins, and sockets, or tails. Dovetail joints are used for fine cabinets, for strong drawers, and for fine jewelry boxes, music boxes, and trays. They are considered by some to be the strongest of all the woodworking joints. They are also time-consuming to make and require a good bit of skill. The pins and tails of dovetail joints fit together, with several possible combinations: the single dovetail joint, which has one pin; the multiple dovetail joint, which has several pins and tails; the through joint, in which the pin goes through the wood of the tail board; and the hidden joint, in which the pin does not go through the tail board and so remains "hidden."

Internationally famous cabinetmaker James Krenov sometimes leaves dovetailing exposed on the fronts of drawers. His execution of the dovetailing is precise, and the effect enhances the overall beauty of whatever he has built, a silver chest, music stand, or cabinet.

Dovetail joints must be measured accurately, cut precisely, and the mortise part cleaned out neatly with a chisel. When they are made right, dovetail joints create tight joints as well as beautiful ones.

Mortise and tenon joints are probably used more than any other joint in the making of cabinets and other furniture. They can be made very, very tight. When made correctly they also guarantee the wood against shifting. Strength and stability, then, are two features of a well-constructed mortise and tenon joint. As with dovetail joints, there are blind mortise and tenon joints and through mortise and tenon joints. There are also double mortises and tenons, where two tenons fit into side-by-side mortises. A pinned mortise and tenon joint has a nail, or pin, driven through both parts to keep them from coming apart. This type of joint is often used by modern millworkers in constructing window sashes for extra strength. It is also used for the frames of bridge-work. Millworkers pride themselves on making "water-tight" joints. If this is so, it is because some form of the mortise and tenon joint is probably used in their construction.

Butt joints occur when two boards are fastened end to end, without any overlapping parts. Butt joints may be glued along the entire length of their adjoining surfaces. More likely than not, they also have dowel rods joining them together. This is also a common form of joining still done in modern millwork. Holes to receive the dowels are drilled with power tools, the dowels are cut to fit, and the boards are joined by inserting the dowels in the holes. Then the joint may be glued together and clamped until it has set.

Another use of the butt joint is for gluing veneers onto furniture. The selected veneers are cut and placed on the tabletop, glued, and clamped. Butt joints are used for fine inlay work with veneers. Pieces of the veneer are cut to fit the pattern, laid in the formation of the pattern, glued to the surface, and clamped. Warping of pieces is prevented when using butt joints by alternating the boards so that every other board faces upside down.

Rabbet joints have been used for a long time. Rabbets,

like dados, are among the grooved joints. In rabbet joints, the groove or cut is along the edge of the board so that a board similarly fashioned can fit right into it. Rabbets have two sides and are at the ends of boards. Rabbets can be cut by hand with a special plane; the trick is to cut the matching rabbet for a perfect fit. Cabinet doors often require rabbet grooves, and where the doors are concave that can pose a real problem. This is just one of the problems that cabinetmaker James Krenov works to overcome in his shop.

The dado groove is three-sided. It is used where one board is set into a groove in another board. Some say this is one of the strongest of all the cabinetmaking joints. The dado is used for shelving. The board is placed within a groove precisely the right size to receive it in another board, and both boards gain in strength by the new construction. If further reinforcement is needed, a toenail is hammered through the joint during the gluing process. Dados are used for leg braces on tables and chairs, for shelving, and for putting panels in frames.

Both rabbets and dados can be used for flooring, for stairs, and for panel installation. Rabbets and dados can be cut with routers or with chisels and hand saws. As with all the other joints mentioned, good workmanship ensures good joints and fine furniture. Good dado joints help to make particularly strong cabinets.

The tongue and groove joint is similar to both the rabbet and dado joints in that a rabbetlike edge is fitted into a matching groove of another board. Tongue and groove joints are commonly used for laying wooden floors and for exterior siding. There is not much warping with tongue and groove joints, and they are virtually watertight and airtight. They are invisible grooves, and that makes them a favorite joint to use in laying floors or for the installation of paneling. Like the rabbet and the dado, the tongue and groove can be made with the router for the groove and a hand saw or plane for the tongue.

The tongue and groove joint is one of a number of joints referred to as lap joints, so called because part of one board overlaps part of another board. Other lap joints are: dovetail joints, cross lap, wedge lap, and end lap joints. Another name for an end lap joint is ship lap. It is a simple and strong joint that resists the damage brought on by shrinkage. Like other lap joints, the two boards gain in strength from the imposition of one over the other. The ship lap jont is good for frames.

In other times, a person first learned the art of joining wood. When he/she had mastered that art, admission was sought into the carpenter's trade. All carpenters knew how to do the skilled work involved in making joints. Carpenters were always expert woodworkers. That is not necessarily so today, when the finish work is done at mills, and the carpenters have other skills. Millworkers today will even tell you that "carpenters" come to the mill for window sashes or door jambs and don't know how to measure for them properly.

There are many fly-by-night carpenters "out there," amateurs who have somehow lucked into doing some work for somebody and who call themselves carpenters. The carpenter's trade is hard to regulate. There is no licensing. There are, however, some excellent schools to attend if one is truly serious about becoming a good carpenter. In these schools finish work is taught as well as the rough work we associate with most carpentry work today.

Chapter IV

The Schools

State-operated vocational schools offer excellent carpentry courses, good teachers, and an abundance of the materials needed to learn carpentry. The state schools may be at the secondary or the postsecondary level. Many high school students have the opportunity to learn carpentry from master craftsmen while still in school. There is a specified curriculum, and the students must progress through certain skill areas during the course. Students in the postsecondary schools have coursework for about two years and the added advantage of possible on-the-job training.

In the postsecondary schools an arrangement is usually in effect that is known as open-entry/open-exit. The coursework is sectioned so that a student may leave at the completion of any section. A typical postsecondary school might have 280 specific tasks for the carpentry student to master; he/she might choose to leave at the completion of any task in the course outline and would be given credit for areas completed. Another postsecondary school might have the carpentry skills divided into several categories, and the student would be expected to complete the requirements of a category before receiving credit for that category. The Indiana Voca-

A class in progress at the Local 64 apprentice school. Basic math is essential to carpentry.

tional Technical School, known in the area simply as Ivy Tech, divides carpentry classwork into these basic skill areas: comprehensive skill/knowledge, concrete form-work, framing, exterior finish, interior finish, interior systems, and supplemental skill areas. There are several skills to master in each division. The Jefferson State Vocational Institute, on the other hand, has 280 skills to be mastered, with open-exit possible at the completion of any skill.

At Ivy Tech each student is given a handout listing:

Course number
Course description
Competencies mastered
Prerequisites, if any
Class hours required
Lab hours required
Practical experience required
Credits offered
Lab shop fee
Names of teachers
Grading procedure
Textbook assignments
Periodicals used
Audiovisual tools used
Tool list
Times of midterm and final exams

Thus, a student entering the cabinetmaking phase of carpentry would see a general course description something like this: Learns the techniques of cabinetmaking, with emphasis on joining, installation of hardware and countertops. The student would see that he/she would learn these competencies:

1. joining techniques: rabbet, dado, dovetail, mortise and tenon, miter, tongue and groove, butt joints
2. use of cabinetmaking tools: hand tools, power tools
3. method of assembling a cabinet
4. method of putting on a cabinet top

The student at Jefferson State Vocational, however, would learn about cabinetmaking in item # 106. Item #69 dealt with joinery, and many other skills were taught prior to #106 that could relate to cabinetmaking. In this school, various aspects of trimwork are taught all along the way, but most of the sophisticated finish work classes come near the end of the two-year course. These students also receive a handout, this one in the form of a checklist for each item studied. There is room for the teacher to mark off and give a grade for every skill as it is mastered. On the back of the form the instructor may write additional comments. There is a note suggesting that the teacher include information about the student's work habits, performance levels, and attendance record.

All vocational schools stress attendance. Nothing jeopardizes a student's continuing education faster than a poor attendance record. The schools regularly put their own credibility on the line by going to employers with requests to hire students as apprentices. They also try to place as many students as possible in jobs upon graduation. They do not want to lose good connections with the business community, especially in hard economic times, because of the inferior quality of students they send on for apprenticeship. One of the most important things to a potential employer is attendance. According to Clyde Huber of the Jefferson State Vocational School, the first things employers ask are:

1. What kind of mechanic is this student?
2. Is he/she dependable?

Huber interprets "dependable" to mean:

1. Does he/she come on time and come regularly?
2. Is he/she reliable?
3. Is he/she interested in the work or just plain lazy?

If Huber or Robert Hardley, the other carpentry instructor at Jefferson State, tells the employer something like: "Well, John doesn't know a whole lot yet, but he's a good worker, and he's dependable," the employer usually responds with, "As long as he comes every day, we'll teach him the rest."

Another excellent school for carpenters is at the union hall. The unions train good carpenters. The union program lasts four years, during which time the student is considered an apprentice, is helped to find on-the-job training, and receives apprentice wages. Those who leave the other postsecondary carpentry schools must still attend the union school if they join the union. They must complete the four-year program and receive apprenticeship pay until they do so. The union carpentry school is a highly structured program, with first-rate teachers and a staff of interested people who follow up on the students on the job and who are constantly searching for effective ways to teach the material. Unions are justly proud of their educational programs. They have put much time, money, and effort into ensuring that high standards of carpentry skills will be taught to many generations. The people who operate the union school are drawn from the union membership. The textbooks, audiovisual materials, and lab materials are all carefully selected by the school's principal and the assistant director. Staff people often travel to job sites, not to check up on the apprentices or to talk to the bosses, but just to let the apprentices know that "they are there" and are interested in them. The quality of education and the standards of excellence at the union carpentry school are such that even nonunion carpenters praise it, and the instructors at the state schools give it excellent ratings. Attitude, attendance, and ability are emphasized here, as at the other carpentry schools, and employers trust apprentices that the union sends them. Very rarely does an employer have a complaint about a union apprentice.

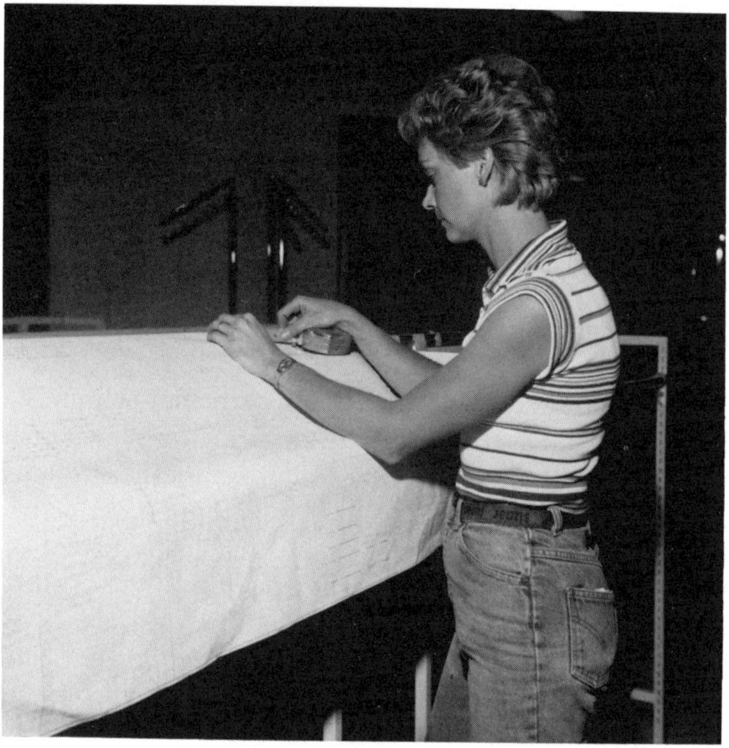

The carpenter who can read blueprints has an advantage in being able to visualize the project in hand.

Veterans take advantage of their G.I. Bill of Rights to go to carpentry schools. The carpentry schools rank second only to auto mechanic schools in popularity with students applying for entrance to vocational schools. There are many CETA workers in carpentry classes. It is to their disadvantage that they are being paid to attend vocational programs. Many of them have excellent skill potential, and the fact that they are paid to attend vocational classes, rather than giving them added incentive, destroys a love for learning. The pay becomes an end in itself, and the real point, the learning of a skill for life, is either overlooked or becomes secondary.

Government grants are also available to make attendance at the vocational schools possible. It is rare that anyone is excluded from vocational training because of money problems.

Both the union schools and the state vocational schools require that students be eighteen years of age and have a high school diploma or a Graduate Equivalency Diploma, a GED. Other requirements are in skill areas and can be learned.

Chapter V

Other Skills

A group of high school seniors are sitting around a table in the lunchroom discussing how terrible the cafeteria food is. It is April, and they have only a couple of weeks left before their school lives are over. They are very different in their outlooks, goals, and personal achievements. Marie, who will be the class valedictorian, does little but study. She is on the school paper, and she uses every spare minute in that class to study for Latin or calculus classes. After the deadlines are met each month, Marie uses newspaper class to prepare for other assignments. She does her newspaper work diligently, however, and does whatever the advisor asks her to do.

Rhonda, the yearbook editor, is also present. Rhonda is not only the yearbook editor: she plays volleyball, runs track, and starts on the basketball team. She is on the honor roll, in the Beta Club, and maintains a B average.

Darin will be glad to get out of school. It has been a hard struggle for him, and he hasn't enjoyed any of it. Last year he was late every day and missed first period. Darin spends part of each day in a class for learning disabled students. He has just gotten his math skills up to an eighth-grade level, and he reads on a seventh-grade level.

Pam is also an LD student, but she attends vocational education for part of each day also. In vocational education she is enrolled in auto mechanics but feels she might like some other skill area better. She receives good grades from her auto mechanics teacher, however.

Phil is in the band and in all regular classes. He is an average student. He took algebra his freshman year and geometry his sophomore year. He hates to write essays, but he enjoys it when the class reads novels in English Literature. He liked reading *Ordinary People* and *1984*. He didn't think he'd like Shakespeare, but he really got into *Othello* and changed his mind about Shakespeare.

André is one of the leaders of this group and also of the school. The kids don't really like him: he cheats in class to maintain a B average, and he pushes himself forward wherever possible. However, it's hard to get away from him. He enters every contest they have at the high school, and, even though he doesn't win, he's probably one of the most visible students in the senior class. He was elected president of the Scholarship Committee because nobody ran against him. The principal thinks André is just the greatest person in the school, and André has even been heard to address the principal by his first name.

Barbara was the manager of the football team. She is a smart girl but often finds something else to do besides go to class. She always seems to be in the halls just when some teacher needs someone to set up the slide projector in the auditorium or to give out roses at an assembly program. She has managed to leave the school grounds for lunch at a nearby fast-food restaurant during her entire senior year, and the fact that she is with these other students in the lunchroom now is because she bought a lunch "to go" and is now munching on her hamburger.

Roger has been caught and suspended for smoking

dope at school twice during his senior year. He has failed most of his academic subjects during his five-year tenure in high school. He will be twenty when he graduates in May. He enjoyed going to vocational school this year in small engine repair. He is in the "basic" program in the regular education program. He was never tested for Special Education.

Ben is the first person in his family to graduate from high school. His father has been unemployed because of a work injury that happened when Ben was very little. The family refused to go on welfare; his mother got a job as a nurse's aide, and she supports the family. Ben works nights at a fast-food restaurant. On weekends he gets a little drunk with his friends. He is often so tired he falls asleep in class. He bought himself a used car and likes to work on it.

Paul is probably the smartest student in the entire school. He just understands whatever is put in front of him. He is in the computer math class, on the math team, and in advanced calculus. He hardly ever gets to homeroom on time, and he never does his homework for any class until the five minutes before the class starts. He can often be seen doing lessons in the halls. He played football on the high school team but had a hard time "thinking on his feet." He wasn't quick enough in his judgments to make a good football player.

Ruth fights with her teachers. She prides herself on being able to "cuss" a teacher out and get what she wants by bringing her mother in to back her up. Her mother threatens to "go to the Board" if Ruth isn't treated fairly. Ruth is popular with the kids because she acts so crazy. She was voted "Miss Senior Class" at the Homecoming Prom. She gets mostly Cs and Ds in regular program classes. She likes to paint, and art class is the only class in which she does well.

Sharon has a two-year-old son. She has been working after school at a grocery store for a year to help support him. Sometimes her homework has grease stains on it or is wrinkled where the baby grabbed it. She gets her assignments done. Her work is not spectacular, and she is often very tired, but she passes all her classes.

If we were to say that two of these students would go through apprentice training for carpentry, which two would you pick? If only two of them will make it as apprentice carpenters and stay to become journeymen carpenters, which two will it be? What qualities are needed to go into carpentry and make a living at it? Which two of these high school seniors could stick it out to make carpentry a worthwhile profession?

As you go back over the list, take into consideration the negative factors that public schools cause. Some of the "bad qualities" you note may be due more to the fact that these students have been in an atmosphere charged with nonproductivity for most of their lives, than to any significant character flaw in themselves. Remember that they have been in a school environment that restricted their growth as mature human beings rather than helped them develop individuality and creativity. If they seem not to be very responsible or forward-looking, the fault may be the system's, not their own. Assuming, then, that their public education is one additional deterrent, the effects of which they must overcome, which two of these twelve young people could make it as carpenters? What qualities are needed to become a good carpenter?

The people at the carpentry schools say they do not want someone who is overqualified. For some time applicants were given standardized tests when they came to the carpentry schools. Those who scored high in the math areas were considered good material for the program. The school administrators soon found out how wrong they were in judgments based solely on interpretation of test scores. Sometimes the high scorers were also overachievers; they wanted more out of the carpentry field than they were willing to put into it. They were impatient to get ahead; they were unwilling to wait and work for the rewards.

Carpentry is a skill that takes many years to perfect. It is also a field that is subject to the whims and caprices of the economy. Beginning carpenters do not make much more than $5 or $6 an hour. The new apprentice may receive even less than that. It may take many years before the carpenter achieves the status of journeyman and makes $15 an hour.

The schools have found that some of these highly qualified youngsters just didn't understand the correlation between skill acquisition and pay. They wanted to be paid $7 or $8 an hour from the beginning of their apprenticeship. These young people were ambitious and impatient. They possessed skills that should have made them valuable as carpenters, but they just didn't make it in the building field. They wanted too much from the industry.

Also, most of these youngsters were looking for immediate advancement. They were advancement-oriented and were not interested in sticking out a job with one company or with the union when they could leave and find something better. All in all, they were not the type of carpenter material the schools wanted to produce.

However, applicants should possess some skills. Mechanical skills are very high on the list. People who like to work with *things* are generally included in that category. Other indications of mechanical aptitude might be:

1. artistic ability
2. spatial awareness—the ability to "see" things, to visualize
3. fondness for craftwork
4. musical ability
5. ability to reason abstractly
6. ability to do detailed work
7. ability to figure out technical data
8. interest in the finished product of work
9. manual skills
10. creative ability

Which of our dozen students possess qualities in the mechanical area? With training and sufficient motivation, could those qualities be utilized to make a good carpenter out of Pam, or Phil, or Roger? What other qualities are needed? Could Marie make it as a carpenter? Could André?

A carpenter needs to be able to figure mathematically. To do so he/she must possess basic math skills. A carpenter need not have had a course in calculus, but basic math skills might include:

1. fractions
2. decimals
3. percentage
4. algebra
5. geometry

The carpenter has to be able to *think* in one/thirty-second of an inch dimensions. The carpenter must be able to put out work that is correct to the smallest fraction of an inch. He/she MUST be able to get that close.

According to Dale Burchett, who operates his own woodworking shop, Custom Woodworking, a carpenter must be: a salesperson, a bookkeeper/accountant, a draftsman, a designer, a woodworker, a carpenter. Dale says that a carpenter wears many hats, and many skills are required to be a good woodworker.

Mike Andres, an instructor at Ivy Tech, says that a carpenter needs to have manual skills and common sense. The manual skills, he says, can be taught, but it takes more common sense than anything else. You can think your way through any problem, but 60 percent of the youngsters he sees in his program blow their cool if they mess up. If you make a mess of a piece of wood, throw it away and start over, Andres counsels. If something isn't going to hurt a building, leave it and go on to the next thing. Some carpenters will knock out a stud if it's one-eighth of an inch off. Use your judgment, he says. There's a limit to how perfect a thing can be.

Carpenters must be able to read blueprints. In order to do this accurately, they must be able to read the words on the blueprint. Reading and English skills are, believe it or not, important to a carpenter.

The carpenter who goes into business for himself/herself must draw up contracts for customers. Dale Burchett says, "If you hand them a third-grade contract to sign, they'll treat you like a third grader." Burchett says that customers regard your carpentry skill the way they see your grammar. "If you come across looking like a dingbat, that's the respect you'll get for your carpentry. Would you let someone build your kitchen cabinets, which are going to cost thousands of dollars, if that person speaks and writes like a third grader?"

Mike Garrison, the Business Agent for Local 64, feels that a prospective carpenter ought to be able to read well enough to comprehend the textbooks and to pass the tests at the union school. A sixth-grade reading level is probably enough to read and comprehend most written matter. The union school and the state-operated vocational schools have learning centers where students may improve their reading skills.

A minimum of writing skills are probably needed, as Burchett points out. It is important for someone who deals with the public to be able to spell correctly and to write a complete sentence. It is more important for the carpenter in business for himself/herself than for one working for a big company. Those in supervisory capacities in larger companies, however, have opportunities to use writing and reading skills more frequently.

A carpenter must have patience. Patience, like manual skills, can be acquired. The work is exacting and demanding. Someone who gets frustrated easily and gives up when discouraged will not make it as a carpenter. The would-be carpenter must be able to take criticism.

Public relations skills are necessary for one who would be a carpenter. Those who go into business for themselves especially need to know how to get along with the public. Foremen and supervisors of jobs meet the public more than do those who are just working on the job, but the ability to get along with others is important even as a member of the building team.

Can women make it in the field of carpentry? Clyde Huber of the Jefferson State Vocational School says he'll "get crucified for saying so, but they make some of the best carpenters." According to Huber, women are more motivated than men. They're determined to be good at it. Local 64 had a woman who was a journeyman carpenter in 1976. The local regularly trains and sends out women apprentices.

The physically handicapped need to assess their own capabilities as honestly as possible before trying for admittance to carpentry school. Most students with minor learning problems can overcome them and become good carpenters, if that is what they want to do. Some physical handicaps would make carpentry a poor career choice for the handicapped person. Mike Andres points out that a deaf person will be in a dangerous position around power tools. One needs sight and hearing to know when power tools are on. "Sometimes those saws are going so fast," he says, "you don't even see that they are moving. If a deaf person came along and ran a hand over the edge of a saw in motion, he'd lose his fingers." One needs to be able to hear motors running. A totally blind person would not be suited for carpentry, which is a highly visual skill. With other physical handicaps an honest assessment needs to be made by both the handicapped applicant and the vocational school counselor. Carpentry requires a lot of physical stamina. The carpenter must do much lifting, bending, reaching, standing, and walking. There is work that must be done on scaffolds. If one is afraid of heights, carpentry would not be an excellent career choice. There are many repetitious tasks in carpentry. Some days the carpenter does nothing but hammer nails all day long. The hammering arm gets very tired and sore. The carpenter must carry boards and tools every day. The carpenter must work outdoors in heat and cold. Some people with handicaps probably could adjust to carpentry and become good at the profession, but the handicapped person needs to listen to the advice of prudent counselors before making a career decision in this direction. It is a risky business.

Well, which of the twelve students profiled do you think can become career carpenters? If we could choose two, which two would you pick? Even if they are poor in math skills, remember that they can learn those in carpentry school. And with calculators and computers at everyone's disposal, a problem can simply be plugged into the computer and an answer retrieved. Look at the quality of the twelve, the quantity of their output, keeping in mind that they are disadvantaged by being in a sterile learning situation. How was their attendance? Do they display some natural ability? As Clyde Huber says about natural ability, "Some got to work for it; some got it."

The people who enter carpentry schools each year are men and women like yourself. They have some natural abilities that can be developed by sensitive instructors. They possess some qualities that would make them be very good carpenters, if that is what they want to become. There are traits in each of them that could prevent their becoming expert craftsmen in the field of carpentry. Who knows which of them will become good carpenters? It is like working with raw wood. Only after the seasoning, planing, shaping, and finishing is there a truly beautiful product. The same can be said for the carpenter.

Chapter VI

The Apprentice Carpenter

In the Middle Ages, when craftsmen belonged to guilds, a young man considered himself fortunate to be apprenticed to a master artisan. He might spend years learning the craft from a master goldsmith, silversmith, mason, or carpenter. Finally, when his own work was judged of a quality acceptable to the master, he moved up to journeyman rank. At that point he could perform some functions more independently, and the master trusted him with more responsible work. He was acknowledged in the whole guild as a journeyman worker, just one step away from becoming a master. When he became a master in his own right, he could open his own shop, take in and instruct apprentices, and have journeymen working for him. There was great honor attached to belonging to a guild, and each guild adopted standards of excellence for its members.

During the Middle Ages some of the finest workmanship of that time or any time was done. In the thirteenth century, sometimes called the greatest of centuries, great cathedrals, guild halls, and other buildings were constructed. The stained glass windows, the flying buttresses and Gothic towers were all works of love done by craftsmen from guilds. There was a great sense of accomplishment and pride in the beautiful, sturdy, and well-constructed buildings. The whole town might turn out for the dedication of a church, and the workmanship was greatly admired. Even in spite of this admiration, the guild workers did their tasks as perfectly as they could. There was, for them, a relationship between their work and their whole lives. They were who they were because of their work. Their personal identities assumed the characteristics of their trade. They became the products of their crafts. One was a goldsmith, or a carpenter, or a silversmith. What they produced and who they were as persons were inextricably bound together. Thus they took care that what they produced was not shoddy. One's whole life was bound up in one's work, and the judgment on the value of a life might be determined from an appraisal of one's workmanship.

Gottfried Reck, of the Steiner-Reck Organ Company, Louisville, Kentucky, apprenticed in such a situation. Such apprenticeships rarely exist anymore. Reck, who was born in Germany, apprenticed at a school for organ-building in the town of Bielefeld in northern Germany. He received no pay during the four years he attended the school, only a $10 a month allowance and his board while he learned the art of organ-building. He studied under master architects, and he is now one of the few great master architects of organ-building himself. In his shop in the Old Louisville section of the city, he has a few high school students, whom he pays and who are learning how to build great organs.

Possibly any situation in which the young learn from the old may be called a master/apprentice situation. Tom Haile has taught classes in violin-making and has tried to give instruction to youngsters in his own shop. His brother, Haskell Haile, one of the greatest living classical guitar-makers, has taught college-level classes in guitar-making. Haskell has been known as quite a taskmaster, and one time his students complained bitterly to him that he drove them too hard. When he came to class the next day he told them all to put away their work, their notes, and their notebooks. "Today we are going to play music," he said. "Get your instruments." The students and Haskell played their guitars all day, and it was one of the loveliest days of the entire course. When the course was over and the students were to return to their own cities, they all went to Haskell's house for dinner. Many wept upon leaving their master.

Union apprentices spend four years learning the carpentry trade. For their on-the-job training they are paid a percentage of a journeymen's wage. A fair journeymen's wage might be $13 an hour, so a novice apprentice receives 60 percent of that. The apprentice receives an increment of 5 percent every six months until he reaches journeyman pay at the end of four years. However, the union is considering a program paying an entry wage of 40 percent of journeymen's pay, 5 percent increases every six months for two years, and 10 percent increases during the final stages of apprenticeship. According to Mike Garrison, the union's Business Agent, "It is mighty hard to justify to contractors putting a completely inexperienced man on a job for $10 an hour when he's never been on a construction site in his life." The new proposal is one of several options Local 64 is considering, but the union leadership feels that this plan could provide the motivation for some carpenter apprentices to complete the program in 3½ years, making them work faster and harder. The program as it is now, says Garrison, "is gauged to the average Joe and could take five years."

Any student can upgrade his/her apprenticeship. The student can challenge blocks of the curriculum and test out of them. It is a flexible program. Or the student can go back and apply himself/herself and get the schooling done. It is possible to put in eight hours on Saturdays at the Local's education center.

Union apprentices must be eighteen years of age and have a high school diploma or a GED. The union accepts apprentices according to the Equal Opportunity Employment guidelines. When there is room for apprentices in the program the union advertises for two weeks in the local papers. Usually it advertises every six months. It accepts applications from all and advertises for all. It has had female apprentices for many years. Some of its black carpenters have already reached retirement age and retired. Blacks have been in the union for thirty years.

When someone makes application for the union's apprenticeship program the union follows the "intent to hire" procedure:

1. It opens up the program to bring anybody in.
2. The applicant fills out an application.
3. The union interviews for union membership.
4. The apprentice goes out and interviews for his/her own job.

There used to be a top age limit of thirty-two years or, in some schools, twenty-five years for admission to apprentice programs in the state schools. Those limits were challenged in the courts, and it was judged discriminatory to bar someone from carpenter's school for being "too old." Now people of all ages are learning the carpenter's trade. At Vocational Industrial Clubs of America Skills Olympics, apprentice carpenters of every age and from all over the country compete.

You may hear someone referred to as a carpenter's "helper." A helper is not the same as an apprentice. Helpers do the "gofer" work for carpenters. They pick up around the job site, carry lumber for the carpenters, and fetch tools. They are stuck in their jobs. Helpers may receive yearly increments in wages, but nothing like the increments of the apprentices. They don't have to make decisions: they do what they're told. Many helpers are little more than nail pounders, but some of them make a career of being helpers. In time they may pick up certain carpentry skills. There are certain advantages to being a helper, if you are a good one. When a carpenter quits, the best helper may be hired as a replacement. Thus, the helper may work up to wages of $9 to $11 an hour.

The unemployment rate for apprentices is not as great as it is for journeymen. Good apprentices can keep jobs. It costs less to pay them, and they are often getting direct instruction in the exact work that they are doing on site. Most schools accommodate the apprentice's classwork to the type of work he/she is doing. For instance, if an apprentice is doing formwork on the job—let's say this apprentice is a woman—her school instructors would give her instruction in formwork. If an apprentice is studying the installation of acoustical tile—let's say this apprentice is a man—he would be doing acoustical tile installation on the job. The apprentice can skip to those blocks in the instructional program that are relevant to the on-the-job training, rather than proceed in the designated order in the instructional sequence.

Many carpenters learn the trade from someone in

their own family. Their apprenticeship is a family concern. Clyde Huber, the instructor at Jefferson State, learned the trade from his father and brothers. James Erhart, an independent contractor, also picked up carpentry from his father and brothers. Mike Andres, the instructor at Ivy Tech, worked for his brother when he was in high school and picked up many of his skills at that time.

Austin Abell, a former cabinetmaker, is the supervisor of millwork at Cook Lumber Company in Louisville. Abell instructs the men under him in millwork. He supervises their activities and teaches them what he knows about joinery and finish work. He is the master, and they are the apprentices. He is proud of the watertight joints that Cook Lumber manufactures, and he passes on his knowledge to the younger workers.

Dave Ledger has worked at Cook Lumber for several years. He works as a laborer, or helper, loading trucks, putting away the stock, keeping the yard clean, and waiting on customers. However, Dave feels he has learned a lot on the job. He has watched what goes on, listened to Abell and the others, and practiced some of the skills himself. He would like to open a shop in his own garage and make furniture. He has learned to appreciate the look and feel of wood. He is interested in the different types of wood and the varieties of things you can do with it.

Steve Horjus came as a young man to the Steiner-Reck Organ Company. He worked as an apprentice under Gottfried Reck and the others. Now, at twenty-six years of age, he has become an important and valuable part of the organization. He has helped to build several organs.

There are several ways to become an apprentice and work your way up in the carpenter's trade. The best, easiest, and surest route is through one of the schools, either the union school or the vocational schools. You will not be a journeyman when you complete the course-work at a vocational school, but you will be well on your way. We have nothing so fine as the old guilds anymore, but wherever you go you can find skilled carpenters, woodworkers who are masters and who are willing to share their knowledge with you. Apprenticeship is a period for the novice to learn from masters, and there are still plenty of master carpenters around, if one looks for them.

Chapter VII

What Comes First?

Why is it that they always teach safety first? Surely everyone knows about safety. Everyone knows how to take care of person and property on the job. Just visualize an imaginary work site, if you will.

It's early in the morning, and the workers are getting things ready for the day's work. A few are looking through toolboxes, picking over various hammers, hand saws, and squares. Two women are rolling lengths of rope. A couple of apprentices are taking turns rolling each other to the work site on the scaffolding. A woman worker turns on a circular saw and prepares to cut some boards.

It is a usual peaceful morning for this crew. This is their first morning on this particular job. For some reason, they never stay on jobs very long. Well, Larry, their foreman, is in the hospital recuperating from major hand surgery; he nearly sliced his thumb off on the circular saw the day before yesterday. Today Connie is operating the circular saw, and she's not a little scared after having seen Larry's thumb dangling by one piece of skin. She knows enough not to mess around with this saw, even if it is just a portable power saw. That's why she holds it with one hand rather than two while sawing. There's no sense endangering both her hands, is there?

Biff and Joe Tom have rolled to the side of the building where they'll be working. The scaffolding rams into the frame of the building, knocking the planks from the side posts, and Biff crashes to the ground. It was just a few feet, though, so no harm is done. He quickly recovers himself, punches Joe Tom playfully to show what really good spirits he is in, and they both clamber up the cross braces of the scaffolding. However, as neither of the two fellows thought to check the braces before they started out, another calamity takes place. The braces on Biff's side give out, and Biff crashes to the ground again. Joe Tom manages to swing onto the building frame and hangs there, looking like a chimp in the jungle, laughing at Biff. Biff hurt his ankle a little in this fall, but he reasons that it will be all right. He needs this job; he can't take off just to be laid up for some dumb ankle, so he hobbles to the abused scaffolding and decides to try again. First, the scaffold must be put back together.

But let's see what Fred and Lamont are doing. They have found the tools they wanted from the toolboxes and have proceeded to the pile of lumber they stacked last evening. They were in a hurry then, so they piled some old lumber with nails in it along with the new lumber. They had challenged each other to a contest to see who could stack the highest pile of lumber in the shortest time. Lamont won easily: he stacked a twenty-eight-foot pile in thirty-three minutes while Fred had only piled twenty-three feet. They had called it quits then and left the yard. They had not bothered to pick up any of the wood scraps lying around the yard; that was for a helper, they figured. Fred and Lamont considered themselves journeyman carpenters, and they surely weren't going to pick up scraps.

Connie leaned across her saw blade to reach one of the wood scraps on the other side of the machine. She misjudged her distance from the blade, and a whole hank of her waist-length hair was sliced off as she leaned over. Connie was disconsolate: she had been growing that hair since she was ten years old.

Meanwhile, Lamont and Fred were running into a little difficulty with the wood they had piled the night before. It seems that you really shouldn't stack wood higher than sixteen feet. Fred and Lamont, who were at the bottom of a pile of fallen boards, remembered this now. A slight bump of Lamont's shoulder had caused the disaster.

"Hey, man, you ever hear anything about not stacking wood with nails in it with new lumber?" Lamont complained to Fred.

"Why?"

"Well, just look at me, man." Lamont stuck his scratched face out from under three or four boards with nails emerging from the ends. When he saw Fred he burst out laughing.

Fred was miserable. He demanded to know what was so funny. He could hardly move where he was. Points of nails were sticking into his body from every angle.

"I'm sorry," Lamont choked back his laughter, "it's just that you look like one of those gurus on a bed of nails."

Jeanine and Tawny were over at the building fixing their length of rope to some beams to send up to Biff and Joe Tom. Both boys were now on the scaffold at about the second-story level. Jeanine threw the rope over a supporting beam of the building, and she and Tawny yanked on the rope. The beams had risen just above the level of the boys' heads when the rope broke. The beams fell and knocked Biff to the ground.

"Didn't you check that rope?" Jeanine said to Tawny.

"No, I thought you did," Tawny said to Jeanine.

Meanwhile, back at the circular saw, Connie tripped over one of the wood scraps next to the machine and tried to catch herself by grabbing hold of the saw blade. If the machine had been running, she would have lost her hand.

"Darn," she muttered to herself, "now I've got a nasty cut on my hand."

Tawny and Jeanine knotted their rope this time and passed their beams back up to Joe Tom. Joe Tom stood atop a ladder he had placed on the scaffolding so he could reach the boards better.

Fred and Lamont were busy restacking the fallen boards in smaller piles. Fred stopped and looked at his hands.

"Can I borrow your gloves, Lamont?"

"What do you mean, can you borrow my gloves? You know I lost my gloves on the last job when they dropped into the concrete forms. Splinters is just the way of life, man."

Connie was actually sawing some wood now. She was pushing a piece of board toward the blade. Because she hadn't checked out her saw before she started using it that morning, though, she had failed to notice the chip in the blade. As her hands got close to the blade, it caught on the board, causing splinters to fly up into her face. Connie wore no goggles. She rubbed her hands across her eyes.

Biff, Joe Tom, Jeanine, and Tawny stopped what they were doing as the noon whistle blew. They were joined on their way to Kentucky Fried Chicken by Fred and

Lamont. Connie hurried up to the group, her eyes wet and red.

"What's the matter with you?" Tawny asked her.

"Oh, nothing. I thought I got something in my eye, but I was lucky," Connie told her.

"No, I mean your *hair*. What did you do to it? It looks really wild."

"I'm glad you like it, Tawny. Thank you."

A car going through a yellow light passed close to the edge of their group as they stepped off the curb. Biff, limping along behind the others, shook his fist after the driver.

"Get off the road if you can't drive right. We could've been killed," he yelled.

Any number of times that morning any or all of the "carpenters" in this group could have been killed. How many safety violations did you count? What would be a good name for this company? Why do they move on to new jobs so often?

Take the scaffolding crew. What are safety measures regarding scaffolds?

1. Do you use damaged scaffolds?
2. Do you assume scaffolds are in good shape when you use them, or do you check them out?
3. Do you fasten the braces securely?
4. Do you climb the cross braces?
5. Do you ride rolling scaffolds?
6. Do you put ladders on scaffolds to extend your reach?

These are just some of the things to keep in mind when using scaffolds. It is also important to see that the planks extend over the edges of the supports and that you don't run into power lines with scaffolding.

Connie didn't know anything about operating a power tool safely, particularly a power saw. She didn't check it out before starting the motor; she didn't hold the portable saw with two hands. Other safety violations committed by Connie were:

1. Failure to clean up work site before starting to work.
2. Failure to wear eye protection.
3. Reaching over the saw to pick up material.

Tawny and Jeanine didn't check out their rope before using it. Once it had broken they should have discarded it; they never should have tied it together to use again.

Lamont and Fred should have known not to pile lumber so high. Sixteen feet is as high as safety standards permit. Boards should never be stacked with nails in them. Fred and Lamont also failed to clean up the work area, and when working with wood they should have worn gloves.

No one on the crew wore goggles, which is one of the first safety requirements in working with lumber.

There are many other safety measures that you learn as soon as you start classes in carpentry. Safety measures will be repeated in each area you study. It may seem like common sense to you, but common sense fails you when you are inexperienced and under pressure to perform your best at something new. Until safety measures become as familiar to you as hammering nails, you have to be reminded of them. Every step of the way, then, your instructors will recommend safety measures in their classes. Even common sense needs to be learned. When you automatically think about procedures in carpentry in the safest way possible, then your *real* common sense will be in effect. Until that time, you need to learn safety first.

George Franke, a union carpenter working at the Marble Hill Nuclear Plant in Madison, Indiana, says he's taken his falls in carpentry. He's had his share of broken bones.

Robert Silliman knows what it is like almost to lose a thumb on a power saw. He actually did trip, as Connie did in our story, on scraps of wood. He reached out to catch himself, and what he caught hold of was the moving blade of a circular saw. His thumb was hanging by one thin piece of skin when his wife rushed him to the emergency room. "I thought for sure my thumb was gone, but those doctors saved it. Not much you can do without a thumb, I've heard."

Austin Abell considers himself lucky that he still has all his fingers, and he's been doing millwork for thirty years. "The best thing is I've still got all my fingers. That's unusual for someone working in a mill," says Abell.

Why is safety so important a part of any carpentry curriculum? So you will be able to be a carpenter all your life. Without your limbs and fingers you would have to give up carpentry. So that you can stay alive.

Even with all the safety precautions in the world, there is still the chance that you could be hurt on the job. Many risks are involved in carpentry. Besides scaffolding, power saws, and splinters, there are risks involved with pneumatic equipment. The air pressure has to be checked; hoses need to be inspected for wear. You must wear eye protection when using pneumatic tools.

Chains and cables have to be kept in good condition,

as well as ropes. You have to be sure that power tools have safety guards. You can't work with power tools with wet hands or feet. Hammers and chisels and knives need to be checked to ensure that they are in good working order, sharp enough and secure enough.

Common sense? Maybe so. But when you are busy and involved with blueprints and building, formwork and framing, you sometimes need an extra nudge in the area of safety precautions. Don't expect too much of yourself. Safety is a learned technique. When it is learned well, it will be part of your "common sense."

Chapter VIII

Formwork and Framing Work

José is a roughwork artist. He builds the forms for hospitals, shopping malls, libraries, and office buildings. He loves his work. He likes formwork better than any other area of carpentry, and he usually tells an employer when he goes job-hunting that he does his best work at building forms. He has worked in formwork for twelve years. Once he taught a class in formwork at the state vocational school, but he didn't like teaching as much as he liked doing, so he quit and went back to formwork. Even in the worst of the recession, José was able to keep working; he has built quite a reputation for himself as an expert form builder.

José works with a variety of materials: plywood, steel, reinforced concrete, fiberboard, and lumber. José works close to the earth, as some forms are built on the ground. The earth may be used for one side of the form. José works in excavations, with the earth forming the floor and one side of his forms. He enjoys working so close to the earth; it makes him feel almost like a farmer, only he is planting buildings instead of seeds. His people have always been close to the land; his father and brothers had been farmers in Mexico. José came here looking for work to support his family. When he became an American citizen he joined the union, learned carpentry, and

Building forms for concrete is a major part of "rough" carpentry.

sent for his wife and children, and he has been supporting them well ever since.

So José feels at home working where he can smell and feel the earth. It gets a little hard in cold weather and in the blistering heat of summer, but on most days José takes a minute or two to look up from his work at the blue sky and realize how lucky he is. He is also very attentive to his work. He knows exactly how to construct the forms for each particular job. He makes beautiful tongue and groove joints for plywood where the forms will show in the finished structure. He also makes tongue and groove joints in undressed lumber for forms that will be exposed in the finished building. José can make tongue and groove joints expertly with hand tools, but he often uses a portable circular saw for greater speed.

José is noted for making tight concrete forms. Contractors like to have him on the job because they know their formwork will pass inspection. His forms are so tight that none of the concrete paste is lost, nor any of the water. His forms have enough rigidity and strength so that they will not burst from the pressure of the concrete.

Steel is what made concrete the durable material it is. Reinforced concrete has iron mesh or iron I-bars in it to give it extra strength. The concrete is consolidated to get rid of air bubbles that would weaken the bonding of concrete and steel. This consolidation is similar to stirring the layers of concrete to work out the air bubbles. A vibrator or spading tool is used to do this.

When José pours a basement at 7:30 on Tuesday morning, he knows his forms will be ready to come off on Friday morning. It takes three days for the concrete to set. However, it will take twenty-one days for the concrete to cure.

When José first started working in formwork he had trouble removing the forms so that the concrete didn't stick to them. He made quite a few messes stripping forms off concrete in the early days of his career. He was helped by a journeyman carpenter on the job, who explained about oiling the wooden forms before pouring the concrete into them. This journeyman also recommended the use of lacquer or paint for forms that were going to be used over and over again.

Another technique of good framework that initially

puzzled José was the need to keep the concrete wet. He nearly got himself fired from his first job for arguing with the foreman over the stupidity, as he called it, of putting water on concrete that you wanted to set. The foreman was patient with José, and José learned that it was important that the concrete not dry out before it was cured. Hydration is what occurs to cause concrete to harden. Hydration is the chemical reaction of the concrete mixture and the water. It is absolutely necessary that the concrete be kept wet during the drying process. José was amused at how ignorant he once had been and at how much he had learned when he flooded his first concrete slabs. To do this he and the other carpenters built a dike in the earth around the slab and flooded it. Usually José uses strips of wet burlap to keep the concrete moist. Concrete that is to be exposed to direct sunlight, such as pavements, is sometimes sprayed with a hose. Hay and stray also make good wet covers for concrete.

By the time the concrete is ready for wetting it has already been screeded. José screeds the surface of the concrete just before the "wet blanket" is applied. Screeding smooths out the surface of the mixture and makes it level. To do this José may use a trowel, a wooden floating device, or a mechanical screeder.

José has built forms for basements, sidewalks, the sides of driveways, patios, stairways, steps, and floors. He has done "heavy highway" work, building the forms for roads.

Like José, Paula has done her share of formwork. Paula, however, prefers to do the framing. She is also considered a rough carpenter. Rough carpenters do the support work for all kinds of buildings, from homes to high rises, from cottages to condominiums. Paula and her crew put in the subflooring, the inside wall studs, the exterior studding and siding, the ceiling joists, and the roof rafters.

Paula likes her work so much because she sees framework as the "shell" of a building. She is excited by the idea that she is creating a shell for someone else to dress up and make beautiful. She often tries to imagine the people who will inhabit the shell she is working on. What will they be like? Can they ever love this structure as much as she loves and cares about it? Sometimes she pretends she is a Mongolian herder building his yurt. Yurts have been around for centuries and are wonderfully adaptable structures. At other times, Paula fantasizes about being in the space program and building living structures on a space satellite. In her spare time she studies how to construct passive solar homes.

Paula never finished high school. She found high school to be incredibly boring and meaningless. She dropped out when she was sixteen and sat around at home watching television. That was even more boring. Just how much energy can one put into watching three hundred sixty-five episodes of Monica Quartermain's life on *General Hospital*? A friend encouraged her to go to the State Vocational School to get her GED and a career, all in one. Paula did so. She obtained her GED, graduated from the Carpentry School, and got a job working for a contractor. She has worked for that same contractor for five years now and makes top journeyman pay, $15 an hour. And she loves her work!

Paula reads blueprints well, but she also knows that the contractor will tell her exactly what he wants her to do. Sometimes she has acted as foreman of jobs, but she prefers to be more directly involved with the building. She likes being able to spend long hours doing her job, alone with her thoughts.

Her favorite work is in the "superstructure" of a building, the part that rises up from the foundation. She knows how important it is to get the sill framing done correctly: the whole building rests on this construction, which may go all around the building. The sills rest on the foundation piers, and the foundation joists rest on the sills. From that point on, there is nowhere to go but up.

The joists are reinforced. They are framed to steel girders, and bridging is done between joists to keep them aligned and to help distribute weight evenly among them. They are further strengthened by the subflooring, especially when the subflooring is laid at an angle.

The wall framing goes up next, and this is the part that Paula gets most excited about. It is when she puts up the wall studs, the vertical supports for everything above the floor, that her imagination takes over. Of course, when the partition walls are constructed, and the door frames and window frames added, it becomes a challenge to Paula to envision what each room will be used for, how it will be decorated, and who will live or work there. Her company has a reputation for putting up fine, durable buildings, and Paula has learned a lot about bracing walls from her contractor. When the interior wall sheathing goes up and the rooms take shape, it is much easier to visualize actual space filled with bodies and furniture. Sometimes Paula thinks she ought to round out her career by going into interior decorating for a few years. She feels she knows so much about how buildings are put together that she would be very good at designing the furnishings to go into them.

Paula's crew puts on the exterior siding next. Usually they work with wood, but they do put up aluminum siding too. They have installed vinyl siding. Even though they are not always working with wood, it is the carpenters' job to put up the siding.

The crew finishes their work on this house by putting up the roof rafters, allowing for two dormers, and then shingling the roof. Paula is no longer afraid of roof work; she has done so many of them that she feels at home on a roof. Paula is one of those journeyman carpenters who can take a plan, study it, and go ahead and build it. She is very visually oriented; she can "see" the finished product when she studies the plan.

Both these carpenters, José and Paula, are journeymen carpenters who are at the top of their trade. They are professionals. And, though they are both carpenters, each of them is a specialist in a certain phase of the trade. There are other areas of specialization in carpentry. There is something for everyone. Formwork and framing are but examples of a varied and interesting trade; they are both aspects of the rough work of carpentry. There is also finish work, sometimes called trimwork.

Chapter IX

Finish Work

To be precise, the finish work is whatever is applied to the frame of a building as well as the interior trim and cabinet work. The exterior siding can be considered part of the finish work. The application of tar paper, tiles, asphalt, or shingles to a roof is also finish work. The framework is the rough work, and whatever goes onto the frame is the finish.

Daniel does finish work for Paula's contractor. Although Paula and her crew often put up the siding and do all the work on a roof, Daniel usually does all the finish work to doors and windows by himself. He has been doing finish work for this contractor for fourteen years now, and he does some cabinetmaking on the side. He works quickly and expertly, and he sometimes is finished with the trimwork about the same time that the roofing is completed.

After all, a door or a window is just a hole in the framework until Daniel is done. Daniel's work must stand the test of time, perhaps even more rigorously than that of Paula and the others. Doors and windows are built-in weaknesses in an edifice that is constructed to protect people from the elements. Doors and windows have cracks around them that let in wind, cold air, hot air, and moisture. Walls and floors provide thick layers

Fixtures are assembled and installed in a local department store.

of insulation from the outside world, but doors and windows are vulnerable to the weather and to hostile people who break into houses. In a structure that is otherwise wholly stationary, doors and windows are unique: they move. Double-hung windows move up and down; doors swing in and out. There is more wear and tear on these movable parts than on the stationary features of the house in normal circumstances.

Therefore, Daniel tries to make the trimwork on his windows and doors as substantial as possible. His boss could order the trim from a mill for Daniel to install, but he knows the quality of the joinery that Daniel does and how close a fit he makes of door jambs and window casings.

Daniel is careful that the door jamb is wedged evenly and that it is not out of plumb. Then he nails the trim material, or casing, onto the jamb. He makes mitered joints that are watertight. He uses a plane, miter box, bench saw, and radial arm saw. Daniel usually reinforces his mitered joints for door and window casings with a triangular spline.

Daniel then carefully measures the door opening so that he may hang the door. This opening should be perfectly rectangular, but that is not always the case. Any irregularities in the door jambs must be transferred to the door before it is hung, if it is to hang properly. He hangs the door with side hinges that have a removable pin, and are thus called loose pin-butt mortise hinges. Daniel installs the doorknobs, and on the exterior doors of the house he puts in dead-bolt locks. When the doors are finished, he moves on to the windows.

The windows are hung in much the same way as doors. A doublehung window has two sashes, the upper sash and the lower sash. From the 1600s until shortly after World War II sashes were supported by pulleys, one for each sash, which were installed in the sides of the window, behind the jamb. By the 1950s, channel balances replaced many of the old sash pulleys. The channel balances have a spring-type action, and they are also hidden behind the jamb. Daniel stocks glass panes for all the different types of fits he needs. He hangs the sashes, making sure that they are not out of plumb, and installs the glass. He putties the panes in firmly to make them as airtight as possible.

Carpeting is considered part of the carpenter's domain because it has to do with the floors, which in the long-gone days were always of wood.

Other interior trim that Daniel does includes the baseboards and the stairs. The specifications for this house require chair rail molding in the kitchen. The builder also wants Daniel to install tiles in the bathroom, the kitchen and bathroom linoleum, and the carpeting in the living and dining rooms. By the time Daniel is finished with this house, Paula's crew will be working on another frame somewhere else.

When Daniel returns home in the evening he finds relaxation doing woodwork in his basement. He makes

Finish work includes everything that is applied to the interior of a building. Here wood paneling is installed.

bookcases, cabinets, tables, and chairs. Sometimes he installs built-in kitchen cabinets for his contractor, but on this particular job the owners are getting the cabinets from another company. At present he is building new kitchen cabinets for his wife. He and his wife are completely remodeling the kitchen, so Daniel purchased some white oak and set to work making new cabinets in his basement workshop. He has a variety of hand tools and has made most of his own clamps and chisels. Besides these, he has a lathe, a circular saw, a radial arm saw, and a jointer plane. He has made blueprints, which Caroline approves, and is trying to give her more cabinet space in the new kitchen. Sometimes she helps him do some of the work on the cabinets.

They have made all the frames, or subassemblies, and most of the drawers. Daniel has fitted the drawers so that his excellent dovetailing is visible on the front and sides of each drawer. He feels that good joinery ought to be shown off, not hidden on the inside tracks of the drawer frames. He has used rabbet joints and dados on the cabinets. When he makes the door panels, he will use a mortise and tenon construction in fitting the panel boards into grooves all along the frame. Daniel has also made all the hinges and hardware for the cabinets. He is justifiably proud of the workmanship in them; they will be real works of art when he is finished and greatly increase the property value of the house.

He and his wife lacquer all the finished parts. They chose to stain the white oak a blond color to give the kitchen a lighter, airier look. Daniel's wife went to a good paint store and showed the clerk a picture of some cabinets that she liked from a magazine. The clerk helped her find just the light yellow stain she wanted. She did much of the staining and sealing while Daniel was at work. She wore a filter mask to protect herself from fumes as much as possible. She applied a thin coat of lacquer to the surface after she had done the staining. When that had dried, usually in a matter of seconds, she applied several more thin coats before putting on the final coat. Then she used some powdered pumice to rub down and polish the wood, giving it a special sheen.

When all the subassemblies are ready, Daniel and Caroline will move the units up to the kitchen. That will

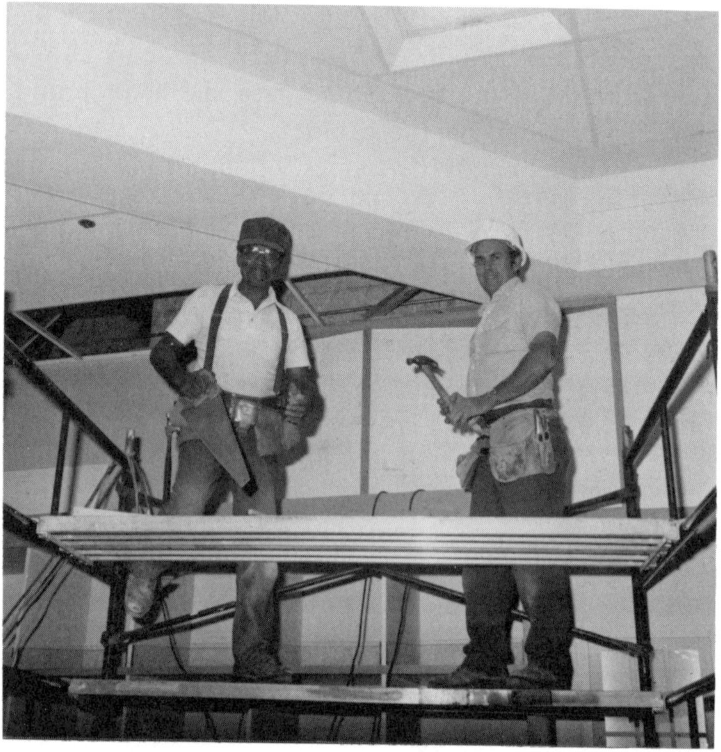

Installation of drywall is part of finish work.

entail a lot of mess and a lot of work, because all the old cabinets must be removed and their contents stored elsewhere. They will then install the cabinets, and Daniel will get the final measurements for the formica top he is going to make. He does all the final trim work on the cabinets after they are installed and fits and hangs the doors at that time.

Daniel and Caroline do a lot of cabinetmaking together. Using his lathe he made a beautiful crib for their baby. The side posts were turned out especially beautifully. They made all their baby furniture and most of the furniture in the rest of the house. One of their big projects was making a high-rise deck off their back door, which led down stairs to a patio that they built. They made all the patio furniture, including chairs, chaises, and a picnic table, out of redwood boards. Daniel made some big planter boxes out of the redwood scraps, and his wife made a sandbox for the baby. It took them a long time, but they succeeded one summer in making a white picket fence that totally enclosed their property. Daniel figures they have saved thousands of dollars by doing all their own building.

They have become proficient enough as a husband-wife team to think about going into business on a more serious basis. At present, they do repair work for friends and relatives and have even built some cabinets and bookcases for people. Their reputation has spread, and more and more people call asking Daniel to make an article of furniture for them. Caroline would like to open a shop where she could sell small handmade wooden articles while Daniel took orders for furniture making. They would do caning on chairs, refinish old furniture, and make repairs. Daniel has even thought of leaving the construction company if business goes well. He and Caroline have an appointment at the local Federal Building to discuss opening up a small business. The consultants are retired businessmen who help others starting out in business to get answers to their questions. They also advise people starting businesses on how to apply for loans.

There are many opportunities for the trimwork specialist. If the worker does a really good job, there are ways to make lots of money. Besides being in demand in construction, the finish worker who does cabinetmaking is in demand by the general public. Especially nowadays, people feel they are always being cheated. They do not trust the materials or the workmanship of goods they buy in the stores. They may not know quality when they see it, but they have come to expect to get less value than they are paying for. When a hand craftsman comes along who does obviously beautiful work, they will pay to get what he can make. When they can actually go into Daniel's shop and see the wood that he uses and talk to him about the way he puts things together, they will become hungry for the products he makes. When they can watch Caroline at work refinishing something or caning a chair bottom, they will feel that here is a place where their money will purchase things of value.

Daniel may learn to make grandfather clocks. Always a consumer favorite, they can be sold for more than two thousand dollars. Robert Silliman has made such grandfather clocks. His are made of solid walnut, and, as he says, "They will last forever." When he first started making them, it cost him about $250 for the materials. The clocks are worth well over $2,000 now.

The finish artist possesses rare skills that are much sought after by the general public. If one is good and manages to capture the public's fancy, a lifetime of rewards is promised.

Although José, Paula, Daniel, and Caroline are fictional characters, they represent possibilities for real people in the carpentry trade. Anyone *could* practice carpentry skills, as they do, in a career choice. There are skilled carpenters who, like José, prefer to do formwork over anything else. It is possible to specialize in formwork, and when there is a market for new construction the formworker is busy. Like Paula, many carpenters enjoy framing and are very good at it. They can install insulation and dry wall as well as joists and studs. Their work is always a little different, and there is a new challenge to each frame they build.

People like Daniel and Caroline have a lot going for them. They are the carpenters who can supply things that people want to buy, handcrafted furniture: beautiful cabinets, chairs, coffee tables, patio furniture, bedposts,

A grandfather clock built by Robert Silliman.

and bookshelves. Their work is like that of artists, sculptors, and musicians. They are truly artists, and the products of their creativity can be used by other folks in their living and working environments.

Dale Burchett of Custom Woodworking, Louisville, offers a word of caution, however: "Woodworkers are generally like starving artists. They may make a ton of money. On the other hand, they may do beautiful work and be starving. Woodworkers go in and out of business every day."

Nothing is guaranteed. When you go to carpentry school you will learn all that you need to know to become an expert craftsman. Years of on-the-job practice will enable you to perfect your skills and become a master artisan. The market for your skills may fluctuate with the economy, but, as Clyde Huber says, "The real professional is going to work. The most unskilled will go first in a recession. The highly trained will be the last to go."

It is a risky business, and one has only one's own abilities to fall back on. Job tenure is dependent on job skills.

Chapter X

"I Want to Be a Carpenter"

"You want to be a what?" Tony's mother yelled over the din of the electric dishwasher.

"A carpenter."

"You're joking, aren't you? I know you're joking."

"I'm not joking, Mother. I really want to be a carpenter. I've made up my mind."

"I know your sense of humor. I remember the time when you were in first grade and went out of here without any clothes on and told the neighbors we were too poor to buy you..."

"This isn't a joke, Mother. I'm really serious about becoming a carpenter..."

"And, darling, do you remember the time you stayed up in your treehouse till we promised to take you to see that Woody Allen picture?"

"Mother, will you please listen to me? I'm trying to tell you I've made up my mind. I want to go to carpentry school when I graduate."

"And there was the time you tape-recorded the minister on *Sunday Sermon on the Air*, hid it in the cabinet, and played it when we had your father's boss and her new husband over for dinner. There we sat, listening to this sermon on "Employers, Be Fair to Your Employees," and we didn't even know where the voice was coming from. I thought your father would die before he found where you'd hidden it."

"Mother, I've already made application for carpentry school in the fall. See, here are my acceptance papers." Tony handed his mother two of the papers he held in his hand. She glanced through them and threw them angrily on the table.

"The answer is no, Tony. I don't know what you're trying to do to us this time, but you'll go to carpentry school over my dead body. No son of mine is going to be a *carpenter*. Wait till your father hears about this."

"What have you got against carpenters?"

"What have you got against being a lawyer? You could be a corporate liar—lawyer—and make millions every year."

"You were right the first time—corporate liar. I'm going to do something I feel good about, Mother, something I can be proud of."

"And you couldn't feel good about defending some crook who'd pay you part of his hard-earned thousands to get him off with plea bargaining?"

"When I'm a carpenter, Mother, I can see what I make; I can stand back and look at things I've done with my own two hands."

"Tony, fine. So you want to look at your work? Be a millionaire doctor, a surgeon. You can look at those stiches and just see the money come rolling in. You could see five or six office patients in an afternoon, and, at fifty dollars a visit, you'd have a substantial income."

"I can make furniture, Mother. Do you know how exciting it would be to make my own furniture for my house?"

"Where are you going to live—in a barn?"

"Mother, handmade wooden furniture is beautiful. I want to be a cabinetmaker and work in mahogany and spalted maple."

"Spalted maple! Good grief, Tony, what on earth is spalted maple? And who would want your ugly furniture anyway? Look at the lovely plastic and chrome we have here. It took your father and me years to save enough to buy this modern furniture. Of course, it would have helped if he'd gotten that promotion he wanted when we had the boss and her husband over for dinner. That tape recording . . ."

"Mother, he was better off without that promotion. I did him a favor. He would have been on the road three weeks out of every four. His quality of life would have been diminished."

"What do you know about the quality of life—you, who lives in treehouses and goes to Woody Allen movies. What do you know about the quality of life?"

"I know that I want to work with wood, Mother. I want to see and feel and smell wood, to form it into lovely things that will please people. I want to have a closer share of my environment. I want my work life to be part of my total environment. I want to help people understand their place in the world, on earth. I want to build things that will make people happy they're alive and living on such a wonderful planet."

"You're talking nonsense, Tony, and you know it. Are you high?"

"It isn't nonsense, Mother, and, no, I'm not high. Won't you listen to me—please?"

"I've been listening to you for twenty minutes, Tony, and you're not making any sense. If you want to change people, why don't you just become a computer programmer? You could make software that would change people. You could make computer games. That would give people enjoyment."

"I don't want to just give people fun times, Mother. Can't you see? I want to do something real with my life. Builders are like architects and artists. We can help people become more human, become better humans."

"You're talking like a preacher. Do you still tape those Sunday Sermons from the radio?"

"Mother, if we're going to have a world with no more Auschwitzes and Buchenwalds, with no more reservations for Indians, with no discrimination against women and minorities, we're going to have to do something about the way we *think* about living on this planet. We're becoming more and more dehumanized, Mother, the more civilized we get. We need creative people, people working with the things of the earth to help us remember who we are."

"Where did you learn all this stuff, Tony? At school? We've sent you to good, typical, nonprogressive public schools. Is this where you've learned this garbage?"

"It isn't garbage, Mother. And, no, I never picked up anything like this from any school I've ever gone to. I've done a lot of reading on my own, talked to some people, listened, and just done a lot of thinking, that's all."

"Tony, Tony, this isn't the kind of world for woodworkers. That stuff went out with the Middle Ages. This is a different kind of world, honey." His mother ran her hand over Tony's forehead, touched his shoulders. "This is a plastic world, and people just need to get along as best they can in the world they've created for themselves. You can't go back, Tony, not any more."

"I hate plastic, Mother. Plastic sticks to your butt

when you try to get up from a chair. It just isn't natural. I believe there's a way to bring more natural things back into people's lives. I believe that if we had more natural things in our lives, we'd be better people. We ought to be able to run our hands over a table and think of the hundreds of years it took to grow this wood. We ought to be able to look at a cabinet and recall the tree that made it."

"I should have bought you Legos instead of those Lincoln Logs you had in your tree house."

"Mother, I would have turned out this way, anyway. What does Legos have to do with anything?"

"They're plastic. You could have learned to love plastic, I know you could." She sat down in a chair at the table and rested her head in her hands. The dishwasher rumbled.

Tony went to the window and stared into the backyard. How could he tell her how he felt? How could he make her see the way he looked at things? He glanced up at the treehouse his father had built him when he was just a little boy. His mother had helped by handing his father the boards and tools when he needed them. When it was all finished the three of them had climbed the tree and had a picnic lunch to "dedicate" Tony's Treehouse. Often in the summers they ate up there, just the three of them. During bad heat spells they all three had slept up there.

"We should've invited Dad's boss and her husband up there. I wonder what she'd have thought of that?"

"What are you muttering, Tony?" She looked at him quizzically.

"What I'm trying to say, Mother, is that you and Dad helped me to become the person I am. I don't know if anyone else would like me for the way I am, any more than Dad's boss ever seemed to appreciate who he really was. She never had enough sense to see what a quality person he is. I don't want to waste my life working for someone like that. I want to do my work and be proud of what I have to offer. Some people will like it and buy my stuff, and that's good. You and Dad gave me the chance to be free, to play in a natural environment. That's really why I turned out the way I did. Hell, Mom, that's probably why I took all my clothes off and ran around."

"Who did you think you were, Tarzan?"

"I don't think the neighbors thought I looked like Tarzan." They both laughed, and Tony got another sheet of paper from among the several in his hand. He handed it to his mother. The dishwasher clicked off.

"Here, Mother, I want you to read this."

She took it and read silently. Tony watched and waited for her to finish. It was a selection called:

THE CARPENTER

There is a rare characteristic inherent in men whose guild or craft is that of carpenter. I have occasionally known and remonstrated with surly, unreliable and careless workmen of just about all other crafts and trades. I never have known a genuine carpenter who was not prideful in his work; gentle, forthright and humane in his nature. Carpenters are mysteriously likely to be men of intelligence and integrity; they are at once visionary and realistic. Perhaps the working with wood has something to do with all this. Sawing, cutting, hammering, nailing, the scent of clean wood is always in his nostrils. Perhaps still lurking in the wood is something of the quiet fragrant forest whence it came. It just could be that the still living tonic of the long-gelled trees clears the workman's brain and steadies his nerves and makes his hand sure and deft. Carpenters talk little above the tap of the hammer, the buzz of the saw, but when they do speak they are likely to be unloquacious and dryly humorous. All this fancied explanation could be false and probably is. Doubtless the fundamental explanation for the characteristic of the genuine carpenter is that he is descended from the carpenter who possessed all these qualities—the carpenter craftsman, Jesus Christ.

—Edna Ferber

It was a long time before his mother looked up from the paper and spoke to Tony, but when she did she was smiling. A tear crested at the corner of her eye and spilled onto her cheek. She took his hand in hers.

"It's because of you and Dad that I love the outdoors and trees and wood so much, Mom. You taught me how to enjoy and love the real world. I just want to share that with other people."

She squeezed his hand tighter. Now there were two tears on her cheeks. "OK," she said, "just don't run around in the nude anymore, all right?"

Tony got up and hugged his mother's face tightly against his chest.

Chapter XI

Good Things and Bad Things

Aside from the fact that sometimes carpenters are like starving artists, are there any other bad features to the trade? Yes. Like everything else, there are good things and bad things about being a carpenter. First the bad things.

According to Mike Andres of Ivy Tech, many carpenters leave the trade by the time they're forty years old. It gets to be very hard work, and there are those who get out altogether or who go into business for themselves. Besides arthritis in the hammering arm and shoulder, carpenters can sustain injuries from bad falls. Andres himself has fallen off three or four roofs and still suffers from the damage done to one elbow in a fall. Carpenters can be electrocuted if they fall into live wires or handle them with wet hands. There is the danger of standing in water and working with power tools. Sawdust and wood chips can get in the carpenter's eyes. Loss of eyesight is not just a remote possibility or something that happens to "someone else." There are accident-related deaths in carpentry. Fatalities are not numerous. "They don't happen every day," says Andres. But they do occur.

Mike Garrison points out that carpenters are vulnerable to hearing loss because of working around pneumatic drills. Dust gets into lungs. For years carpenters worked around asbestos before it was found to be linked to cancer. Treated lumber is also a hazard. There is formaldehyde in particle board. Carpenters handle insulation material, fiberglass, mineral wool. Carpenters are constantly exposed to the elements; only in bad rainstorms do they quit, or when the snow makes it temporarily impossible to work.

George Franke, who works at Marble Hill Nuclear Plant, says, "You have no control over the weather. It's pretty tough sometimes, all the sun and all the cold." Franke also says that you have to work whether your arm or leg hurts; you just have to keep going.

Of course, there are always broken or cut fingers to worry about. As James Erhart, of Erhart and Recktenwald Construction Company, says, "It's not as bad when you're working for a small company as it is working for the big commercial companies. There, you're usually up high on a scaffolding." There is always the chance of losing one's footing on heights. Erhart mentions that many carpenters spend time in back braces at one time or another in their careers.

The physical risks are plenty bad. Carpenters also have to face unemployment due to plant closures and generally poor economic conditions in the country. Mike Garrison is saddened by what he has seen in the economic recession. "There are more ramifications of a bad economy than just the loss of jobs," Garrison warns. He has seen a lot of the bad effects: suicides, an increase in alcoholism, more child abuse and wife beating. When people are out of work, the pressure builds to an unbearable point. There is no way out for some but self-abuse or abuse of those around them. It hits the older ones worst.

"Guys who have been around for twenty, thirty years are not going to get anything when they're let go," Garrison continues. A fifty-year-old carpenter out of work is not likely to find something else. Employers hire the young. "When people aren't working, they can't pay their taxes," says Garrison, "and there's an increase in the loads on the courts. Many go on welfare; their kids are on free breakfast programs in school. People lose their buying power; the merchants suffer from lack of business."

In Local 64 about 35 percent of the carpenters didn't work more than two months during a recent two-year period. The inflation hit the builders and contractors hard. There was no work for construction workers for months and months. Says Garrison, "They'd rather have inflation and a paycheck than no paycheck and no inflation." Builders were unemployed and unimpressed with administration reports that the inflation was being brought under control. The carpenters and other construction people often felt as if they were the sacrificial lambs to the government's economic program. If inflation was broken, it was broken over the backs of thousands of unemployed construction workers.

Are there any good things to say about being a carpenter? Yes. In spite of the troubles carpenters have to face in the performance of their careers, there are compensations. Even in the bleakest of economic times, most carpenters were able to find jobs moonlighting. Garrison knows this, and although the union does not endorse moonlighting—even condemns it as a practice— he has ignored it during hard times. "If things were different, I'd go after them," he says of the moonlighters. But he knows they have to eat; they have mortgage payments to meet and other obligations to fulfill.

People do need repairs done to their homes even if they are not going to do large-scale remodeling until interest rates come down. There is always a need for skilled carpenters. Bob Hardley, who with Clyde Huber teaches carpentry at Jefferson State, says, "There has been a need for builders since the Stone Age; there will always be a need for builders."

Both Hardley and Huber feel that skilled workers will always have jobs. Huber says, "The most unskilled is the first to go in a recession; the highly trained worker is the last to go."

There are also some aspects of carpentry that provide more job security than others. Maintenance work in factories offers a carpenter pretty stable employment. There are often jobs in shipyards and on road crews.

Another benefit of being a carpenter, as Hardley suggests, is that, "You can save on home improvement." A lot of money for furniture, room additions, and repairs can be saved when there is an expert in the home who can build what is needed. The expert remodeling and repair work can increase the value of the property investment for the carpenter's family.

Carpenters can be more independent than many people in other careers. They have the opportunity to set themselves up in business, to start their own shop. They have a valuable commodity to offer the public, their own handiwork. They can work for themselves and expand—with trucks, more tools, and people who will work for them. Once in business, carpenters can bid on jobs.

Dale Burchett tells how risky this can be: "You might have to eat some bids in the beginning. If you underbid, you're not only not going to get paid for your work, you have to subsidize it."

When there is work and employment is steady, carpentry is a fine profession. The wages are good. Clyde Huber says he always tells students, however, that: "High wages can bring out the best in a lot of people—the best way to get around their work and avoid what they have to do."

George Franke sums up his feelings about the work he has done all his life: "I don't work to live; I love to work, and I love to get off. I love my job. I take pride in it even if it's going to be covered up. I want it to be done right so the people I work for will make their profit." Franke enjoys working outside. And even though there are dangers involved in carpentry, Franke, who helped build locks in the middle of the Ohio River in 1961, says: "You've got to block danger out of your mind, or you won't be able to do your job, and that's when you really will get hurt."

Franke likes to see things go up. He likes to visualize what it's going to be like from the "blues." He could build something as he went along, just from instinct.

Mike Andres finds a lot of satisfaction in being a carpenter. He says: "When I drive by a job I've done, I stop and look at it and think, 'I did that. I did that with my own two hands.' "

Chapter XII

The Union

The unions have made it possible for American workers to enjoy the standard of living they do now. The unions have brought the American laborer out of the Dark Ages of labor, when workers were treated like serfs or slaves. The American laborer now earns wages that compensate him for the work he does; he receives benefits that make the condition of his life more satisfying. The hours he works are short enough so that he has time for himself and his family.

The United Brotherhood of Carpenters and Joiners was established on August 12, 1881. Peter J. McGuire of St. Louis urged the carpenters to unite and is the union's founder. He is also the founder of Labor Day and a co-founder of the A.F.L. Even in colonial times there had been organizations of carpenters. It just needed the leadership of McGuire to unionize these builders.

The early carpenters brought their skills with them from Europe. During the Middle Ages carpentry had become one of the finest skills, and carpenters were valued members of society. Their craft was widely recognized, and they were held in honor. Other unskilled craftsmen bought the opportunity to come to America with seven years of their lives. These indentured servants were bound out to carpenters and other builders until their seven years were up. More than half of the white working force in early America was made up of indentured servants. Carpenters built the homes, the meeting halls, and the churches of colonial America. Carpenter's Hall in Philadelphia, where the First and Second Continental Congresses met, is one example of early workmanship. A flurry of building went on early in the nineteenth century. Carpenters raised barns and helped in the move westward. When railroads were built, it was the carpenters who built the trestles and laid the railroad ties. Carpenters had always been involved in shipbuilding.

There were carpenters, joiners, and cabinetmakers back then. The carpenters put up the frames and did the rough work. The joiners did the finish work. The cabinetmakers made the furniture. It was a step up from carpenter to joiner, and another step up from joiner to cabinetmaker. With the spread of the industrial revolution, more furniture was made in factories. Handwork was replaced by machine work, and the joiner became a millworker. After the Civil War journeymen carpenters were in a much different situation. No longer were they so much in demand to make bedposts, newels, mantels, and cabinets. No longer were they in demand to finish lovely bay windows and carved doors. It was quicker and cheaper to get the furniture from a factory and the trim work from a mill. The carpentry trade was being threatened by technology. Not only was industrialization threatening carpentry, but the use of materials other than wood for building faced carpenters with another serious threat. Steel was one of the first of the industrial-age products to replace wood. When the Brotherhood was organized, one of its first tenets was: "Once wood, it is always the right of the carpenter to install it no matter what the material now used may be." This is why carpenters consider it their right to install insulation, aluminum siding, linoleum, and carpet. "Once wood," the installations are still done by carpenters "no matter what the material now used may be." That is a union rule, a rule to protect carpenters.

Women, children, minorities, and immigrants found help from the U.B., the United Brotherhood. Women and children were hired, as was immigrant labor, in the factories because they were cheap. They were called "green hands" because, working for less than half carpenters' wages, they put carpenters out of work in the mills. The union's efforts helped to bring about child labor reform and brought women and immigrants into the union. In the early twentieth century the composition of the carpentry union was stretched to include: carpenters, joiners, boxmakers, shipwrights, millworkers, caulkers, stairbuilders, car builders, railroad workers, shinglers, shorers, pile drivers, casket makers, floor layers, bench hands, and finishers.

The U.B.C.J.A. union label was adopted in 1900. Carpenters were urged to purchase only goods that carried union labels. An article in *The Carpenter* in 1897 said: "Union men can afford to pay more for label goods. The label enables them to make more and they should always see that the label is on articles used by them, as well as by all other members of their craft." If a shop paid at least $.25 an hour and complied with union rules, the label was issued to the shop.

The rise of unionism frightened employers. The employers succeeded in getting the courts to back them, and in 1890 the Sherman Antitrust Act, which had been passed to block business monopolies, became a weapon to use against organized labor. In 1912, one of U.B.C.J.A.'s strongest presidents took office. He was "Big Bill" Hutcheson. It was because of the efforts of Hutcheson that one anti-union campaign was wrecked in the 1920s. The American Plan, as it was called, had as its secret purpose the destruction of unionism in America. It did away with the closed shop and encouraged the conduct of business only with nonunion shops. Contractors were unable to purchase building materials if they hired union workers. Hutcheson put the American Plan out of business; he had the carpenter's union buy their own construction and supply company. They provided materials to any contractors who hired union workers. The American Plan gave up in confusion. Hutcheson won a Supreme Court ruling in 1941 against the Sherman Antitrust Act. He had been the only labor leader to oppose it, and the victory exempted organized labor from the antitrust laws.

In 1935 Congress passed the Wagner Act, guaranteeing workers the right to organize and bargain collectively. Labor unions had come to the end of their fight—so they thought. In 1947 the Taft-Hartley Amendment said that where states passed open-shop laws, the closed shop, or union shop, was illegal. Thus, where the open shop was in effect, union and nonunion workers would work side by side. The nonunion workers would not pay union dues but would receive all the benefits of union workers. They could cross picket lines in a strike. The Taft-Hartley Act greatly angered the U.B.C. They had maintained a position of nonpartisan politics since the beginning of the union in 1881; now they adopted a resolution that allowed them to endorse political candidates. The Taft-Hartley Act was called the "right-to wreck" law and the "slave labor act". Closed shops could be outlawed and bargaining rights weakened under Taft-Hartley. Organized labor knew that their troubles were far from over.

During World War II carpenters performed outstanding service to the country. They worked so speedily at building ships that two ships were named after carpenter "heroes," the *Peter J. Mcguire* and the *Santiago Iglesias*, after the carpenter who had led the labor movement in Puerto Rico. It is said that on December 7, 1941, the station master of the Pearl Harbor shipyard put out an emergency call to the carpenters after the first Japanese attack. The carpenters ran to the shipyards, raising their fists at the Japanese planes that were coming back for their second strike.

After the war carpenters were called upon for big government projects, such as the Manhattan Project. They worked on the St. Lawrence Seaway and for Hughes Tool Co., among others. Carpenters work in the space program.

The union faces different tactics from union-busters now. Violence is not used against them so much as marketing techniques. They are fought by teams of professionals in three-piece suits carrying briefcases. They are fought in plant sites by professionals using de-unionizing strategies, including:

1. seminars given by psychologists and public relations personnel that alarm workers about the effects of becoming unionized
2. advice from anti-union law firms that coach employers on "legal" union-busting maneuvers
3. surveys and industrial testing done by psycholo-

gists and the use of positive reinforcement techniques to steer workers away from union ideas
4. active anti-union campaigning by a consultant in the industry
5. the use of all the above techniques by trade associations that are not union associations; for example, a carpenters' group or builders' organization outside the union.

In some shops workers are terrified to be caught talking to someone about unions, afraid that if they are even seen listening to union talk by another employee they will be fired. The unions charge that freedom of choice for the worker is jeopardized by these high-power techniques. The workers are manipulated by experts into attitudes and actions they would not otherwise adopt. The unions charge that the institution of collective bargaining is seriously weakened by these manipulative activities.

However, more and more carpenters and others go into open shops or nonunion shops every year. Why do they do it? Why do union carpenters "put their cards in their shoes" and go nonunion?

They have found work. They have found steady work. Sometimes they would get jobs only a few months out of every year when they were with the union. By joining a nonunion shop they may have improved their chances of keeping a job. They may not be paid as much per hour, but it evens out in the long run.

Union people who go nonunion often find that they are the best-trained workers in the outfit. The union does a good job of training its people. In fact, they may wind up sharing their skill-knowledge with someone else, so, in effect, the unions are teaching their competitors. Union people who go nonunion find that sometimes it's much easier to get the job done outside the union. Instead of calling in a pipefitter to take off a pipe or an electrician to fix a socket, the nonunion carpenter can go ahead and do it himself. The area of jurisdiction, where each union has to allow only union workers from other trades to do the jobs of their trades, results in loss of time and money. It is a tedious anachronism in the late twentieth century.

The common remark is that, "We are where we are today because of the unions; now, however, they're destructive." Or you hear that, "They've gone too far. The pendulum has swung too far." You even occasionally hear it said that "The unions are a rip-off."

Twenty or thirty years ago the unions were in the housing industry; the unions built most of the new housing. But the wage scale went out, unions lost control of the market, and nonunions took over the housing industry. Commercial work was more dangerous, and there was more money in it. The unions went to commercial work; the nonunion companies took over the housing construction.

Unions lose members because construction is a family-oriented industry. The first-generation carpenters in a family build up the business and are strong union supporters. The second-generation carpenters in that family may stay in the business and stay in the union. The third generation, however, has other ideas, wants to do something else. That person breaks away from the carpentry trade and from the union. The business closes down, and the union has lost a member. When this happens on a large scale, it becomes noticeable.

It has now become hard for unions to change the labor laws. For a while the unions had the upper hand when it came to labor legislation. That has changed. One of the last major triumphs of the U.B. was in 1964 when Congress passed, and Lyndon Baines Johnson signed, the Davis-Bacon Fringe Benefit Bill. This bill forced successful bidders on government contracts to match prevailing wage scales in an area as well as the prevailing fringe benefits, or to give workers the cash equivalent. The Davis-Bacon Act has been one of the principal targets of the union-busters. They have tried to have the act repealed in Congress. They try to tell women and minorities that Davis-Bacon is against them, that wage cutting would mean more work for them.

The NAACP has gone on record supporting Davis-Bacon. American Indians and Mexican Americans came out in favor of Davis-Bacon. The construction industry has drawn minority workers and women for many years for precisely the reason that they are treated fairly there. They can be reasonably sure of a good standard of living, and they will be taught the skills of the trade efficiently. Davis-Bacon proponents feel that it has been good for minority hiring.

Proposed amendments to the Hobbs Act illustrate the trend of government away from unions. When the Hobbs Act was passed in 1946, it was a measure to curb racketeering and extortion in connection with interstate commerce. The Hobbs Act was a strengthening of the 1934 Anti-Racketeering Act. The Hobbs Act also covered labor racketeering. In the early seventies, federal prosecutors tried to use the Hobbs Act to nail some unionists who were charged with violence and destruction of property during contract negotiations. This activity, the prosecutors said, was extortion because it forced the employer to negotiate in favor of the unionists out of fear. In a Supreme Court verdict, *United States* vs. *Enmons*, the Justices ruled that this was not a case of extortion. The unionists who had engaged in violence were punished for those acts, but this 1973 decision ruled out extortion under the Hobbs Act in their actions. It was a victory for the unions. However, since then activity has been intense on Capitol Hill to pass an amendment to the Hobbs Act. Under one possible amendment, if a striker yelled, "We'll see you about this later," to a scab, he could be tried in federal court for threatening the worker. He could be fined up to $20,000 or given a twenty-year term in federal prison, or both. In addition, the leadership of his union could be charged with conspiracy and be prosecuted under the Hobbs Act. On the other hand, if management got involved in pushing and shoving some of the picketers, they would be charged with misdemeanors in the local courts. Is it any wonder the unions feel discouraged?

The argument has been made that many big industries are closing their shops in the North because of union practices, that they are moving to the South where there are more open-shop states. The unions argue that these industries are leaving the North because:

1. There is so much competition that they have been forced to move out of sheer economic necessity.
2. There is an older work force in their present plants. Older workers get more benefits, more vacation time, and higher wages. If they move elsewhere and start over again with new employees, it will be cheaper.

3. There are often no inducements for industry to stay in an area. If a community offers a twenty-year tax break to an industry to relocate there, that is a good reason to move.
4. Specialization makes it easy to move a plant. In piecemeal operations, where one plant builds one part for something that is assembled elsewhere, it is convenient to close that plant up and move it.

Plants also close down and people lose their jobs because Congress passed a law giving tax breaks to companies for renovation purposes. It became a reinvestment inducement for companies to go out and acquire other companies, closing them down to gain the assets of the old corporations.

Mike Garrison feels that his union people know they have to give more than they're taking. He feels they know that "If work is good, labor gets all it can; if work slows down, labor suffers." His union has negotiated excellent contracts with several large companies in the area, including Philip Morris. When the contract negotiations were completed, management was satisfied that there were not going to be any strikes or work slowdowns. It was a nine-year contract with a possibility for an opener every three years. Both labor and management were, as Garrison puts it, "tickled to death with the contract."

Prior to the signing of this contract, workers could go on strike if there were enough cigarettes stockpiled. The new contract provides for a guaranteed minimum 3% percent yearly increment, and the carpenters in the plant get a $300 yearly cash bonus. Every three years they negotiate everything above 3 percent and a cost-of-living increase. The nine carpenters in the Philip Morris plant make $15 an hour, with vacations, holidays, and a better medical plan than the union offers.

Garrison says a contract is a two-way street. "You hammer it out in negotiations. In the meantime, you live with it. If it's bad, you shouldn't have agreed to it." Garrison thinks his local is way ahead of the game in comparison to unions in other parts of the country. The capenters' union drew up an agreement with light commercial contractors in which the carpenters agreed to $2.10 less per hour than they had been receiving. The 10 cents was earmarked for contribution to an industry fund to be jointly managed by the local and the contractors.

The union offers an excellent health and welfare program for the carpenter, his wife, and his children. The benefits of this plan come primarily from employer contributions as a result of bargaining agreements. The health and welfare fund is supervised by a ten-member Board of Trustees, five from the union, five from management. The Board of Trustees also supervises the administration of the pension fund. Union members may choose the pension plan they want, and there is a disability benefits fund also. The apprenticeship program is one of the things the union is most proud of. The union has adopted the Performance Evaluated Training System, PETS, as it is called, in which the apprentice studies under master carpenters over a four-year period. The apprentice school is also funded by contributions from employers. There is no fee for any student in the program, also as a result of collective bargaining. The union has an active retirement club that meets regularly. The retirees donate time and service to other union members when called upon.

Mike Garrison says: "The unions are an essential part

of this country and why it is what it is today. Lots of people who enjoy a certain standard of living don't understand how they got that way. Unions need insight now, enough to know what's good for them. A couple of months ago they got too much on one contract. If they get more than what's good for them, they can price themselves right out of the market. Union politics can be vicious politics. On the other hand, they can be more democratic than American democracy. It's one man, one vote. There has to be a real leadership job in a context like that. You can't do what's popular all the time. You have to do what's best for the organization overall, for all its members."

He recalls the selling job he had to do on the light commercial agreement. He met with a lot of adversity on that $2.10 decrease in wages. He had to do a good advertising job to get the union to accept the agreement. "Some full-time members don't even understand that 35 percent of their brothers are not even working. I'm more aware than the guy in the field of what's going on. It's an information process. I'm exposed to more of the inner workings of the problems."

In the 1915 edition of *The Carpenter*, the union magazine, appeared:

THE CARPENTER'S TEN COMMANDMENTS
(JOHN J. FLYNN'S "TEN COMMANDMENTS"
FOR U.B.C. MEMBERS)

FIRST: Thou shalt be a union carpenter, spreading its teachings, advancing its interests and making converts at all times and places.

SECOND: Thou shalt not belong to any other organization of carpenters.

THIRD: Thou shalt keep whole the Saturday half-holiday and all holidays.

FOURTH: Thou shalt honor and respect thy officers.

FIFTH: Thou shall not become "boisterous" in the meetings of thy local unions and want to lick anyone who may disagree with thy opinions.

SIXTH: Thou shalt not commit offenses against the laws of the U.B.

SEVENTH: Thou shalt not steal time from the boss, but keep in mind the principle of unionism, "A fair day's work for a fair day's wages." Show him it pays to employ U.B. members.

EIGHTH: Thou shalt be charitable toward fellow members. Thou shalt not try to gain favor with the foreman by pointing out their shortcomings, nor shalt thou use their edged tools to cut old, gritty lumber with while thine own saw or chisel lies close by.

NINTH: Thou shalt not be envious at thy fellow member if he should happen to be working while thou art on the sidewalk. He may need the money as much as thyself.

TENTH: Thou shalt not covet thy fellow member's good fortune if he should happen to own his little home.

Finally, let us remember that the U.B. is a "fraternal organization" where we should [be brothers] in fact as well as in name.

Chapter **XIII**

Your Résumé? Throw It Away

There are several current books that deal with successful techniques for getting jobs. One of these is titled *Throw Away Your Resume.* The author, Robert Hochheiser, advocates interview techniques rather than the use of a résumé for the aggressive job hunter. He says that résumés just don't get the job for you; they are too long to interest a busy boss and contain too much irrelevant information. Hochheiser advocates a systematic approach to job-getting in which you are in control of the process from the start. A résumé tends to be more like a list of things, dull and boring.

Hochheiser does suggest the use of letter-writing in order to get a job. He cautions the job seeker to be concise and creative in the definition of abilities. For instance, a carpenter might possibly be called a framework producer, or a furniture engineer, or a building effector. If you have done building effecting, or furniture engineering, or framework producing, then you should say so in your letter. It is important to know exactly what this particular boss wants: a furniture engineer, a building effector, or a framework producer. You need to do research in order to reach that conclusion.

Of course, you can always say that you have done work with cosmetic covering materials (paneling) or that you are a ferroconcrete specialist (formworker). You may be a machine tool technician or an industrial instrumentation artisan.

The plain fact of the matter is that you are a carpenter. Do not write an employer a letter. Those who are encouraging concentration on interviewing techniques are right. You need to get out, go see a contractor, a dozen contractors, and state what you can do.

Clyde Huber tells his students: "Take a day off, take your car and go around to construction sites. Tell the boss, 'Hey, I need a job—bad.'" He tells them to go back often, to go back until the boss is tired of seeing them. Eventually they will get a job. Then they need to prove they can do the work and agree on pay. Huber ran his own construction business for years, and he says, "These guys will come and tell you they've done everything. So you put 'em to work for a few hours, and you see just how much they can't do."

Mike Andres says: "If a guy handed me a résumé, I'd tell him, 'No, you're probably overqualified and won't stay in this field.'" Andres says guys like that will leave as soon as they find a job in the area they're trained for. He'd rather hire a youngster right out of high school and train him/her. Young men and women right out of the service are fine, too. It's easier than trying to retrain someone who has worked for someone else. "Everyone does the job different, and I'd rather train a guy myself than retrain him. I'd rather hire someone with no skills at all than someone who thinks he knows everything."

Interviewing for a job when you're right on a work site can be a little bit different from interviewing for jobs in paneled offices. Don't wear a three-piece suit. Chances are the boss may say: "When can you start?" Imagine your confusion if you had to say: "As soon as I go home and change my clothes." Dress for the job. That doesn't mean you have to be dirty. You'll always make a better impression if you're neat.

Some interview techniques are readily adaptable to interviewing for a construction job. Let's say this particular interviewee is a woman. One suggestion is for her to make herself a "partner" of the boss. This can be done by moving to a position so that she and the boss are side by side. In fact, this is an easier feat for a prospective carpenter on a job site than for an interviewee in an office. It is extremely awkward to get one's chair behind the desk with the boss, but it can work perfectly and naturally on the construction site. Once the two of them are "on the same side" surveying the works together, it is a simpler task for her to convince the boss that they would make a "great team." Already they are reviewing the work being done together, and she needs only to be able to make him see that with her at his side the efficiency of his construction work would be greatly improved. She can help herself along by using phrases such as, "We'll be able to get the formwork done by Friday," or "We'll certainly do a great job with this building." She's instilling into his mind that she is already part of his team and working effectively to accomplish his goals.

Interviewing has become a highly skilled art. Go to any book store and look at the "how-to" books on the art of interviewing. The best person does not always get the job; the best interviewee usually does. No matter how skilled you know you are, if you cannot put yourself across as a valuable asset to this boss, you will never be hired. It simply takes a lot of courage and an enormous amount of belief in self. Or, it takes being awfully hungry.

One young man went back to a job site seventeen times and filled out an application each time. Finally one day the supervisor called him in and said: "Look, you've got the job. You're costing me a fortune in applications. Come back tomorrow and start work."

Carpentry work, of all construction work, is highly competitive, especially with the economy in a slump and thousands of workers laid off. If you are going to get a job you will have to be like shoppers at bargain-basement sale; go early and hang in there. Be prepared for a little damage to your ego from time to time. Be prepared to go after your job aggressively.

It might help to know exactly what the boss needs before you approach him for a job. Your research can be conducted easily enough around the construction site before you ever introduce yourself to him. Talk to some of the other workers. Ask them if he has enough workers, or enough of certain specialty workers. Ask if he needs some trim workers or roofers. Find out if he needs someone to do the jobs you know how to do.

When you meet the boss, be honest. Don't pretend you're an expert at every aspect of carpentry if all you've ever done is build frames. It is suggested that you look the boss, the interviewer, straight in the eyes and tell him your story. If you tell him things that are patently not true about yourself, he will probably know it. If he's been in business any length of time he will know how to read you. James Erhart says he can tell right away which customers will pay him and which won't. He says it's something he's learned over the years. He's been a contractor for twenty-five years and had only two bad debts in that time. "You get so you can tell about people," he says. "I don't know what it is, but I always know."

What have you got to lose? If he says no, that he

doesn't want to hire you, you won't be any worse off than before. You'll still just be without a job. If you keep trying, you'll get work sooner or later.

All the interview books suggest that the interviewee take control of the interviewing process. That may be a little more difficult when interviewing for a job at the work site. The boss will be busy; you'll have to catch him on the run. He may have time to ask you a few questions and listen to a few answers. It is unlikely that you will get the chance to play some of the sophisticated verbal games that interviewees for white-collar jobs can try. What you can do, however, is take the initiative and ask some questions yourself. The idea is for you to learn enough from his responses that you can form an idea of what he wants. Then you draw a picture of yourself as the person who can get his job done. For instance, if you ask him, "When do you want this building finished?", you may get him started on something he wants to talk about: his schedules, his work loads, his commitment to the owner, his troubles with the subcontractors. Then you know what to say to him. You will know how to fit yourself into the pattern of his needs. Do it skillfully, and you will have a job.

The good thing about interviewing in a situation like this is that the boss isn't concentrating on the techniques of interviewing. He isn't thinking, "What should I say next to this person? How do I know if this person is right or not for my outfit?" He's too busy for that kind of concentration in the middle of a building going up. If you can manage to pin him down long enough to discuss what he's doing, you may have an even better chance than the interviewee in the paneled office. After all, he's right there on site, with all that work to be done all around him. It's up to you to make him see that you can help him do it.

Of course, some construction interviews are held in offices. Sometimes you catch a contractor at his desk. The same methods suggested can work here. This is a busy man, one who probably has to have his secretary hold calls from subcontractors, suppliers, and customers just so he can talk to you. He isn't going to keep you long. If you're going to take the initiative, do so as soon as possible. If you can't accomplish that, you probably can't work efficiently for him either. If you can get him to hire you when he perhaps wasn't planning on hiring anyone, he will be impressed with your strength and skillfulness. All you have to do then is prove to him how right he was.

Integrity is one of the most important aspects of interviewing. Promise what you know you can give, and then do all in your power to deliver what you've promised. If you're desperate enough for work, you may become a good carpenter just to live up to your promises.

As Clyde Huber says: "Times couldn't get rough enough if you're good. If you're good, you're going to work."

When you interview, that's what you have to let the boss know—just how valuable you are. Be sure of yourself and interview aggressively. Make the boss see that you will be a good member of a winning team. Just don't tell him you are a sound effects producer when what you do is install acoustical tiles.

Chapter XIV

A Carpenter's Self-evaluation

George Franke sat in the little kitchen of his trailer home, sun coming in the east-facing window and enhancing the yellows, browns, and orange hues in the decor. Two long-haired cats studied the scene from various perches, then went to sleep. His wife had died ten weeks previously. "They were hers," he said, pointing to the cats. "I'd never get rid of them. She'd have a fit. They're good company."

Franke was now working the night shift. After his wife had died, Mike Garrison had called him asking him if he'd like to take the night shift at the Marble Hill Nuclear Plant in Madison, Indiana. It meant a long drive from Louisville, but he was grateful to Garrison for trying to do something to help him get through his grief and loneliness. He pondered over his prescription for self-evaluation. These are his ideas:

1. Take pride in anything you do.
2. Be neat about your work.
3. Go back to school to improve your skills. (He intends to go back to the union hall in the fall to take classes in blueprint reading and the use of the transit and level.)
4. Listen to people around you.

5. Sometimes bad advice is good advice. Take something from what a person tells you and use it; you can get something from it.
6. It takes cooperation to be a carpenter. There are so many people doing so many different things. You've all got to work together. You may put part of a wall up; another crew comes in and takes it up to the finish point.
7. Every individual is important, even if he's just picking up a piece of wood and handing it to you. Someone's got to pick it up, and if he didn't you might have to.
8. Listen to what he or she tells you. At that point that person may be a little smarter than you, but you may get to that point.
9. I make sure I know what I'm doing. Youngsters want to get there too fast.
10. Every move I make I'm doing something to accomplish the job I was put on.
11. No matter how much experience you get, you'll make mistakes.
12. It takes a better carpenter to correct mistakes than to make one. Get so you can correct it in the least amount of time.
13. You can't get frustrated. Use your rule, tape, etc. and be exact.
14. Learn your math. I haven't done too much designing, but I could. I wasn't too interested in it in school; I could have used more math.
15. If you take shortcuts, you're bound to be caught. Kids don't pay attention to authority. You don't hold a job very long if you have that tendency. Some of them are in too big a hurry to get the job done right. They aren't going to hurt me.

16. Get so you can do your job eyes closed. I can just about read a rule with my eyes closed.
17. You can judge a good job. I know how many square feet or pieces of board I should get up in a day. If there are mistakes in the way it's designed, I tell my boss; he calls the architect.
18. There's always someone looking at you to help you if you let them help you. Another carpenter will always help you. Supervisors and foremen don't have much time to teach you, except when materials change. When new materials comc in, the foreman and supervisors show you how to use them.
19. Do it right. Somebody's going to build that job. It might not be you, but somebody's going to build it. The job's going to be done, even if somebody has to take your place.
20. Be sociable. I've made a lot of friends, a world of them. When I go out, there's always somebody hollering at me. I like people, and I think people like me. Work together; you can't be a loner.
21. Jealousy will catch up with you. I would confront any individual who acted that way to me. There can be a lot of it any place.
22. You don't accomplish much when you're all uptight, and accomplishment's the name of the game. There's always a lot of bantering and kidding. You shout to each other. It kindly makes the day go; it makes a relaxed atmosphere. It keeps you going.
23. Some teams are faster and can do the job better. It's the job of the foreman to determine if a man really belongs. One individual may be a little sharper than someone else.

24. If you're caught fighting, you go to civil court, and you're fired. That's automatic.
25. If you're drunk or use drugs on the job, you're warned first, then fired if it happens again.
26. You get points against you if you're sick and don't call up and tell them. Every man-hour is figured. You want to hold the man-hours down to hold the profit margin as high as you can. The wage/price scale is important to all of us.
27. It's possible to get a mean foreman, but he's one of us. You've got to learn to live with it, but he's got to learn to live with you, too. It takes two to tangle. He's got to have you to get the job done. Of course, if you're not union you've got no protection.
28. The supervisors hold down lewd remarks around the women. Some of the women are good workers; some are not.
29. There's no place for troublemakers on the job. You've got to be together to get the job done.
30. You've got to believe in yourself because the next man did it, and I know I can do it.
31. I've never turned down a job in my life.
32. I put enough initiative in it that I know I can do it.
33. I like to get down on a job and just go right on up with it. Most of the time I stay on a job till the end. I may not be the last one on the job, but I'm close to the last.
34. I have a good attitude on life; carpentry's part of your life really.
35. I hold the bad times to a minimum.
36. You've got to talk to someone; I always talked to my wife.

37. I find out what the individual wants before I start working.
38. Anything anyone else can do, I can do in a matter of time.
39. I believe in equal work for equal pay, but we do do some charitable things in the union.
40. I've faced daily crises in my work, just like in my life.
41. I'll go till I'm sixty-five or seventy. If I wasn't working on a job, I'd pick up a little work; it occupies my mind.

The phone rings and Franke's daughter invites him over for lunch. His daughter and his sister keep pretty close tabs on him now that his wife is dead. They see to it that he eats right and isn't too lonely. The cats stir, stretch, and come rubbing against his leg. There is a faint smell of coffee in the bright little kitchen that looks as if another presence, another hand had tidied it up again, just as in all the days gone by.

Chapter XV

Real People

Dale Burchett

Dale Burchett of Custom Woodworking builds wall units, cabinets, anything people want. He is a custom builder. If people see something in a magazine that they like, he'll put it together for them. Sometimes it's a composite of ideas from various places. The customer gives him the idea of what she wants, and Dale goes to the drawing board and designs it. He says it involves problem-solving, getting an idea of what you want, and then going ahead and doing it.

Dale has patented the *Silhouette* chalice, a wooden chalice carved in the likeness of a person's profile. Each chalice is different, a reproduction of someone else's profile. The chalices may be made from ash, cherry, walnut, or mahogany. He designed a machine to hollow out the cup part of the chalice when he was told he couldn't do it with existing machines. He adapted a millworking machine so that the blade comes down through a solid four-by-four block and hollows it out to paper-thin dimensions of about one-sixteenth of an inch. A silversmith in Boston makes silver cups that are glued to the insides of the chalices. Burchett advertises the chalices as excellent wedding gifts. The bride and groom toast each other with chalices containing their own images and engraved with their names and the date of their wedding on the bottom.

When Dale has many similar cabinets to make for a customer, he builds one from his drawing to see that the measurements and all the mechanics are exactly right. Then he goes ahead and builds the rest of the units. He cuts the wood, assembles the cabinet, puts on the molding, stains, seals, and lacquers it. Then he puts on the knobs and decoration. For pieces that are built in sections, he must transport them and assemble them at the site. He says it is like working a big jigsaw puzzle, especially for wall units that cover a wall-to-wall area. Another problem is that you must allow for a room being out of square. A high building has to have sway, like a tree in a windstorm, or it would snap in half. It has to give. However, this condition causes problems for the cabinetmaker. Cabinet doors may be flush one day and off the next day, having shifted after installation because of the building's sway. He ran into this problem with a recreation room he installed on the twenty-fifth floor of a condominium. He had built the bar, a back-bar display with tiers and leaded glass, an entertainment center with raised panel doors, and the room's wainscoting with chair rail and raised panels. He had to readjust the cabinet doors in the room several times because of the sway in the building.

Dale attended Western Kentucky University to study electrical engineering. The electric and electronics courses were held in the industrial education building. He enjoyed what he saw going on there so much that he changed his major to industrial technology, hoping to become a technical illustrator. Then he switched to industrial education because he decided he wanted to teach. He taught school for seven years. He says it was challenging at first, but he became very discouraged. Finally he quit and started his own business with a saw, a hammer, a screwdriver, and his garage for a workshop. Business picked up. People began to hear about Dale Burchett's workmanship, and he moved from his 100 square feet in the garage to 4,000 square feet in a store front. He bought the building; then he sold it at a profit and with a good lease for himself. Now he's looking for a place with more space. He usually has three to five people working for him, sometimes six. Burchett does work for interior designers and large hotel firms. He has had his work shipped as far away as California. He is nonunion.

Dale Burchett is a custom–work expert. Even now he says he learns something new from every job. His only regret is that he didn't apprentice out when he was younger. He lost out on what someone could have taught him.

Mike Andres

When Mike Andres was in high school he worked for his brother in the construction business. At that time he said, "No way," to the construction field and went into military service. On his discharge he got a job, but he was soon laid off. He needed a job, so he went to Ivy Tech to learn carpentry. He's never left Ivy Tech, although now he's the instructor in carpentry.

Mike is constantly busy outside of school time building things for other people. He takes a job every weekend and is busy three-fourths of the weekends every year. He sets walls, puts on roofs, puts up interior walls, and does the exterior finish, which may be siding or paint.

He says two of the most important classes for carpentry students are estimating and specifications. A carpenter has to know how much material he will need to do a job and what it will cost the customer. You need to be able to approach the customer with the right answers the first time. With practice you become a professional at this, but it is wise for students to take these classes a few times before they finish school.

The carpentry business is changing just like everything else, Mike notes. There are air guns that can hammer in short nails; there are robots with eight- or nine-foot arms that can hammer short nails. There are computers that do just about everything; they can make a perfect design for you every time.

Mike says there is a cost factor involved in hiring a cabinetmaker. It is too expensive for most people. Cabinetmakers are pricing themselves right out of the market.

A nonunion carpenter, Mike has definite ideas about unionization. He says that a nonunion contractor must pay prevailing nonunion wages. Anybody can bid on contracts, and in the nonunion shop there is more chance for the contractor to make money because he doesn't have to pay such high wages.

However, Mike does admit the advantages of dealing with the union. When you hire union workers, the union has already done the screening for you; if you need a hundred workers and they are not union, you must go to the trouble of interviewing all of them. You then run the risk of taking someone's word that they know how to do the work, and sometimes they don't.

Jackie June

Jackie June is another former teacher. When her father died, Jackie inherited all his woodworking tools and his love of working with wood. Now she builds cabinets and makes rocking unicorns.

At first Jackie intended to make rocking giraffes, but when she heard the story of the unicorn, she made rocking unicorns her specialty. Unicorns, it was said, were afraid of people. They would only come near women; they were afraid of men, who killed them. Old tapestries show unicorns and women in fenced-in gardens. Because it made men so angry that unicorns would go only to women, they imprisoned them both. Unicorns are supposed to be mystical and magical; they point up the gentleness of women. In the movie *The Last Unicorn* men couldn't see the horn on the unicorn; what they saw instead was a white horse.

For her rocking unicorns Jackie uses pine. The hardwoods are too expensive. She sands it down a lot. She says there is something about working with wood that feels really good. The grain, the texture feels satiny smooth, and it smells good. It can certainly be a noisy business, though, she concedes. Working with power tools is not a quiet operation.

Jackie has a dremel tool, a hand tool with which she can do carving. It also routs in order to do inlay work. She has become interested in carving faces of crones in blocks of wood. She sells these and hand-carved mirrors at various fairs. She also makes candlesticks and small wooden boxes.

She says people become almost childlike when they get on a rocking unicorn. It makes them smile a little just to look at it. Jackie says it saves on therapy bills: you can come home and rock your stress away. It goes back to the idea of nurturing; rocking has always been important for infants.

Most of Jackie's time is spent working in people's homes. She and two partners do construction work. They put up dry wall, paint, lay linoleum and install handmade cabinets. The cabinet tops are made commercially, but they install them. Jackie uses hardwood veneers for doors; they won't warp, they're cheap, and they're beautiful. She makes the frame and sets the veneer in.

Jackie is a very visual person. It is easy for her to listen to someone's ideas of what they want and to say whether or not she thinks it would look well. She likes the planning part of construction; she doesn't make drawings except for the benefit of customers. She says she used to think everyone was visual, but she has learned that that isn't so. She can see where all the pieces are going to fit together, and she also sees when something won't fit. She likes creating the best, whether it's cabinets or unicorns.

Sometimes she works fourteen-hour days; it depends on the job. Some people hire them because they're women; some won't hire them because they're women. Older women trust them; working women trust them with their animals or homes when they're at work. On the other hand, there are those who feel that because they are women they don't know enough to do this kind of work.

Jackie was a Vista volunteer when she graduated from the University of Kentucky. She served in an alternative school in Louisville for a year, working with an exceptionally gifted teacher, and she learned much from his example with students. Jackie worked as a counselor at the Easter Seal Society summer camp one year. Several years ago she was fortunate enough to be placed in one of the most creative learning environments in the public school systems; but things changed and the school was closed and replaced by a typical public school. Jackie quit and is using her creative energies in building with wood.

Mike Garrison

Mike Garrison is the Business Agent for Local 64 of the United Brotherhood of Carpenters and Joiners of America. His dad was a union carpenter and a florist in New Albany, Indiana. They had an eighteen-acre farm, so Mike was exposed to hard work very early in life. Because he was so involved in farm work of all kinds, he never took woodworking or carpentry in school. He won a partial scholarship in agriculture at Purdue when he graduated from high school, but he passed it up. He worked at various jobs during and after high school, including pumping gas and working in the family florist shop. He also built houses for nonunion contractors. He lied about his age to get a job with Willett Furniture in Louisville, one of the finest furniture-making companies in the area. When he was eighteen he went to work at General Electric but was laid off. As he says: "They built a superior product, like the unions, and had to charge too much."

Then he took a job in construction in an A&P warehouse. He worked the second shift for several years. During this time he was a member of the Teamsters union. He obtained a license and sold insurance until the bottom dropped out of the stock market in 1968–69. He

Mike Garrison, Business Agent of Local 64, United Brotherhood of Carpenters and Joiners.

was a firefighter and security guard at an ammunition plant for a while.

When he'd been out of high school many years and was starting a family, he passed a billboard one day that read: "It's what you learn after you know it all that counts."

He worked a while for his brother who was a carpenter, took the journeyman test at the Louisville union hall, and has been working in carpentry ever since. He continued working for his brother or out of the union hall. That was when Garrison began attending union meetings. As he says: "I attended too many meetings, and that got me where I am now."

He has mixed emotions about being Business Agent. It's a job that's got to be done. "I'm doing as good a job as I can in view of what the unions and industry are facing now," he says, "but if I knew then what I know now, I wouldn't have taken it." He is committed to the union cause, but he does feel the unions have to make adjustments if they are going to survive. He would like to see Saturday become a time-and-a-half day instead of double-time. He is very cautious about overtime and would like to be sure it was always an emergency situation and not something that was planned. Garrison advocates a make-up day on Saturdays to compensate for rainy days during the week. That is part of his philosophy of "giving more than you're taking."

He talks about problems in the industry. There is a code, but it's hard to implement. Fire marshals and building inspectors don't always get out to a site. You don't have to be licensed to be a contractor or a carpenter, and he sees a problem with that. "There have to be some criteria somewhere," he states. "A floor ought not fall out." He feels that licensing would eliminate many abuses in home repair and in commercial work.

"I don't discourage moonlighting. People are losing homes, cars, families. If they can find work, let them. If I had plenty of work for them, I might feel differently. It is detrimental to the cause, and we're cutting our own throats in the long run."

Garrison is the grievance committee, he says. He negotiates individually with each contractor. The complaining employee meets with the shop steward, who attempts to correct the grievance. If it's not corrected, either the employee or the shop steward comes to Garrison, who goes to the higher-level supervisor. If it is still warranted, the matter goes to arbitration.

Garrison does fire people from the union when he feels it is warranted. In most instances members are warned first. If the problem does not improve, firing may become necessary.

Austin Abell

Austin Abell has been a supervisor in a mill for nineteen years. He was a millwork supervisor in New Albany, Indiana, before coming to the Cook Lumber Company in Louisville. Before that he did construction work. Abell has also made furniture. He is nonunion. He likes working with small crews. He has worked steadily all his life. "I've never been laid off an hour, never drawn unemployment in twenty-nine years of working," he says.

Austin Abell was born on a farm in Larue County, Kentucky. He learned woodworking from others, picking it up while he was growing up. All in all, he spent about fourteen years doing cabinetmaking. He fought in World War II.

Abell finds carpentry very rewarding. He especially likes building cabinets and measuring and building complete kitchens. He says: "I've met a lot of interesting people—and some I'd just as soon not have met."

He does a lot of teaching now. Although many high school kids get jobs in the mills, they are not called apprentices. "They can come in off the street and learn, but not many are qualified. We train 'em, train kids right out of high school." According to Abell, the older fellows around the shop take over the new kids and help them learn the trade.

Not many people like millwork, Abell admits. Sawdust and wood chips are always flying. You can get splinters easily. The wood warps on you, and you have to make a new piece. "It's just the nature of wood to warp," he says, holding up a length of board for inspection. It is slightly bowed out of shape.

Millwork requires skill. You have to be able to run the cut-off saw and the ripsaw, make sashes and shelving, and cut paneling. You have to know how to operate the pallet machine, how to drill holes in sashes for grooved dowels, and how to insert the dowels so that no air pressure will build up behind the dowel in the joint. Millwork is inside work; it is day work; it is regular work. The pay is less than on construction and less than in a union shop.

George Franke

George Franke started in carpentry in 1952. He had been in military service and found that there were not too many jobs around after the war. His whole family had been in construction, so George joined Local 64 and began his life's work. He has done formwork, framing, and finish work. He has worked on office buildings, shopping malls, and river locks. He has laid carpet, put in acoustical tiles, and done pile-driving. He has worked on forms where the concrete was poured eight feet thick, poured continuously for a day and a half. One of his most dangerous jobs was the building of the locks in the

An inlaid veneer picture created by Robert Silliman.

Ohio River at the north end of Louisville. A crane used for that job had a 100-foot stick boom.

Franke loves to work outside. He is fiercely loyal to the union. He worked steadily until the last few years when the economy was so bad. He had been out of work for five months when his wife died and Mike Garrison called him about the job at the Marble Hill Nuclear plant.

Robert Silliman

Woodworking is a hobby for Robert Silliman. He got started in it as a kid making model airplanes. He started reading everything he could find about making things out of wood. He kept going to the library to check out a certain book on guitar building, and finally he bought the book. From it he learned to make a guitar.

He had to build his own form for bending the wood to take the shape of the guitar. He may use different woods for the sides and bottoms of his guitars, but he always uses white spruce for the tops and for the ribs and struts that make up the fan bracing on the inside. The quality of sound produced depends on the fan bracing. He has made all his own hand tools, his chisels and knives. You can't really buy ready-made knives, he finds; you have to design your own. Silliman does hand sanding on his guitars, which are all classical instruments. He says that the sanding is delicate; you can sand a bit too much and go right through the wood and ruin six months' work. The crucial thing is for the surface and all the pieces to be perfectly flat. He gives an instrument several wash coats to keep the grain down, then a final coat of lacquer. He uses rubbing oil or a compound of water and pumice powder to give it a hand-rubbed finish. It may take him two months to make all his tools before he ever begins work on a guitar. He has made his own round-bottom plane, purfling cutter, and workboard with clamps. He has a hygrometer in his shop to tell him what the heat and humidity are. He never puts finish on when the humidity is greater than 50 percent. Silliman's classical guitars are works of art. From the boiling of the rosewood sides for four hours before they are put on bending forms, to the point when he puts the ebony macassar and ivory, the German silver fretboard and nylon strings on the finished guitar, it is a work of love and patience.

Silliman has always liked the smell and feel of wood, he says, especially when he uses the lathe and the whole room fills with wood aroma. He loves being able to take a raw hunk of wood and make something beautiful out of it.

Silliman has a drawer full of blue ribbons he has won at State Fairs for his woodwork. He has done inlay work on jewelry boxes, made veneer pictures, and built cabinets and grandfather clocks. He does a lot of hand carving for his cabinets and small boxes. He loves to work with mahogany. "It's the best wood for anything," he says. "It's fine-grained, it sands well, and I love to work with it." He especially loves Honduras mahogany. Silliman likes to talk about his work and will show you lovely drawers with beautifully made dovetail joints, a mahogany table with cabriole legs, and a prize-winning venecr picture of a Japanese lady he made years ago. He carves rosettes, flowers, birds, and butterflies for his furniture. He makes inlaid flowers, butterflies, and initials.

James Erhart

"Besides eating and sleeping it's the biggest part of my life," says James Erhart of his work. He warns that people shouldn't go into carpentry or constuction if they think they're going to make big money. It's hard work, and you do it because it's satisfying. You look at something you've done—a room, a house, or a pretty mitered joint—and you can tell if it's straight and true, if it's a good job.

"There's only so many hours a week you can work," he says, "and when a day's gone, it's gone. It's not like running a store. If you have a bad day you can make up for it by selling your stock on another day. When you're in construction you're selling your services for an hourly wage. You work, you get paid."

Erhart has been in the construction business for twenty-five years. His dad, brothers, and grandfather were also in the business. His grandfather was really a jack-of-all-trades and could do just about anything. His father worked for the A&P Company, then around World War II started doing small repairs. His older brothers began to branch out in the trade. Erhart has had no formal training, just picked it up. He feels it certainly wouldn't hurt anybody to try construction; even if they didn't stick with it, they'd learn a lot while they were in it. They could learn to fix up their own homes, if nothing else. He does feel it takes someone who is mechanically inclined to be a carpenter. "Some people can't drive a nail straight," he says. He learned from his dad and from a woodworking class in high school.

Erhart says you work harder being your own boss. You can't put in a forty-hour week. You might be out at night doing estimates and other nights doing the figuring for the estimates, and that's all free time. You don't get paid to give estimates. It has to be done, though, and you do it. You have to be the type of person who will work harder when you're your own boss than you would in another situation. You have to be responsible; you can't go fishing or goof off.

He wonders if people working for big companies appreciate their benefits. It gets harder and harder to afford your own insurance. He has one income and seven children, and it is difficult sometimes.

But Erhart enjoys his work. He likes working in his shop making cabinets. He likes the variety in the construction field. It would be hard for him to do a factory job day in and day out, the same thing every day. It's a pleasure for him to go into a run-down place and fix it up. Even if it isn't run down, it's fun to fix up the kitchen, say, and make it look nice.

He has had no real trouble with customers in twenty-five years. Only twice in all that time has he had bad debts. He requires so much at the start of a job, another payment in the middle, and the balance when the job is finished. If you lose money, at least your materials are covered; it's just the labor you lose on. He tells prospective customers to talk to people for whom he's done work. He also tells them to check at the stores where he charges for materials. "I've got charges all over town. They can check and see if I'm paying my bills and if I've got good credit." He thinks this is a better way for people to find out about a contractor than by phoning the Better Business Bureau. "As long as you settle your complaints you're as good as someone with no complaints," he says of the way the Bureau reports findings to callers.

Erhart makes a shop out of his two-car garage. His table saws are kept in the shop; his electric hand tools are kept in his truck, which has been robbed twice.

To him the unions are a big rip-off. Although they were needed at one time, he feels that now they demand more than the pay scale can manage. He remembers when his father's house was built; carpenters made twenty cents a hour, and the foreman made forty cents an hour. He realizes how much the unions have done to change all that, but he also feels they have been irresponsible in their demands.

He has been busy through all the bad economic times. There is always work, if not in building, then in repairing. His reputation as a good carpenter has spread, usually by word of mouth, and he has steady work. There might be more chance for advancement out of the union hall, but Erhart is quick to point out that you need to check on the duration of union jobs. When a man is done with a job for the union hall, that's that. Erhart, on the other hand, may finish building a home in three months, but he has something else waiting for him to start working on.

His work is not as boring as if he were doing one or two jobs a year. There are, however, a lot of headaches in construction, more than there used to be. Things are priced so high that it has taken some of the fun out of it.

Still, James Erhart figures he'll be hanging in there twenty years from now. He may not be any better off financially, but he'll be hanging in there. He never was interested in being a big outfit or in becoming a millionaire. He lives in a home that bears the marks of his craftsmanship in the furniture, the interior trim, and the exterior finish. He lives in a neighborhood that many others fled during the past twenty or so years. It is in one of the oldest sections of the city. He works in partnership with his brother and Jerry Recktenwald.

Clyde Huber

Clyde Huber was in the union for thirty-nine years and ten months. When he took a job as instructor at Jefferson state he saw no reason to stay in the union any longer. His dad was a union man for forty-three years. He says of union carpenters, "They are top-notch men, really good craftsmen." However, he feels that after World War II the unions took in too many inadequate men. Huber has been working in carpentry since he "was a little bitty kid, from the time I could walk." Altogether he's been involved in the industry for forty-three years. He did commercial and residential work. He once worked with an architect who was building $200,000 homes and found that to be a "different ball game." It really topped off his experience. He went to night school to learn blueprint reading and how to use the steel square. He had his own company, Huber & Sons.

Bob Hardley

Hardley likes teaching. He also was in the union, and says: "The union treated me fair. I worked real well out of it." He worked for a large commercial construction company. He has done formwork, put up hospital walls, set fixtures, installed glass cases in department stores, installed paneling, and laid tile and carpet. You finish one job and go to the next. He says: "When you look around and see that the crew is getting smaller and smaller every day, you put out feelers and start looking for a new job. It won't be long before that one is over."

The best job he ever had was at the new Blue Cross office building. The job was supposed to last a month, and it lasted a year. "Some guys won't work a job that is just for a couple of days. You never can tell; some of those turn into longer jobs."

Hardley, who teaches at Jefferson State with Clyde Huber, says you have to want to do carpentry. You can save on home improvements with what you learn. You are more independent; you might be able to start your own shop, work for yourself, get a truck. There are times when Hardley misses picking up his tools and going to work, even though he likes teaching. He liked formwork and setting fixtures best, then doing ceilings, floors, and trim work.

He gestures to the kids in the classroom. "A lot of these kids will never realize the satisfaction of hanging a door by hand rather than with power equipment."

Power equipment, he says, has replaced a large percentage of handwork. "So much of the manual labor has gone out of the trade. You used to have to lift everything by hand; now cranes and lifts do it all for you. Nail guns take the place of regular hammers. Power planes do the work we did by hand." The trade is much simpler than it used to be.

He, Huber, and the students built an animal convalescent home at the zoo. They were allowed to do this in a volunteer capacity for a charitable purpose. They cut every piece of wood and metal, built the doors, and put up the siding.

Hardley recalls the day Huber got the first paycheck of his life and saw money taken out for income tax. Huber, as owner of his own company, had paid all his own taxes all his life. He took one look at that paycheck, says Hardley, and yelled, *"What is this? What have they done with my pay?"*

Thomas Haile

Thomas Haile makes $4,000 violins. Actually, he calls them fiddles, but then he clarifies his use of labels by saying: "It's the person that's got a hold of it that determines whether it's a fiddle or a violin." It takes him about two weeks to make a fine violin and about two months to put the varnish on it. And there you have a $4,000 violin.

It's all in the craftsmanship. It's much like his distinction between a fiddle and a violin. "An amateur fiddle," he says, "will play like the devil. A fine violin's like a person with a strong character."

Haile makes all his own machinery. He uses the finest woods. He uses only white spruce for the violin tops.

A banjo valued at $4,000, built by Tom Haile.

White spruce, he says, will vibrate properly; it's even, close, and straight-grained. He says it takes time to learn to use the tools properly, but then Thomas Haile has had a lot of time and a lot of practice.

He was raised near a sawmill in Tompkinsville, Kentucky. He learned a great deal about wood there, that you can't rush it to dry properly. If you do rush it, he says, it will honeycomb, pull moisture right out of the air and wind up as moist as before. Wood should be time-seasoned for about a year and then kiln-dried for about three weeks. White oak should be time-seasoned for ten years and stacked in tiers with strips between them for air to get at the oak. Lumber has to have some moisture in it, about 10 percent, or it will come apart. He tells people who buy his violins to keep a sweet potato in the case to hold some moisture. Apples, oranges, or lemons will also help retain moisture. When he stores dry lumber in his attic, he keeps a can of water there to control the moisture in the air.

Haile has been with lumber in every phase of the industry. He has felled trees, run them on a raft down river, and run the logs through the planing mill to slice them into boards. He had his own cabinetmaking shop in Tompkinsville. He and his brother, Haskell, who is probably the best guitar-maker in the country, made cabinets that they sold and personally delivered all over the country. He refers to their work as "a lock and key job." They knew the precise measurements, everything was specified. They knew exactly what was going to go into their cabinets and exactly what it was going to cost them.

He tells of the time he and Haskell were eating at the old Maxwell House in Salinas, Tennessee. The cook there, "the finest cook I ever ate after in my life," told the Haile brothers that there was something wrong with his kitchen cabinet. He couldn't get around the cabinet without tripping. So the Hailes set to work and, as Tom tells it, invented the kitchen cabinet with a recessed foot. "That was sixty years ago. Everybody copied our idea then, but we developed it through trial and error. We started building built-in kitchen cabinets before anyone even knew what they were."

Haile came to Louisville and went to work for the Anderson Woodworking Company. There he made doors, window casings, paneling, and cornices. He and a co-worker named Amos made all the molding and cornice work for the Justice Department building in

Washington, D.C. They made black walnut paneling for the judges' chambers and a desk that required one whole boxcar to carry it to Washington. The two of them, with their three big bags of carving chisels, also carved an eagle that was nine feet wide and eight feet tall and stood on a huge ball. It took them three months to complete. He and Amos worked well together even though Amos wouldn't talk when working. The Amos/Tom team made the carved doors that hang in the Speed School of the University of Louisville.

Tom tells of the time a crabbed old fellow at Anderson's approached him and tried to find something Tom couldn't do.

"Can you turn out round two-inch balls for cornices?"

"Sure." Tom filled up a whole box of them.

"What in hell is it you can't do?"

During World War II Tom worked at a plant that made B-24 bombers. He made prototypes, templates, and molds for a device that went on the wings and made it possible to hunt subs.

Tom Haile has done his share of teaching too. He taught night classes in Tompkinsville. He's taught blacksmithing, carpentry, sheet metal work, and cabinetmaking.

After the war Tom worked for Shackleton's Music Store repairing violins. The owners recognized his talent and apprenticed him for eight years to a master violinmaker from Paris, Robert DelPrato, who came to Louisville to teach Haile. When Shackleton's sold out their music business, Haile made preparations to go into business for himself. Now he makes and repairs violins and makes dulcimers and banjos. The last banjo he made sold for $4,000.

Haile is surrounded in his Louisville shop by cabinets

full of things for his craft. He has drawers full of cello parts, guitar and banjo parts, violin pegs, strings, and necks. There are metronomes, a gavel he made by hand, little band saws and big band saws, spokeshaves, spoon chisels, skew chisels, and knives for every different shape he wants to make. He has lizard skins for the grips on bows and willow blocks for the insides of violins.

It has been a long and full career for Tom Haile from the time he built a pine schoolhouse in Tompkinsville to his precision-made violins of the present. He made that little schoolhouse with as much care as he does his fine instruments, though. He drove his nails deep into the floor so they wouldn't puncture any small bare feet. He made the slates the children used. Now he is one of the finest violin-makers in the world, who understands about the wedding of wood, the dimensions, thicknesses, and fits that go to make a perfect instrument. His brother Haskell tells people, however, that the "next guitar will be the best one." And Tom would probably say the same about his violins, that the next one will be even better.

Tom says if you play the fiddle for tomatoes they'll grow higher, and he has a picture of some sixteen-foot tomato vines to prove his point. He also insists that cows will give more milk if you play the fiddle for them.

Gottfried Reck

"Organs from scratch" is what the vibrant young lady calls them as she takes you through the factory of Louisville's Steiner-Reck Organ Company. The factory is located above a garage in "Old Louisville," a section that has been set aside as a preservation area. It is hard even

A pipe organ built by the Steiner-Reck Organ Company.

to find the factory; the sign has recently been stolen. You have to ask other shopkeepers in the area where the organ place is, turn the corner into an alley, and climb narrow iron stairs that resemble a fire escape to get to the second-floor workshop. Across the alley a young drunk with a paper bag-covered bottle lies asleep in a doorway.

Inside the factory a magnificent Steiner-Reck organ is being dismantled to go to Columbus, Ohio, on the following day. It stands thirty-seven feet tall, and people are actually walking around in the casework. A woman is cutting holes in pipes according to exact specifications.

The designer of this organ is Gottfried Reck. Reck was born in Germany and lived there most of his life. As a young man he apprenticed at Bielefeld, the only school in the world for organ-building. He received $10 a month as spending money during his four years there while he learned to design and build organs. Circumstances brought Reck into contact with Phares L. Steiner, an organ builder in Louisville; he moved here from Germany, and the company is now the Steiner-Reck Organ Company.

This is the sixty-fourth organ the company has built, and they already have assignments for more. It takes from eight months to a year to build one of these organs. They are called tracker action organs because they have mechanical keyboards and stops, although sometimes only the keyboard is operated mechanically. Some of the organs are fitted with electric stops for the pipes.

Reck calls himself an amateur musician. He likes to sing and play the violin. There are beautiful sketches on his easel of organs not yet built. The sketches themselves are reminiscent of Gothic cathedrals, towering, majestic, and wonderful. Gottfried pulls from a drawer a picture of one of his finest achievements, a portatife, the only one like it in the world. The portatife is an organ small enough to fit in one's lap; it is played with the right hand while the left pumps the bellows. There is fine inlay work in the wood. Gottfried made this portatife by studying oil paintings by the Flemish painter Hans Memling, who died in 1494. Reck found that Memling's paintings were astonishingly accurate; he was able to draw precise conclusions as to the tuning and the length of the pipes.

Reck likes to use white oak for his organ cabinets. He calls it a nice stable wood with no capillary openings. Even some of the pipes are made from white oak. In every organ there are some stops made of wood, which makes a special sound. There are all kinds of joints in the

A portatife copied by Gottfried Reck from oil paintings by Hans Memling.

organ: mitered joints, dowels, tongue and groove. You will find anything but a perfect right angle, even though it may look as if there are right angles.

The pipes are a zinc alloy that comes from Germany. They are very fragile. Three voicings are done on the organ pipes. Reck has a moisture- and temperature-controlled sound room where he does the pre-voicing and second voicing, but the final voicing is done upon installation at the site.

Only about fifteen to twenty people work at this organ factory at any given time. Roy is the chief cabinetmaker. Roy built organs in the twenties, then went into mill-work. Two years ago he read an ad in the paper for an organ builder and applied for the job. He is now the one responsible for getting the woodworking done. There are always several young people about, apprentices perhaps they could be called. Steve Horjus came when he was nineteen. Now, at twenty-six, he is a valuable part of the organization. Some who are working are high school students. People advance here because they feel they are learning new skills all the time.

Gottfried hand carves the pipe shades, sometimes from basewood, sometimes from spruce. Gottfried occasionally does his own kind of wood staining in the closed-up factory with absolutely no one else around. He does what is called fuming; he sets a pot of ammonia in front of a fan and lets it blow the fumes onto the wood. This makes, he says, a nice dark wood.

Gottfried says there is a sense of intimacy, a response of feeling, when you press the keyboard manually. It takes a patient, thorough, mechanically minded person to work on organs. His organs carry a ten-year warranty; everything in them is built to last a hundred years.

Outside the crew is getting ready to load the parts onto the moving van. Six or seven of them will go to Columbus with the organ tomorrow and stay there until the dedication is held in seven weeks. During that time they will reassemble the organ, joint by joint, pipe by pipe, and do the final voicing.

From the alley doorway opposite, the young drunk rubs his eyes, sits up, and stares at the activity.

David Wilding

Architect David Wilding has built a table for two out of mahogany. It is a table for two because two crossbeams form the table top. These crossbeams are movable. David fashioned the brackets that hold the crossbeams so that the boards could move. In summer, with increased humidity, the wood swells and the crossbeams actually come closer together. There is a period in the drier winter weather when they tend to move apart.

Wilding claims this is much like human relationships, the moving closer together, the withdrawal. There are times, he says, when greater intimacy is achievable, but there are also times when we need a time apart. His table defines a space for each person seated there. Each person is seated at his/her own crossbeam, part of the whole table, yet apart enough to be individual. It is, Wilding speculates, the ideal way for relationships to work. There is a definite unity, but also a remarkable sense of the individual.

Wilding is very proud of the tools he used for the table, which is of two kinds of mahogany. He has a mallet of lignum vitae, the head from the pith of the tree trunk. He has a scribe for marking the mortise and tenon joints, a wood chisel with which he carved the mortises, and a small chisel. He has a Sandvik scraper, a kerfed-edged Scandinavian scraping tool. He has an Oriental saw that operates quite differently from American saws: it cuts on the pulling motion rather than on the pushing motion. The tool that was the most fun for him to use was the spokeshave, which he says is basically a plane, but is more sensitive. He carved the legs from sturdy bases to slender tops with spokeshave. Wilding also used a drawknife on the table.

The table is made of Honduras mahogany, but some of the parts on the underside he made of African mahogany. He considers the African mahogany more valuable, so he used it for the interior, the soul, of his table.

Wilding tells of the man who showed him how to run the ten-ton press where he formed his brackets. He first approached this workman as he was hidden behind a newspaper he was reading. When Wilding asked him for help, he dropped the paper, and Wilding saw two bandages covering the places where fingers had been. The whole floor moves when this press is on, and it cuts through a quarter inch of steel like scissors through paper. The workman laughed, held up the bandaged stumps, and said: "Why? You afraid of getting one of these?"

Chapter XVI

Wood

Wood cook stoves are fashionable again. If you want baked goods that rise just right, use birch. Beech is good for slow cooking, but for really slow cooking, for roasts, oak is the best. We gather kindling for our campfires. Wood smells good in the fireplace or stove.

We love to smell the blankets when they come from the cedar chest. The woods of yuletide charm us with their scents. We love wood.

The man in the park carves an African drum out of a big log. There are splashes of barbecue sauce and three or four Campbell's beans from last night's picnickers covering some of his chisel marks. He intends to leave this drum here for the people, in their park.

Riding or jogging through the park, you see playground equipment made of logs, and the wooden bleachers around the baseball diamonds. There are more bleachers around the basketball court where the summer Dirt Bowl classics are held every year. This is "run and gun" basketball, under the trees and on blacktop courts.

Notes are tacked to every other tree along the path. They read: Car Wash at 34th and Broadway Sat.; All Night Skating Party at the Broadway Roller Rink Fri.; Dirt Bowl sign-up Fri., Sat., Sun.

Farther along there is the blackened tree stump with

huge gouges in it where the firemen hacked at it in dousing the blaze set by careless youths. Around the bend is the grandstand with wooden bleachers in front of the stage. It was here, under the trees, that the fireworks display was held last Saturday night. They followed the rock concert given on this stage, the same stage on which a church service was performed on Sunday morning. All under the trees.

Trees make us more human. Trees provide us with good things for our whole lives: beautiful sights, good smells, jobs, means of cooking food, recreational things. They are pleasant to touch, to carve, to rub oil into, to cook with.

Wood can bring out the creativity in most people. Trees force us to look upward, away from ourselves. It's fun to watch them change with the seasons, to watch squirrels at play in the branches, and to glimpse patches of blue and sunlight between the leaves.

People who work with wood are nice people, noteworthy people. Usually they are more visual and mechanical than the rest of us. Usually they have more insight about structures, design, and purpose than do the rest of us.

They are builders, the kind of people who do things constructively. They may be the ones to give us ideas about becoming more human, about making education more human and more efficient, about making our society more livable.

Wood. It improves our lives. Trees from around the world: maple, makore, Hawaiian koa, butternut, beech, birch, tupelo, palao, myrtle burl, limba, cherry, rosewood . . .

Periodicals of Interest to Woodworkers

American Forests
1319 Eighteenth Street NW
Washington, DC

The Business Roundtable
The Taunton Press
52 Church Hill Road
Newton, CT 06470

Fine Homebuilding
200 Park Avenue
New York, NY 10166

Professional Builder
270 St. Paul Street
Denver, CO 80206

Professional Remodeler
P.O. Box 6170
Dublin, MN

Suggested Reading

Bealer, Alex W. *The Tools That Built America.* Barre, MA: Barre Publishing, 1976.

Bureau of Naval Personnel. *Basic Construction Techniques for Houses and Small Buildings.* New York: Dover Publications, 1972.

Burke, Arthur J. et al. *Architectural and Building Trades Dictionary.* Chicago: American Technical Society, 1950.

Chaney, Len. *Build a Yurt.* New York: Macmillan Publishing Co., Inc. 1974.

Doors and Windows. Alexandria, VA: Time-Life Books, 1978.

Encyclopedia International, Vol. 4. Lexicon Publications, Inc., 1980.

Floors and Stairways. Alexandria, VA: Time-Life Books, 1978.

Garrison, Clifford B. *Finding a Job You Feel Good About.* Allen, TX: Argus Communications, 1977.

Hochheiser, Robert. *Throw Away Your Resume.* Woodbury, NY: Barron's Educational Series, 1982.

Krenov, James. *The Impractical Cabinetmaker.* New York: Van Nostrand Reinhold Company, 1979.

Maguire, Byron W. *The Complete Book of Woodworking and Cabinetmaking.* Reston, VA: Reston Publishing Company, Inc., 1974.

Medley, H. Anthony. *Sweaty Palms.* Belmont, CA: Lifetime Learning Publications, 1978.

Nervi, Pier Luigi. *Structures.* New York: F. W. Dodge Corporation, 1956.

Noyes, William. *Handwork in Wood.* Peoria, IL: The Manual Arts Press, 1910.

Scharff, Robert. *Complete Book of Wood Finishing.* New York: McGraw-Hill Book Company, 1956.

Sloane, Eric. *Reverence for Wood.* New York: Ballantine Books, 1978.

Ulrey, Harry F. *Carpentry and Building.* Indianapolis: Theodore Audel & Co., 1972.

Working with Wood. Alexandria, VA: Time-Life Books, 1979.

World Book Encyclopedia, Vol. 3. World Book-Childcraft International, Inc., 1981.

Wyatt. E. M. *Common Woodworking Tools.* Milwaukee: The Bruce Publishing Company, 1936.